PENTHOUSE AND PAVEMENT

MAINSTREAM SPORT

PENTHOUSE AND PAVEMENT

HOW TO SURVIVE IN FOOTBALL WITHOUT SUCKING UP TO THE OLD FIRM

BILL LECKIE

MAINSTREAM
PUBLISHING

EDINBURGH AND LONDON

First published in Great Britain in 1999 by
MAINSTREAM PUBLISHING COMPANY (EDINBURGH) LTD
7 Albany Street
Edinburgh EH1 3UG

ISBN 1 84018 219 9

A catalogue record for this book is available from the British Library

Typeset in Garamond
Printed and bound in Finland by WSOY

STUFF THAT'S IN THIS BOOK

*For my dad, who taught me everything
I know about decency in football and
in life and whom I miss every day*

PREFACE

We're in the press room at Parkhead before the 5–1 Old Firm game of November 1998, the one where Lubomir Moravcik scored two and celebrated like his dog had just died.

I'm having a cup of tea, talking to Mark Guidi from the *Sunday Mail* and Kenny MacDonald from the *News of the Screws*, when cuddly little Graham Speirs of *SoS* comes in.

He walks by us, stops, turns and fixes me with that bendy-necked, furrowed-browed expression he wears when he's being asked a question on *Scotsport*. That look somewhere between utter bafflement and chronic constipation.

Then he says: 'Where is it you actually *live?*'

So I say: 'Falkirk. Why?'

And he bends his neck to the other side and screws his face up even more than usual and says: 'It's just that I keep seeing your byline from places like Dumfries and Cowdenbeath and . . . and . . . *Dingwall.*'

Except he pronouces the word 'Dingwall' to rhyme with 'syphilis'.

'Yeah?' I say. 'So what's your point, caller?'

'Well . . . I just wondered . . . like . . . erm . . . *why?*'

'Why what?'

'Why do you *go* to all those places?'

So I stood with an ever-so-slight riddy and tried to justify why, by saying that I liked going there and the people were nice and they made you lots of cups of tea and I need the money.

Then, when he had unscrewed his neck and wandered off, I was angry with myself, not for spending my midweek nights and rainy Saturdays at Third Division grounds, but for standing there justifying why.

Truth is, I'll go anywhere there's a game of football on. For work or for fun. I love watching it, love writing about it. Football's football, isn't it?

Or is it?

Until I started moving through the journalism business, I'd never thought it unusual for someone who grew up loving the game – and who is unutterably lucky enough to be paid to write about it – to actually choose to go and watch it wherever it's being played.

It's how I was brought up. Dad and I went to see St Mirren home and away, except when we couldn't get transport to the odd away game. When that happened, we'd go to Linwood to see his works team or even – check this – jump a train to Cartsdyke and see Morton. *That's* how much we loved the game.

Often on Sundays we'd walk three miles over the back roads from Paisley to see Johnstone Burgh play in the juniors. On midweek summer nights we'd go down to the Racecourse and cruise between amateur games. I'll still watch any game, anywhere.

And yet I was well aware long before being grilled expertly by Speirsy-y that there are far too few people in the national media willing to move out of their little sphere of Rangers-Celtic-Scotland-Celtic-Rangers and dirty their hands seeing what's happening in the rest of the world.

Yet many of these guys are the same ones first on with the tacketies to slaughter the lower divisions. This seems something of an anomaly, he hinted diplomatically. It also has to be said that within this band there are some who would not even think about going to a game unless they had to, which is a worry.

At midweek games played at windy Second and Third Division grounds you see all sorts: Premier League bosses, club chairmen, players from clubs all over the country. But very rarely do you see any media stars checking the talent or, for that matter, do you see the people who run football in this country. This is sad and it is also scary for the future of the game.

I'd hold my hands up if writers and broadcasters took in the full picture of the game before deciding it was guff, but they don't. They sit in little cliques at Ibrox and Parkhead and write off the rest as diddy teams.

What chance is there for a fair assessment of football as a whole when the prospect of having to spend ninety minutes at Stair Park, Stranraer, makes so many noses wrinkle like someone just pooed in their pocket?

I suppose it's become a bit of a mission of mine to publicise the lower divisions, to highlight the personalities and try to make players and managers and fans feel like they're not shouting into the wind about their very existence. But they are, really, and so am I.

The clubs at the very top don't really give a monkey's whether Cowdenbeath and Dumbarton live or die any more and some of my own profession wouldn't be that bothered either – at least then it would guarantee them never having to soil their Guccis at Central Park or Boghead by some horrible accident of a cup draw.

The snobbery which has poisoned Scottish football since the Souness revolution kicked in at Rangers means the best that those who love the whole game can hope for is that all the clubs down the bottom end get to survive and do their own thing in happiness and harmony.

It's all they want, really. To be self-sufficient, except maybe for the odd player sold on to the big boys. Scottish football looking after its own talent – you must remember that?

So this book is about these clubs and the people who love them. It's about the kind of fan who doesn't go to games *expecting* to win . . . or, worse, *demanding* it. This book is about being willing to accept a lifetime of frustration in return for one day of utter wonderment. Days like your team winning the Scottish Cup. Or lifting a title against all odds. Or even just turning one of the Old Firm over.

The title of this book is also the name of Heaven 17's first album, which came out when I was just getting into journalism, and it kind of sums up the game today. There are a few lucky people in football who lord it in towers in the air, while the other 99 per cent are on the street. All they can do is dream that one day they'll be up there.

I'm lucky. I get to see both sides. I love it at pavement level – it's where I grew up and it's still where you feel people really love football. But I'm also lucky enough to get in among the rich boys, to go to cup finals and internationals and meet the stars. I won't kid on being up there isn't brilliant sometimes. But the fresh air is at ground level.

There's a lot of different stuff in this book: from a day spent far away from your team when they are on the brink of relegation, to how different London fans are from ours. From a week spent training with a team fighting for survival, to life with a boss who returned to the little clubs where it all started before going off to be famous. And, of course, there's a chapter on the greatest suffering of all – being a Scotland punter at the World Cup.

This book doesn't pretend to be some great insight into the psyche of the oppressed football fan. It's just a series of rants and attempts to make you laugh and maybe, occasionally, to get something in your eye.

So thank you for reading and look out soon for the follow-up – a hilarious collection of out-takes from the making of this book.

Yes, sports fans, all the best bloopers, bleepers, Droopers and Snorks (*whoops – there goes another one; the sharp-eyed may have noticed those last two were actually from the Banana Splits!*) which lightened the serious business of producing a top-class football publication.

Laugh along as:

*I mean to type Ron Atkinson in Chapter One – but somehow it comes out as ROWAN Atkinson instead! Boy, was *my* face red!

*I'm halfway through page 11 of Chapter Five when I completely forget the next line! But don't worry, mums – we've bleeped out the sweary-words!

*The simple operation – or so you'd think! – of using a semi-colon in the chapter about France '98 needs 17 TAKES as the key sticks! We can laugh now, but at the time . . .

These and many more are all available in paperback early in 1001 – oh, damn, there I go AGAIN! That should of course read 2001!

Waap-waap-waap-waaaaaaah!

Bill Leckie
June 1999

ONE

THE SEVEN AGES OF A FOOTBALL FAN

1. GOING WITH DAD

In the beginning was the word.

And the word was Humped.

For, lo, did a man take his infant son unto the city of Dun-dee; and therein to the temple of Dens, where did play the men called Gil-zean and Ure and even sometimes, when they were really strapped, Craig Brown.

And the man was sore afraid, but he did hide this fear from his infant son and did tell the child of how they would whup unto Dun-dee's ass and even unto their oxen.

But verily he was only kidding himself.

The infant son, though, would not have known the difference had it given him a haircut. For he was 16 months old and knew nothing of the ways of Foot-Ball.

Then yea did his father show him off to the lads and feed him Ma-ca-roon and the gum of spear-mint and did he place unto his lips the cup of sacred Bovril.

And the infant's tongue was sore burned, like the bush.

Then did the gladiators come out and soon it was clear that Dun-dee were not the whuppees but the whuppers and verily did the infant son learn many of the wisdoms of Foot-Ball. He learned that the keeper was as of one of the five fishes: a Haddie. And he heard phrases like: 'Lo, your father was not known unto your mother, referee.' Then: 'You can play nane, o centre-half.'

And: 'Jesus Wept.'

Then Gil-zean and Pen-man and all of Dun-dee did smite the infant son's father's team and lo, was the father's sore afraidness now as plain as Joseph's dull cousin Colin's Monochrome Dreamcoat.

In the end did Dun-dee have Nine and the father's lot none but Two. But the father did store away this day as a parable with which to enlighten his infant son as he grew.

So did the infant become a toddler and the toddler a snottery-nosed schoolboy well versed in the ways of Foot-Ball. One day did he with his father witness their team get Humped again, with none but One against the enemy's Four.

And the snottery-nosed schoolboy wiped the silvery trail like the snail's on the sleeve of his an-o-rak and sayeth unto his father: 'Sod this for a game of soldiers.'

His father smote him for knowing such phrases, then becalmed and replyeth: 'No, but do ye not recall the day of the Nine against our none but Two at the temple of Dens when you were but 16 months old?'

The schoolboy, whose nose was again well snottery, sniffed hard and sayeth: 'No.'

So did his father recount the story of Dun-dee and what a towsing his side did get there. And then he chastiseth: 'So, my snottery-nosed son, surely this must forever put into perspective your wailing and gnashing over the guff our team produces. For did Saint Mirren himself not once say: "In my ground are many shades of pish"?'

And the schoolboy, now blinded by snotters and bemusement, said: 'What does that mean?'

His father took up a hanky and did wipe the snotters and rub the schoolboy's nose far too hard the way dads do outdoors and he looked at his son and said: 'It means that nothing can ever be as bad again, bogey features . . .'

And lo, he was darn tooting. Because nothing ever was or is or will be, unless someday, somewhere, we manage to lose 10–2.

It riles me when I hear people come away from a 0–0 draw or a 1–0 defeat or sometimes even a *win* – go to any Scotland game and you'll know it's true – whingeing that they've just watched the worst *ever* and they'll *never* be back. Trust me, sports fans, when your first-ever game ends in a 9–2 defeat you learn a little perspective.

Not that I remember a sausage about the day back in February

1964. I only know I was there and that, as the years went on, Dad used it as the yardstick for unhappiness in football and that was one of the greatest things he ever did for me. Which is saying something.

Thus, on days when we lost 6–0 at home to Airdrie or 5–0 at home to Queen of the South or 5–0 at East Stirling or 7–0 at Parkhead, he could always turn to me and say: 'It could have been worse.'

And I always knew he was right.

Weekends were my time with Dad. Monday to Friday he'd work shifts in Watson's papermill at Linwood, sometimes twelve hours at a time. The job had its perks; I had the best-covered books in school. But when he came home he'd really just have his tea and doze off watching the box, then hit the sack to sleep deeper than anyone I know. He could have slept on a razor blade.

Come the weekend, though, it was me and him. Sundays he'd let me lie in while he fried breakfast after Mum went off to church. Then we'd sit and munch and drink mugs of tea while we read the *Sunday Mail*, the *Sunday Post* and the *Sunday People*, poring over what we'd already seen the day before.

Saturday for us *was* St Mirren. Dad made it a ritual, from waking up until we got picked up by my Uncle Sam. He wasn't a real uncle, just a friend of the family, but he was uncle to me; and he and his sons Gordon and Richard would roll up and peep the horn and we'd be off.

By then we'd have done the same things every Saturday. Watch telly, read the *Daily Record* and the *Daily Express* – he stuck by it long after they pulled out of Scotland just because he loved the crossword.

Then lunch, same thing every time. Had to be right – any athlete will tell you that – and I still have the same as Dad and I always did: the energy-giving nourishment that is Heinz Beans with Pork Sausages on buttered rolls, plus a mug of tea.

Now, I know many of you have busy lifestyles which don't allow you to prepare for games the way I've been brought up to. So here's a handy guide:

Recipe
(Makes enough for one dad and one kid/or one lonely tubster)
One saucepan (medium)
Two tins Heinz Baked Beans with eight Pork Sausages
Four morning rolls (floury)
Butter (slightly salted)

Method
Pour both tins into saucepan, heat gently
Split rolls, butter both sides well
Remove saucepan from heat
Place two sausages on each roll; mash
Cover with beans; mash
Pour half of remaining sausages/beans into each bowl
Serve with tea and newspapers
Eat while arguing over whether Jackie Copland or John Young is a better sweeper

The final line only actually works if you're a St Mirren fan and it's 1976, but changing the names/team/year will not affect the overall flavour of a tasty and filling pre-football meal.

Our very special *saucissons porc avec haricots en sauce tomate sur pain au beurre* was always best eaten to the accompaniment of *Football Focus*, roly-poly Sam Leitch when I was a kid in the late '60s/turn of the '70s, then Bob Wilson – the worst pretendy Scotsman ever – and today Gary Lineker.

Is it just me or is Lineker:
  (a) wooden,
  (b) incredibly patronising,
  (c) not half as squeaky-clean as he makes out, or,
  (d) all of the above and more that I can't use in a family book?
  You are the ref.

On The Ball or *Saint and Greavsie* were always second best, like *Swap Shop* was to *TISWAS* or HP Beans to Heinz. And second best would have been bad luck in those days when little things mattered so much.

It's odd what you remember about watching football as a kid. Like, every home game the crowd of us who stood together used to put 2p a head into a sweep for first goalscorer, and one day against Hamilton in 1972 I picked Gus McLeod and he scored five and they all gave me extra money.

Or watching Danny Stevenson save a penalty at Alloa and believing he'd never be beaten by one again. Being at a reserve game against Hearts – our first-team keeper Dennis Connaghan played on the left wing, don't ask me why – with my legs dangling over the fence round the track, then the ball hitting the advertising board and jamming the skin behind my knees between the tin hoarding and the wooden frame. I can still feel that.

Or being 4–1 down at home to Dundee – yep, them again – when our big centre-half Andy McFadden (who lived just next to my Uncle Sam and who therefore had an extra *frisson* of mystique) got one back with ten minutes to go and me trying to convince Dad we'd come back and get a draw.

'If we can score one now, we can score another one and then if we do that we can get another one after that. Eh, Dad? Dad? Dad? Eh, Dad?'

And he humoured me and ruffled my hair and said *sure, sure*, knowing all the while there was no chance because it was just a consolation goal. But I was too naïve to know what a consolation goal was and kept believing right up to the whistle.

I've never learned.

No game is over till it's over, in my book. I've never left early, never given up hope. When others around me are telling me that's it, finito, time to go home, I stick my fingers in my ears and go *neeeewhhooooooooowwwwwwaaaawhoooooo.*

I also believe every time I hear 'Old Shep' that he won't get shot in the last verse and Go Where The Good Doggies Go.

Don't get me wrong, I'm not stubborn. Just stupid.

Back then, it was all rituals. We parked in the same spot off Albion Street every home game, bought programmes off the same old bloke, split up outside for me to go in the Boys Gate and then met inside again, walked up the big old steps at the Love Street End, wandered round the old curved open terracing, moving down the same few steps every few yards, then settled in the same spot every time under the roof of the North Bank.

Dad would give me money and I'd go and get a Coke and a Waggon Wheel – these were the days, remember, when Waggon Wheels *were* Waggon Wheels; the size of bin lids and not two-pence pieces the way they are today – from the little wooden stall handily placed just beyond the cover of the shed so you got soaked in the queue.

Then I'd see Big Jim. Every club had a Big Jim then, a harmless loony whom everybody knew and everyone loved and nobody slaughtered. Ours was actually called Peter, but everyone called him Big Jim after Jim Blair, our centre-forward at the turn of the '70s who went on to play for Norwich in the 1973 League Cup final against Spurs. Jim Blair was six-foot-odd and skinny and sharp-nosed and Big Jim was uncannily like him, but much older and with every feature caricatured. On top of which he had no teeth and wore a sombrero.

The day didn't really start until he came over the brow of the Love Street End, sombrero first, then rubbery face, then demob suit jiggling on a boney body and legs that moved like a cross between Bambi and a *Thunderbirds* puppet.

And when he was fully in view he'd sort of stumble-hop-stamp to a halt and he'd yodel. *'Ohleh-ohleh-ohlehohlehohleh-oh-LEH!!!!'*

Even the players would pause their old-fashioned, non-choreographed warm-up and cheer.

Our other Character Fan was Tosh, a binman who stood in a little paddock next to the main stand and abused everything and everyone who went past. Tosh ran a supporters' bus and raised money non-stop for the club and knew everyone, but come kick-off he threw off his ambassadorial robes and gave it pelters. These days he'd be banned, nicked or both five minutes into the first pre-season friendly at most grounds.

There's no room in football for Toshes or Big Jims nowadays. Their faces don't fit. Take Fergie at Hamilton. He's a simple old bloke, a tubby, gumsy soul with an over-severe haircut and a scarf wrapped round like a muffler beneath his battered tweed coat. He swears like a lorryload of drunken navvies. He swears at the players, the ref, the managers, himself, the pies. He swears at the air. But he's harmless, except to people with stuck-up ideas about what their clubs are. God knows how many times he's been banned. I wrote about it when they banned him once, about five years ago, and he phoned me at *The Sun* in tears that someone had bothered to take his side. He didn't have much in his life, not much more than his Saturdays watching the Accies, and they kept on taking that away from him.

Professional football was invented to give ordinary punters something to do with their spare time. Clubs were a focus for the community. They're not churches or libraries, places where you sit down and shut up. They're places full of life and hope and excitement and – yes – rough language, because ordinary punters use rough language sometimes.

My dad didn't swear, but he rarely went out of his way to stop me hearing others use bad language. He trusted me to know what was right and wrong and that was cool. I've tried to do the same with my son.

The only games he usually wouldn't take me to were those when the Old Firm came to town. He never in his life went to see us play Rangers or Celtic away. He loathed their bigotry, their songs of hate, and wouldn't expose me to it all. That stood me in better stead for a life in football than anything else that happened in my childhood, because I never came to accept religious division as part of life.

Yet the people who run football weed out the Fergies of the world, blokes who wouldn't hurt a fly, and let Old Firm fans away with promoting genocide from the terracings. It's easier that way.

Only twice did Dad take me to see either of them before I was old enough to make up my own mind, and both times were in 1972. First we drew Rangers in the fourth round of the Scottish Cup and for once we went, just me and him, up on the Caledonia Street End. Can't remember why.

Anyway, we were 3–0 down with half an hour to go when he decided we'd heard enough of all their guff and took me away. We got the bus home and just when we were getting off, I heard on the driver's radio that we'd scored and I was heartbroken at not having seen the goal.

Then, in May, we faced them in the final of a charity shield that used to be played to help raise money for local hospitals. It was the last game Rangers played before the Cup-Winners' Cup final and Dad asked if I wanted to go. I said yes and this time I saw us score, twice, but they scored five.

Still, eh?

We were on the Caledonia End that night as well and again I don't know why. Maybe he thought I'd hear less of their nonsense and, if so, I thank him again.

When I was wee and still snottery-nosed, I'd leave the grown-ups and go down to the front to stand with the other snot-noses at the fence. Sometimes we'd dangle our legs over and clang our heels against the metal ad boards until the police came by and motioned for us to get back over. After my pain-behind-the-knees reserve game escapade I knew it was for the best. And I never ever wore shorts again to the football, at least not until I got into my thirties and thought it was cool.

But when I was older and wiser and into secondary school, I stood a few steps back from the kids and hung out with Dad and the rest. In those days, long before segregation fences, we'd wait for the toss then walk to the same spot at the other end of the shed if need be. When we did, we always fancied our chances more. We always preferred attacking the Love Street End in the second half.

As you can see from our record over many years, we lost many tosses.

The fear of not getting to the football then was one of the worst feelings of my childhood. We were playing Forfar at home at the start of February 1973 and whatever had happened between us that morning he was in a real huff with me. Dad in a huff was a nightmare. He never, ever in his life laid a finger on me but sometimes I really, really wished he would. Get it out in the open, get it over with.

But, no. Instead, he just fumed. Went silent, knitted his eyebrows and huffed and puffed. About lunchtime he told me I had no chance of going to the game that day, that he'd phone Uncle Sam and tell him not to bother coming round. He probably had no intention of doing it, but he kept me going all the same and it was torture, watching the clock and watching him and saying nothing in case it made it worse.

Then, at ten to two, the car pulled up and he said: 'Right, that's us. Let's go.'

And not another thing was said about it. I was relieved and chuffed and upset and all warm at the same time.

We drew 0–0. But we had a top day, because it was our day.

2. GOING WITH YOUR MATES

Your average child born in the early '60s started going to games alone in an era when the most lucrative job to have in football was a scarf-maker. Because everyone wore four each. One knotted round your neck, one round each wrist and one tied onto your belt and hanging down your side. You wore a flag like Superman's cape, a bobble hat, badges and patches on every scarf. You put on half a stone every time you went to a game.

This was the bizarre fashion era after the Bay City Rollers but before punk, the sad vacuum of time dominated by Brotherhood of Man. This was 1976.

I was thirteen, still young and stupid enough to believe I had looked cool at my sister's wedding the year before. Me, in my light-blue and dark-blue checked suit picked for me by my soon-to-be brother-in-law, with its hang-glider lapels, more buttons than a Pearly King could throw a stick at, and windsock flares. Windsock? Wind-*tunnel*, more like. So wide and flappy that when I walked you couldn't see my shoes – and *they* had three-inch rolling platforms. I looked like I was on castors. The trousers had a three-button waistband, with two of the three sets of buttons purely decorative.

Add to the suit and the shoes – brown, by the way, just to set off the two shades of blue – a shirt in a third shade of blue and a purple bowtie and you're talking 1000 per cent fashion.

Add in the hairdo and you're talking a right shag, if only I'd known what that meant back then.

Mum took me to where she got hers done down Broomlands Street and got my over-the-collar hair put into a pageboy like Brian Connolly from the Sweet or Brian Little from Villa. They washed it, tidied the ends, then turned it all under beautifully. It cost £3.50 and I was sworn to secrecy from my dad, who never paid that much at the barber's in an entire year.

However, this was Friday, the wedding was on Saturday and I had to get through the night without wrecking the look. It was the longest night of my life. I slept with my head three inches off the pillow so the pageboy stayed intact, and woke like a chicken with a broken neck.

Pictures of me at that wedding remain locked in a lead-lined casket inside an eight-foot-thick steel vault two leagues beneath a secret spot in a forbidden wood somewhere in Albania.

At the time, though, I thought I was the bee's danglies and, after seeing myself in a suit for the first time, I travelled to Fashion Adventureworld. I went into Second Year in huge Oxford bags with pockets at the knees, two-inch turn-ups and a *four*-button waistband, kipper school tie five inches wide at the knot but only three inches long, a lilac shirt with the flappy penny collar out over the rounded lapels of a Barathea blazer and the same brown roller platforms. *Hey, ladieeeeez . . .*

Soon it would be time to take the next step and break away from Dad and the rest and go to home games on my own. That time came at the start of the 1976–77 season, which was to be the most momentous in my young, clothes-afflicted life. Alex Ferguson would take us on a thrill-a-minute ride to the Premier League. We would win the First Division title by a street, score a hundred goals, multiply our crowds five-fold, captivate the nation's imagination and have scouts flocking to covet our long-haired, skinny-shirted pin-ups.

And I would be there, in all my scarves and badges and flags and hats, flares flapping, platforms clumping, giving it plenty.

I wish I could say that I picked the Dundee game in October '76 as my first solo mission because it had a fitting juxtaposition with my début as a St Mirren fan 14 and a bit years before, but sadly it would not be true.

I went without my dad that day because it was the first time he let me. Jumped on the bus to Smithhills Street, swaggered through the Piazza like a king, up onto Moss Street, under the railway bridge and over the Sneddon to Love Street. I went through the gate that day a young dude in four scarves with the world at my feet and a quarter of Sports Mixtures in my pocket. I was no longer a child, apart from the Sports Mixtures.

We were 3–0 up in no time against a team which included Gordon Strachan. Rubber-legged Frank McGarvey tormented their left-back so badly I remember him being hooked off before the break.

It finished 4–0 and the legend of Fergie's Furies was born. As was my life as an independent St Mirren supporter.

Pretty soon when we went to away games I cut the next string by disappearing off to meet my mates when we got there then meeting Dad and the rest back at the car. Then finally I went on the road myself: 8 January 1977 at Brockville.

We sang our lungs out, there were handbags at twelve paces as fans swapped ends at half-time and we drew 1–1. Falkirk were one of only two sides to beat us in the league that season, 2–0 in the second game.

The other defeat was at – *ptooo!* – Cappielow. We'd just come off the back of the Scottish Cup-tie when we took 13,000 to Fir Park in a 27,000 crowd and got kicked off the park as we lost 2–1. On the Wednesday we played St Johnstone at home and scrambled a 1–1 draw but come Saturday we were right up for it again. Morton? We'd whupped them 5–1 at home then 6–3 down there on New Year's Day after we'd been 2–0 down on a skating-rink pitch before Billy Stark and Fitz tore them to bits.

The final meeting (there were fourteen in the league and we played each other three times, wacky funsters that the Scottish League were) would be a canter. But we got hoofed 3–0 and could hardly believe it. Nightmare. Between that and haring back to the bus to avoid a kicking then keeping our heads down in case bricks came in, I hated it. That was a day to be with your dad.

By the triumphal end of the season, though, I was thoroughly independent, home and away. I only body-swerved the mates once, for the last home game when we wrapped up the title against Montrose. Well, you couldn't go to football all that time with your old boy and not celebrate together when you finally won something.

Then, in the midweek, I went to Dundee with the mates and we won 4–0 and somehow there seemed something beautifully symmetrical about being there under my own steam and avenging the hidings of old.

You think some amount of cobblers when you're thirteen, eh?

3. SNEAKING DRINK IN

It was only when you reached bevvying age that you realised why flares were invented.

It is also at this point I realise I'm in for a thick ear from my mother, because I have to confess to:

(a) drinking under age,

(b) sneaking drink into football matches,

(c) having appalling dress sense.

The last one I'm sure she remembers. And possibly still believes.

Actually, it's remarkable to think there was a day not so long ago when taking bevvy into the game was allowed. Thousands and thousands carted bottles of whisky and vodka and wine and whole cases of beer through the turnstiles with them and got tanked up and the authorities scratched their heads for reasons why the fans generally then started fighting.

You wonder why it took a televised riot at the Old Firm Scottish Cup final in 1980 to make police and MPs sit down and go: 'Hey, you know how there's always bottles and cans getting thrown about at games, yeah?'

'*Yeeeessss . . .*'

'And, well, you know how loads of people get their heads caved in with them?'

'*Uhhhhhuuuuu . . .*'

'And, like, you know how 99.999 per cent of the people nicked at games are howling drunk?'

'*Hmmmmmmm . . .*'

'Well, just let me throw this in here, run it up the flagpole and see who salutes it, pop it in the toaster and see if it comes out brown – but what do you think might happen if we *didn't* let punters bring drink in?'

'*You mean, like . . . not give them a way to further fuel their aggression and frustration during the game?*'

'Yep.'

'*And take away the opportunity to hurl sharp-edged metal at innocent people or stick broken bottles in the faces of others?*'

'Sounds good to me.'

'*Radical. But, hey, don't you think it might turn people off coming to games?*'

'Maybe, maybe . . . but here's the spin. We *still* let them smuggle in Stanley knives and tomahawks and golf balls with nails in them, at least until we eventually realise the damage they do.'

'*Agreed unanimously!*'

Thus, in 1980, taking bevvy into football matches was banned and suddenly fans had to use the toilets instead of peeing in empty lager cans and adding a subtle twist to the joy of being whapped on the skull.

'*Hey – not only have I suffered severe concussion and lacerations, but I smell like a public lavvy as well. Hurrah!*'

It was such a magnificently obvious move, yet it took us a hundred years to think of it. That's football. Yet I'll admit I regarded it as part of my education that in the final years of drink being an integral part of matchday I, as a minor, was able to outwit the law and take mine with me illegally.

It was Ibrox, December 1978. I was sixteen. I was in a sky-blue zipper hooded top with my Saints strip underneath, the obligatory bobble hat weighed down with badges and the four scarves. Flat-soled, wide, heavily segged brown Frank Wright tassled Weejins, for shoes had moved onwards and downwards. And even more enormously flared, high-waist Brutus jeans, for trousers had moved onwards and outwards.

How wide were those jeans? Wide enough to stuff a can of Tennent's down each side of each football sock and still have the legs blow freely in the chill wind of Edminston Drive.

With the new Broomloan Stand under construction, we were given not only the west end of the enclosure under the main stand but also the privilege of being spat on from above by people who cunningly disguised their moronity by wearing decent clothes.

It was around this time that I came out of a League Cup quarter-final at Ibrox with my mate John, a rabid Rangers fan. We had lost 3–2 after being 2–0 up and having a third disallowed, and you'd have thought their lot would have been happy as Larry Hagman after his per-show fee on Dallas went up to $1 million and a jacuzzi-ful of naked ladies. But no. Not only did they give me and all the other Saints fans horrendous stick as we headed for the bus back to Paisley, just for being someone other than themselves, but John got it as well for being *with* one of the Other Lot. And so he took off his Rangers scarf, dropped it over the bridge onto the M8 and, come the next Saturday, he went on our bus to a 1–1 draw at Pittodrie and supported us from then on.

I'm digressing, though, probably to lull my mother into missing the bit about me standing in the queue with the beer down my socks. To be honest, it wasn't hard to get away with it. You could have comfortably hidden a piano inside each leg of those jeans and still had room for Liberace's wardrobe.

But I was a church-going BB boy who wore guilt like Gyles Brandreth wears loud knitwear, and I might as well have had one of those signs above my head reading R U 18? R U Bollocks! Even now when I walk through customs with nothing more sinister in my luggage than a stuffed donkey, my face says: 'Search me, I've got a kilo of Charlie stuffed up my bum.' (*I could tell you a nasty story involving that very look, Tangiers Airport and the horrible snap of a rubber glove. But I guess by now you'll have worked it out anyway.*) So instead let me just say I will never be sure how I managed not only to get past the feds outside Ibrox with CRAP CRIMINAL written all over my beaming, bum-fluffed coupon, but also get in the Boys Gate. Result.

After that, drink smuggling was a piece of cheese. I could have got a magnum of Bollinger into a mosque wearing nothing but skin-tight Speedos.

By the time I was eighteen, of course, it was legal for me to drink but illegal to take it into the game. Which was fine by me, as doing it with the approval of adults would have been no fun.

Today, of course, if you want to get howling inside a football ground you can as long as you have the dosh or the right friends. You can get corporate hospitality at just about any club, drink yourself senseless and then annoy real fans by staggering to your seat late, leaving early for half-time snackettes, coming back late again and sodding off five minutes from time to get stuck into the beer again. I know I've already mentioned this elsewhere – and I probably will again – but I really, really loathe these people.

Which is not to say I haven't freeloaded with the best of them. Ibrox, Parkhead, Hampden, Tannadice, Wembley, Love Street, Livingston; you name the stadium, I've eaten on someone else's bill there – but it is my sworn principle to be in my seat in time and to watch the whole game.

Even if I *can* see forty-four players and several balls.

4. TAKING YOUR KID

It is indeed a solemn ritual, baptising your first-born in the ways of Foot-Ball.

I'd have had him at the Cup final if I could have got away with it, but he was three days short of being four months old and it was raining and now that I look back, who knows where he might have ended up when Ian Ferguson scored?

Picture it. Man shoots. Ball bulges net. Lifetime's ambition suddenly achieved. Baby soars towards rafters of Rangers End with thousands of scarves and hats.

So instead he stayed home with his mother and almost ended up through the living-room ceiling instead.

It was two months later before I managed to sneak him out to his first game. He was six and half months old. My grandpa had a paper round by that age. So I wrapped him up against the elements of the Paisley summer and pushed him in his buggy to a pre-season friendly against Stirling Albion. It wasn't even at Love Street. They played it on the Astroturf at Linwood Sports Centre. But it was the Saints and we were there together and it was a profound bonding experience.

I looked into his beautiful blue eyes with a smile that said: 'My son, I love you and this is your birthright. Your mission, should you choose to accept it, is to carry on the great traditions of your father and your father's father and your father's father's father.'

And he looked back into my eyes with a grimace that said: 'I've pooed Napalm. This nappy will self-destruct in five seconds.'

He was not to have the same childhood as mine, going round grounds watching St Mirren being whupped from the minute he could walk; sadly, few clubs are sufficiently enlightened to have creches in the pressroom. Plenty don't even have pressrooms.

So the next time we went together was on a Sunday when he was six and that afternoon he would have been well within his rights to decide never, *ever* to watch football again.

By then his mother and I had parted and I had taken her advice to go and live in Falkirk. At least it sounded like Get Tae Falkirk. By chance we were to play my new local team in the B&Q Cup final – the mini-Scottish Cup for non-Premier League clubs – at Fir Park. Kenny was with me for the weekend and we decided we'd go with some of my Bairns-loving friends.

The advantage of that was we got to sit in the new stand behind the goals, a boon on a day when it rained cats, dogs, elephants and killer whales and when the wind blew like Louis Armstrong. Thousands of poor Saints fans were stuck standing in the open at the other end.

The wind and the rain blew right into our faces, however, and the cold bit deep. The wee man hated it. It didn't help that we got a 3–0 towsing, and with half an hour to go he was crying and wanting to go home and I couldn't blame him. But we'd come in a minibus and the guy with the keys was rows away and all I could do was go for endless Bovrils and try to keep the blubbering lump of anorak beside me from getting hypothermia, a turn of events which might have irked his mother a tad.

Eventually it was over and, once the Falkirk fans had rubbed it in by giving their heroes a standing ovation as they shivered through a lap of honour, we trudged back to the bus. I felt I'd let him down.

It was probably a year until he cracked a light about football again, but suddenly it was as if a lightbulb clicked on above his head. One second he didn't give the square root of a monkey's, the next he was – *da-daaaaaa!* – ST MIRREN MAN!

It started when he went to a pre-season open day at Love Street and won a signed ball in a prize draw. Next thing he wanted the strip. Then to go to games. Then a majority shareholding and a life-presidency and the mineral rights to the soil beneath the pitch. It all happened so fast.

He signed up for the Buddies Girls and Boys (shortened to the BGB, a slightly less sinister set of initials than the Killie Boys and Girls – to join you have to be a bisexual Oxbridge graduate with the negatives of a cabinet minister in bed with two hookers and a goat) and met with dozens of other excitable eight-year-olds before home games for five-a-sides in the gym beneath the new Caledonia Stand. Then they had pies and sat in their own section of the North Bank. He loved it.

Then, out of the blue, the club phoned his mother and asked if he'd like to be a mascot. I don't know who was more chuffed, him or me.

We were playing Dundee, as if you needed to ask. I was covering it for the radio station Scot FM and when he led the team out I was so choked I had to stop in the middle of my preview and hand back to the studio.

So he tossed the coin and the ref let him keep it, and, after the cops had stopped the Saints directors trying to prise it from his grasp with pliers, he went back to the dressing-room to get changed. By the time he came out again we were 1–0 down. Swines.

But from then on he was hooked and whenever we play in midweek I go with him and we have the time of our lives. And, believe me, times don't get better than taking your kid to the football.

5. YOUR KID GOING HIMSELF

Funny, isn't it? We whinged the faces off our folks to get to the football on our own, moaned that we were up to it, streetwise enough, that we were too old to go with Dad any more.

'All the other boys have been going on their own for years and they don't get into trouble.'

'Which other boys?'

'Er . . . Andy and Jim and Graeme and Brian and . . . er . . . Torquil . . . and . . . well, all of them.'

'But I see them there with their dads every week.'

'No, you don't, they just bump into each other.'

'What, on the bus into Paisley? And then again in the queue? And on the same bit of terracing?'

'Yeah, well, anyway . . . they're all starting to go on their own and they'll all laugh at me if I don't get to go on my own as well.'

They resist; but eventually, one magical day, we win the fight and the chains are broken and we go through all the sneaking drink in and being on the edge of the boxing and all the other stuff that turns us from kids into stupid kids.

And many years later, our own children come at us with the same pleas. And do we act groovy about it? Do we ruffle their hair and hand them their gate money and immediately give them our blessing the way our stuffy old folks didn't?

Do we chocolate.

I worried myself sick the first time Kenny went on his own. As I write this, he's in his second full solo season and I'm still not too comfortable with it. I keep worrying that all the things I swore would never, ever happen to *me* might happen to *him*. I have this picture of him as a naïve, lost little lamb; whereas I, of course, was a streetwise dude and king of my own vicious jungle. When, in fact, I couldn't have fought sleep, and got disorientated if Mum switched the bedroom furniture round.

At first, his mother would take him down to Love Street and go back for him at full-time. Then he talked her into leaving him at the bus stop. Then he started leaving her in the house and met his mates at the end of the street. He had stopped going with the kiddies club crowd long ago. Now he wanted to stand behind the goals, because if they got there before half two they got in for three pounds. He wanted to go down the front and shout the players over for their autographs while they warmed up, to queue for his own pie, to run with the lads.

By early last season I was just starting to get used to the idea when he phoned and said he was going away that Saturday. On the bus. *To Greenock!*

I mean, Greenock. The polis walk about in threes there. Jehovah's Witnesses tell *you* to get stuffed. I mean, Greenock, of all places.

He assured me his mate Sean's dad was going and that they'd be looked after and it'd be no sweat, but I'd been there many, many times and never once was it any less hairy than the back of Anne Widdicombe's hand.

That day I fretted and sweated and my mind wandered to all sorts of scenarios – especially when I heard on the tranny that we were winning and then that we had won. I couldn't relax till he came on the phone, still high as a kite from his big day out.

'Dad,' he said, 'you'll never guess what they did to us.'

My heart sank. Chased them? Threw bricks? Chopped up one of his friends for kebabs?

'They charged us *seven pounds* to go on the open end in the rain, Dad. How terrible is that?'

I had to say that, at that very moment, it was not so terrible at all.

6. GETTING MIDDLE-AGED AND BORED

It is to my everlasting regret that my dad wasn't at Hampden to see us win the Scottish Cup in 1987. But by then he had grown tired of going to the football, of getting soaked and disappointed and seeing the crowd's tolerance levels shrink and prices soar way beyond inflation.

He lost faith in St Mirren after they sacked Fergie. But, then, didn't we all? There are as-yet-undiscovered tribes in the depths of the Amazon jungle who wrote letters of protest the day the Great Man got the push.

Dad kept going for a while, though, because he always had and he saw us win the Anglo-Scottish Cup and qualify for Europe for the first time and sign players for a hundred grand and start acting the Big-Time Charlies. By then I had even started going to home games with him again. But on the day Chas and Di got hitched I started work, and when the new season began a couple of weeks later I got sent to cover Clydebank's games and pretty soon Dad started spending Saturdays in front of the fire.

In a way, I think he felt his job was done. He'd taken me when I was a kid and baptised me in the mysterious ways of Foot-Ball, fulfilled the rituals of the Sausages and the Beans, then watched me go off into the world on my own and was happy. Then again, maybe by then he just thought football was keech. A lot of blokes feel that way in their forties and fifties, when they take stock of their lives and don't like what they see. Suddenly nothing's as good as it used to be; not telly, not food, not movies. Kids don't have the same respect, neighbours aren't friendly any more, summer's are cold and beer's too warm. And bloody Waggon Wheels aren't as big. Or is that just me?

So they're looking at their life and the huge part in it that football has always played, and it's not good enough either. There's not the same characters, there's not the same skill, they're not allowed to tackle the way they used to, the ball's too light, the wages too heavy.

There's no proof of most of these things. Football's no worse today than it was when I was a kid. If anything, the players are fitter and faster and goalies no longer dive out of the way of shots like they used to; watch Real Madrid *v* Eintracht, allegedly the greatest game ever played, if you don't believe me. (If it is the greatest game ever, why do the goalkeepers dive entirely the wrong way every time a shot comes near them, or when a passback comes their way, or when they're tossing the coin before the start or when they're going for a slice of orange at half-time?) Keepers sucked then, even the keeper of the great Real Madrid side. They wore polonecks and bunnets as huge as poos laid by cows outside Sellafield, and when they *did* by some miracle go the right way for a shot, they dived *under* it.

Defenders? They didn't tackle; they put their foot against the ball and forced it against the opponent's foot and stood there, pressing, until their heads burst. When they slid in, they didn't so much telegraph their arrival as write a letter in beautiful copperplate fountain pen and have it delivered on a silver salver by a liveried flunky some several days before they reached the winger.

The winger, out of a sense of fair play, would stand crouched over the ball until the lumbering, shaven-necked oaf ploughed to within a yard or two, then casually flip the ball away with the boot nearest the touchline and gallop nimbly toward the bye-line, leaving the oaf to slide on across the cinder track, through the hoardings advertising Higginbottom's Dubbin (It's Great For Your Boots And Fine In A Stew), up an aisle of the stand, out through the back wall and plunge eighty feet into the carpark.

Teams would kick off and just wander forward for a crack at goal. Well, I say *crack*; with those huge boots and that dull, heavy ball, shots didn't exactly whistle through the air changing directions several times like in the 1986 Mexico World Cup. They sort of waddled goalwards like fat joggers.

Heading: Jimmy McGrory and Nat Lofthouse must have had bricks plastered into their foreheads to get the force they did when they attacked crosses. Every other player in the age of lace-up balls leapt like salmon, met it in full flight and sunk their heads four inches into the leather before watching it fall limply to the turf. At least the lucky ones did; the unlucky ones got the valve in the eye and their lids slashed open with a loose bit of lace. Aye, it were a man's game in them days.

So watch Eintracht *v* Real all the way through, then watch Brazil *v* Italy in the 1982 World Cup and decide which is the better game.

There was no golden age of football. There were probably people who watched Eintracht against Real Madrid who sighed that it was so-so, but wasn't a patch on Clyde beating Motherwell 4–0 in the 1939 Scottish Cup final, at which old-timers longed for a 1903 thriller between Third Lanark and St Bernard's. And the big talking point *that* day was whether or not the game had improved since the introduction of the penalty kick in 1891.

Everyone longs for what they can't have any more. It's like me and proper-sized Waggon Wheels. The fact is, despite any misgivings any of us may have over money or attitudes on the pitch, the environment in which we watch football at the turn of a new century is far superior to that of the 1960s or the 1930s or 1903 or 1891.

Almost every stadium is miles better than in the '60s and '70s when I first toured them. New TV techniques have brought the game to life for those who can't get out to matches. Those who do can take the family in the knowledge they won't be smacked on the head with cans.

When it comes down to it, your average bored fan having a midlife football crisis isn't really looking for the return of goalies in polonecks or the lace-up ball or open sewers for toilets or rattles and rosettes or even bigger Waggon Wheels.

I think they're mostly just looking for their youth.

7. GETTING OLD AND WEARING TWO HATS

Then, in the twilight of their years, many are reawakened to the joy of Foot-Ball. And, just to prove it, they moan their faces off about it to anyone who'll listen. Go to any ground – but especially those outside the Premier League – and you will find rows of whingeing pensioners taking out the frustrations of old age on the young and the fit.

At Arbroath, there is a lady of a certain age who always brings a bag of mixed sweeties for the press box and you think: what a lovely old soul. Then she proceeds to yell and scream at and fight with anyone who crosses her fiery-breathed path. Her eyes burn through the old blokes beside her if they dare disagree with an opinion, she melts the ref's whistle with abuse, puts the fear of death into kids who dare be seen as well as heard. She and her terrified compadres sit a couple of rows in front of the press seats on cushions kindly supplied by the club in an old tea chest.

To their left and down in the little standing paddock are three or four grizzled men of anything between 85 and 143, snarling and snapping and rasping at anything and anyone. They bawl at their own players, the opposition, the officials, the grass, the weather, the programmes. They are so loud, even at an age when their vocal chords should be covered in cobwebs, that their invective carries above the wind that whips Gayfield from August to May. It is the only thing that gets them all on the same side, that wind. Each agrees that old folk shouldn't be out in that weather.

Pensioner fans with sticks are a menace. If you were twenty and dressed like an Aberdeen Casual, there's no way they'd let you in with a three-foot length of knobbled beech tipped with a miniature rubber cosh. Yet at Links Park and Forthbank and Shielfield and all points round the country there are people to whom you wouldn't give the TV remote to being allowed to brandish these lethal weapons. For what is a stick in the trembling hands of an old person if he or she is not to waggle it to the endangerment of everyone within skull-cracking range? There are enough walking aids at Ochilview and Station Park and Palmerston to rope together and make an ark should Scotland ever be flooded as retribution for the excesses of Gerry McNee.

But the greatest example of old punters in full effect at the game has, sadly, been lost to progress. The day Broomfield was bulldozed, part of my education went with it. The stand at Airdrie's old ground was about as shallow as a TV weathergirl. It couldn't have gone back more than eight rows. When wee Doddy got sent off from the dugout – as happened just about every home game – he simply climbed up into the first row and was only four feet further away from the action than before. At the rear of the stand was the press box, a skelf-ridden bench with a desktop nailed on that made it so cramped even a dwarf like myself had his knees up to his chest. And the rest of the rows were taken up by the town's nonagenarian populus. That's ninety-somethings to you, chief. They were there whenever you arrived, even if you got there at half four on Thursday for a Saturday match. I don't think they ever went home. Maybe they were bulldozed along with the rest. If so, God rest their souls along with all their hats.

For just as when I started going to football alone I wore four scarves, none of these ancient Diamonds fans would be seen dead without a minimum of two pieces of headgear. Yes, they wore two coats each as well; but all old people do, *n'est-ce pas?* A woolly one underneath with a pakamac on top; but with the pakamac buttoned only at the neck. Two coats are part of the OAPs Charter (*Clause 25: Never venture into a densely populated public place without having a cat pee on you first*). But their hats . . . their hats made sure some former Airdrie shop owner today reclines on a mink-covered sun lounger on a private Caribbean isle.

First, they put on the bunnet. None of your Fergus McCann soft-wool-mix nonsense, by the way, nor your modern Nike cotton caper. No sirree, these bunnets were of solid Tweed, the kind that grates flesh like parmesan. Their heads must have looked like burst couches after years of polite doffing to passing ladies. These bunnets on their own were magnificent examples of the sadistic milliner's art. But *on top* of them came the Charlie Brown hats. Vinyl ones, corduroy ones, scratchy tartan ones; the material mattered not so long as they had Spaniel ear-flaps which could be securely tied underneath the chin. Not only did this ensure their bunnets were pushed ever further into their scalps like so many thorny crowns, but it also gave the acoustic effect of them wearing headphones. And thus they *shouted* absolutely bloody everything.

You know that horrible moment – and we've all had it at least once – when you're yelling a conversation above the music in a pub or a club and the music stops suddenly just when you get to the bit where you're hollering: '. . . and then I only went and followed through . . .'?

Well, that was every moment of every conversation overheard in the Broomfield stand, with the situation plainly made worse by the fact that the old codgers couldn't hear each other through their hat-flaps.

'HOW'S YER PILES, WULLIE?'

'WHAT??!!?'

'AH SAYS: "HOW'S YER PILES, WULLIE?"'

'QUARTER PAST TWO – BY THE WAY, HOW'S YER OOZING WOUND, TAM?'

'WHIT????'

'YER WAR WOUND – STILL OOZING PUSS, IS IT?'

On calm nights you can still hear their voices ringing around Airdrie's new Shyberry Stadium. They're not dead – just shouting.

I'd like to think that if my dad had got that far he'd have got the bug again and gone back to Love Street. Except without the two hats. But he died in 1995, so he's got to watch them from a seat higher up.

At least one thing's for sure. Wherever I am and whatever the result, he can always whisper in my ear that it could have been worse. And with any luck, he'll always be right.

Mind you, some days really try your faith . . .

TWO

PSYCHO

I'm at the back of the stand in a tiny football ground plonked in the middle of a public park like the Trumpton Bandstand. Away in the distance over the old doll's-house pavilion opposite, a ferry's in port, all big and white and gleaming in the sunshine that sparkles on the water like it's raining diamonds. There's not a ripple on the sea. It lies peacefully at the foot of the hills like a dozing dog.

I've got tea on my boot.

It's dribbled down the side of the poly cup I've chewed to bits round the edges, lemming-ed off the end and plip-plip-plipped onto my toe. And I'm just standing there looking at it, as if staring will make it go away.

Ever get a day like that, a day when you just can't snap out of it? When your heavy heart makes your feet drag and your brain's somewhere you've not been invited? You're in a mood blacker than Linford Christie locked in a coal bunker and nothing will shift it. They couldn't pull good humour out of your leaden soul with a crowbar.

I'd been that way since my eyes first opened. Normally on Saturdays I wake like Renton coming round from his overdose in *Trainspotting*. Only, my shot of adrenaline is football. Then I realise that those are the two cheesiest sentences ever thought of and crawl back under the duvet in embarrassment.

In truth, I wake on Saturdays the way I do every day; like an unusually feckless sloth coming round from a late night of lard-eating and morphine margaritas.

I *wanted* to write: 'From the second my eyes open, all I think about is the game. Mind racing against pulse and heart for World Bed Speed Record.' But that would be a lie.

Just as it takes a substitute twenty minutes to get into a game, it takes me half an hour to realise I'm alive, to un-Araldite the eyes and de-fur the tongue. To do the things guys do, like untangle the bits hair conditioner doesn't work for. Honesty. That's what life is all about.

And so, after half an hour semi-comatose, I swing my tightly muscled body from beneath the leopardskin cover of the heart-shaped vibrating waterbed and slide into the perfumed bath Ulrika has run for me before tiptoeing downstairs to breakfast on scrambled eggs and smoked salmon with my good friend Eddie Izzard.

Sure, so that's also a lie. Did you *really* think I'd have a leopard-skin cover?

That morning, though, I made my normal first-thing self look like Timmy Mallett.

That morning I just wanted it to be all over and for it to be tonight. For all the bad thoughts to disappear and things to have gone our way and to be back to normal. If you can ever *be* normal when you love a game that makes you as mental as football does.

I'd stomped about the house, ignored the papers, chucked half my breakfast in the bin, snarled and snapped and generally been as much fun to live with as a cockroach cloned from the genes of Jeremy Beadle and Pauline Fowler.

By the time I left there were CDs all over the carpet. I'd been on my knees at the rack (never did get round to putting it on the wall, so it's propped at a drunken angle between couch and telly; I'm about as handy as an all-night grocer's in a minefield) scrabbling in freshly ironed suit breeks for sounds. *Miserable sounds.*

Normally I'd listen to the footy previews on the way to the game. Sometimes Radio Scotland, more usually Radio 5. Because Radio 5 has Stuart Hall. Why don't we have a broadcaster in Scotland like Stuart Hall? Someone who can glue you to the tranny with reports like: 'Here at this modern-day Colosseum, the gladiators have torn each other limb from limb, leaving the ballboys to pick up the scraps as we catch our breath and fill our stomachs with finest mead served in pewter flasks by beautiful semi-naked hand-maidens.

'What a half . . . what a game . . . here we saw Blenkinsop bestride the midfield like a skinhead Colossus, there we marvelled as the jiggling and juggling of O'Reilly entertained the gasping crowd like a court jester in cycling shorts.

'Were this game a painting it would be *La Gioconda*, were it an opera it would be *Carmen* in the original French. If I could live my life all over again I should surely while the years away watching this game over and over.

'And with that, back to the studio with the scoreline Bury 0 Wigan 0 . . .'

The man's an artist. Bring him up here and he would make Brechin *v* Stenhousemuir on a wet Tuesday night sound like Man U beating Bayern in Barcelona.

Sadly, you can always *tell* in Scotland when a reporter on radio, TV or in a paper would rather be poking his/her eyes out with a fork than watching the game they've been sent to. Not Stuart, not old Mr *It's A Knockout*, not the man with the mock-Shakespearian delivery and the heartiest laugh since Sid James first saw Babs Windsor in a bikini.

Not enough people see beauty in all football any more but Stuart Hall does and, as far as I'm concerned, they should give him his own daily show on every radio station and TV channel until his message gets through.

This, however, was not a day even for he. This day I didn't want to hear about any other games, anyone else's problems, anyone else's hopes and fears. This was a day for travelling to music; grim music. Sad, morale-sapping, hang-yourself music. The Smiths? Too upbeat. Leonard Cohen is Black Lace. No, this day called for Elvis Costello going through his endless catalogue of songs about desolate love affairs and shattered lives. I took some Smiths anyway, just in case the mood lightened.

Last thing I remember is turning on the engine then flicking through *Blood and Chocolate* to 'I Want You', a searing tale of a man torn apart by images of the woman he loves cheating on him. He's asking if she called out his name as he held her down and pleading for her to say she never did it, not with *that* clown.

After that? I only know I must have gone first right, right and right again, left out of the gates and straight ahead to self-pitying oblivion. I was well past Ayr before I remember anything else. An hour and a bit at the wheel and not a single memory of another car, a traffic light, a roundabout. Blanko.

Anyone with a licence has had one of those drives when you go on to automatic pilot and then suddenly click back to manual and it scares you witless. Anything could have happened while you're somewhere else – or did God give you some hidden trip switch that would bring you back on line if an artic swerved into your path? I hope I never have to find out.

How many times have we come back to the real world with two tons of metal under our control and looked at the cars in front and behind and to the side and wondered how many others were looking at us wondering where *their* last hour had gone? Add to that all the hungover drivers and the drivers who've been E'd up and the drivers who can't sleep or who're as taut as piano wire and who simply can't drive very well, and you wonder how the hell the roads aren't like one big splattered pizza.

That day I could have had Dawn French naked on the bonnet, playing the banjo in a bath of custard and not cracked a light. Which is strange, as the image usually works a treat . . .

But, no, nothing. Square root of *nada*. Squiddly-poo until the middle of Girvan, ninety-odd miles away. I know I must have slid out one CD and banged in another, because when I came to, the miserable sounds had changed, but that's it.

My mind was in Stirling, fast-forwarding through a game that hadn't happened yet. And that, by the way, is no cheesy lie.

I imagined us snatching it in the last minute. No, scrub that – too heart-stopping a scenario. So I pictured us four up and cruising at half-time. Forget that – never going to happen. Then I saw *them* scoring and us piling forward like Zulus but never getting near their goal, like in your dreams when you chase things and never catch them, or try to run away but can't. Now *that* I could believe.

Then we were celebrating and players were dancing with fans, and people were crying with happiness; only then it dawned that the tears weren't of happiness but of anguish. And the players and fans weren't dancing, but holding onto each other for support in their grief.

All day I couldn't get it out of my mind that we were going down. It tore me up that I wasn't going to be there, even though I couldn't have handled being there.

And all the while I was listening to every heart-ripping, gut-wrenching, spleen-bursting, eye-gouging, feels-like-someone-reached-down-your-throat-pulled-your-dangly-bits-out-your-mouth-and-put-them-in-a-whirling-Magimix angstfest song you can think of. There was blood coming out the speakers.

Just by the superb chippy in Girvan I never remember the name of, a steel guitar intro'd the live version of 'Psycho'. The air disaster of songs, the plague of locusts of songs, the Pol Pot of songs.

You don't know it? You've never died. It is *the* most despair-ridden, soul-roasting number of all time – and, in a genre of songs that thrives on torment, that is saying something. It's about this bloke standing in his mother's kitchen, pouring his heart out about a ruined life. His wife's run off leaving him holding the baby and he can't take it any more. Thinks he's going mental and evidence supports the view.

> *You think I'm psycho don't you mama?*
> *I didn't mean to break your cup;*
> *You think I'm psycho don't you mama?*
> *You better let 'em lock me up . . .*

He's telling Mama how he saw his ex and her new man at a dance the night before and how, rather than talk the situation out in a civilised and consiliatory manner, he took the initiative by killing them both and burying them under a tree. As you do. His mama tells him to cuddle little baby Johnny's puppy, that'll cheer him up. But by now he's telling how he's had a dream about strangling little Johnny. Then he realises he's strangled the puppy. And, by the way, little Johnny too.

By verse four he's coughed to Mama that he'd been down the park and banjoed little Betty Clark from next door in a *sitting on a bench/holding a wrench* stylee. Not a bad day's work by any halfwit's reckoning.

And I'm thinking – hey, you think you've got problems? At least your team's not likely to be relegated by teatime, puppy-murderer. Then you click, as the big croaky-voice-and-steel-guitar climax swells, that he's been telling all this to a mama who by now is lying pan bread on the kitchen floor.

You think I'm psycho don't you mama?
Mama why don't you get up . . .?

This, sports fans, is a different kettle of chopped-up body parts altogether. I mean, anyone can lose the rag. Joke between friends, went too far, faults on both sides. But killing his ma? That's serious.

Maybe I've misjudged the boy. Maybe as well as all his other hassles his team are going down if they lose today. In which case I can't wait for 'Psycho II':

Ma team's just suffered relegation,
So ah've been and bludgeoned my remaining relations . . .

I'm just wondering how to get the boy Costello's phone number and do a publishing deal when some red-faced ned in an Astra behind me starts parping that the lights are green. So I go to move off and the car stalls and he parps again and I'm wrestling with the gears and he's going purple and I'm wondering if he realises I've just been listening to some very novel ways of getting rid of people who noise you up like he's noising me up right now.

First gear thuds back into the socket like a dislocated elbow, just in time. Further up the main drag, Astra-Ned turns right with a petulant flash of his lights that's wasted in the brilliant early May sun and I'm flicking the CD back to Track 18 0:00. Again and again and lots more agains.

That song obsessed me all the way to Stranraer. The most beautiful journey in football on a gorgeous lunchtime and I barely saw it. Ailsa Craig, the sparkling water, Ballantrae; usually it's windows down, sunroof up and I inhale them like vintage wines,* but now they went by as unnoticed as motorway lamp-posts.

---

*I say vintage wines, but I wouldn't know a cheeky South African chardonnay from a can of hairspray. But I couldn't think of anything else I inhale regularly. There's those big thick marker pens, I suppose. They're quite cool. So, let's say I usually inhale the beauty of the drive to Stranraer like a vintage thick marker pen, okay?

And all because of a game of football that hadn't happened yet a hundred miles away. That and a cheating wife and her fancy man and a little boy and his doggie and the girl next door and a poor silver-haired mama, each of them dead in a song.

Over and over Elvis wailed, darkening the black with every repeating murder. Outside, others saw the sun splitting the trees and bouncing off chilled-out water. But inside, with me and Elvis and the mass-murderer, it was deepest polar winter.

What kind of game is it that gets you into that state? And what forces you to make the link with mind-numbingly depressing music of the kind I was blaring over and over? What kind of game is it that twists your mind and your guts in equal measure, and knit your brows until Val Doonican could wear them as a cardy? How can it make your heart pound faster, your blood rush and your pulse do Cozy Powell playing 'Dance with the Devil'? How come the more we know about it, the more we love it, the more it involves us, the less we get to enjoy it when the chips are down? Or *is* that us enjoying ourselves? Dearie me, I rather fear it is.

And here I was, wiping the tea-soaked toe of my right boot on the back of my left trouser leg, looking out over the most beautiful scenery in football on a day when the only black cloud was hanging over my head.

Stirling Albion *v* St Mirren. Winner takes all, loser takes the drop. A game to ruin more than your day; it could wreck your season, your summer, your everything.

It had certainly ruined my day so far. Usually I love travelling to games. How else would most of us see so much of Scotland, of Britain, of the *world* without journeys to football? We never had a car when I was a kid. Uncle Sam (the kiddy-on uncle from Chapter One) or Uncle Billy (definitely a real uncle and the best a boy could have) took us everywhere.

Our council house in Foxbar – if you don't know it, a bohemian little hamlet in the hills above trendy Paisley; if you do, how come you still have thumbs with which to hold this book? – was only about twenty-five miles from Loch Lomond as the crow flies, but in Foxbar crows got shot and Luss might as well have been on the moon for all the chance there was of getting there.

Now? I know the streets in towns from Dingwall to Plymouth as long as they either have a football ground or you have to pass through them to get to one. I've been to every stadium in Scotland, to more than forty in England and have watched games in eleven other countries.

There's no point doing all that travelling, going to all those place and not enjoying it, not soaking it up. I love the whole thing, normally.

The first sight of the floodlights is always a buzz; think of how many skylines they dominate. Think of how many towns you know only because you've been to their football ground. Would the world know Stenhousemuir if not for football? Would fat, bearded men from Oslo go there and ring cowbells for any other reason?

Doesn't matter if it's the Stade de France or Cliftonhill: there's nothing quite like walking into a football ground, taking the stairs two at a time, desperate to get in and see it even if you've been there a hundred times before and there's not much worth seeing anyway.

I love watching empty stands fill, seeing the players warm up. It's as much a part of the day as the game itself. That's why watching on TV will never beat actually being there. Love seeing players prepare, sharing the whole thing from as near an hour before kick off as possible.

This day it was Stair Park, the little bandstand within a park. And I'm looking out over the sparkly sea and the big white ferry and the sunbathing hills and I should be as happy as any man could possibly be at his work. But I'm not. I'm going mental with worry, and I'm not alone. It's not just my team who are in trouble today. All over Scotland, all over Britain, Europe, the world and on any other planets with a sufficiently developed culture to have invented such a brilliantly simple addiction as football, thousands upon thousands are feeling the same as I am.

Everywhere the game is played they buzz awake without an alarm clock on matchday, they live the action a dozen times in their heads before a ball is kicked, scream and gasp and sweat and swear through ninety minutes where all but one of the players is helpless at any one time and even then he might not be too sure.

They're willing to suffer eighty-nine minutes and fifty-nine seconds of miserable, mundane, flaccid, grey, desperate awfulness in the hope of one second of magic which makes their afternoon, their day, their week – sometimes their *life* – worth while.

Yes, their very *life*.

(*Warning: The following subject may well crop up at many other points in this book.*)

Saturday, 16 May 1987, was wet, with the kind of drizzle that soaks right through to your bones. The game was grim, without pattern or excitement or flow. Then a long ball over the top sent a nineteen-year-old bottle-blond from up a close in Parkhead sprinting away from his marker and in one second he had hammered his shot into the roof of the net in front of us. If I had dropped dead then, they would have buried me with a smile on my face.

That goal won my team the Scottish Cup for the first time in my life and the moment will never leave me, not until the day I really *do* die. Ever since the first game I saw, I had wanted them to win the Cup and now they had.

You may be one of those people who say football is just a lot of men in daft shorts chasing a bag of wind about. In which case, my advice would be not to say it within M15 listening-device-range of someone who suffers the emotions described above. Although if you do think that way, it's unlikely you're reading this anyway, so I'm probably ranting at no one. But what's new?

If football *is* just men-shorts-and-bag-of-wind, then 'Yesterday' is just a Scouser singing a lot of words while three men accompany him on bits of wood and metal. Or TV is just a box with pictures coming out of it.

People who have no interest in football are free to like and dislike what they . . . well, like; people who claim to *know* absolutely nothing about the game are beyond me. How can something so huge, with so much media coverage and populist interest, with so much history and social influence, go on around them every day of their lives and not a single atom of its being touch them?

For instance, I have no interest in the computer on which I am writing this book apart from its use as a typewriter with a telly. But I still know roughly how it works and that it has things called RAM and memory and that it can be linked to something called the Internet even though I have no intention of ever being a Web-geek. It's called Being Alive. You don't think of the air in your lungs every time you breathe, but you at least know it's there. For me, football is as important as breathing. Now that *was* cheesy . . .

Anyway, if you're one of those people, you won't understand why seeing my team win the Cup meant so much to me. But what else does a working-class kid get to look forward to all his life? Losing his virginity? Getting a job? Marriage? Mortgage? Children? False teeth? Retirement? Death?

Football gives whole communities something else to dream of, something that touches you as deeply as any of the great milestones of human existence. Something you don't need to be rich or privileged to be part of. It is the only kind of socialism that truly works.

And now here I was eleven years on from our cup win, give or take a fortnight, and the point of all this angst is that our team was now on the brink of relegation to the Second Division. Which would be the end. Full stop. They would JCB us into oblivion and make Love Street a carpark.

Next week's final game was at home to Dundee, already crowned champions. Today, Stirling needed the win to have any chance of staying up. A draw did no one any good.

Never once did I even contemplate asking to cover that game. As a fan, yes, no danger. But working . . . I've had a phobia about covering our games since the '87 semi when Frank McGarvey beat Hearts in the last five minutes and I was almost out the press box window before someone grabbed my jacket. Remember the old Hampden press box? It was suspended something like two hundred feet above the track. You could have taken out a sub with a well-aimed pea from that height . . .

I couldn't go up there for the final. Stood on the terracing in my suit and coat, never taking the notebook in pocket out. It would all be etched in the mind. Still is. I've got it on video, but I never watch it. If I did I'd see how duff the game was. Memory's better than Memorex.

Our Cup final and the 1966 World Cup final are the only two

videos I have which I've never watched, but 1966 stays in the box for different reasons. Bought it so I could tell Englishmen I had it; wouldn't give them the satisfaction of putting it on.

You too, eh? Told you football made us mental . . .

So where am I? That's right, Stranraer. Only my mind's taken a wrong turning and headed for Stirling. Even by my standards I'd got here early, half past one. At Ballantrae I'd passed the Livingston team coming out of a restaurant after lunch.

Why Stranraer? Just because, okay. Because it's the biggest game of their season. If they beat Livingston, who will be promoted if *they* win today, a little miracle is on the cards.

On the first Saturday in February, when they lost at home to Stenhousemuir, Stranraer had been second bottom of the league. Their manager, Campbell Money, called it the lowest point of his career. He was ready to accept the sack.

Money is one of my heroes; that is to say he played in that 1987 Scottish Cup final (yes, it's that game again). One of the bravest and most-kicked-in-the-head keepers I ever saw. Carted off seven times for us at the last count. Used to be a cop, so they call him Dibble. He gave eighteen years to St Mirren, but they only ended up doing to him what all football clubs do. They called him in, told him someone or other had asked to sign him and that they had accepted. The message was clear: take it or leave us. Then he found out that Stranraer, for it was they, actually wanted him as manager. He didn't fancy it one bit, but took it because he read the gypsy's warning that he had no future with the club for whom he'd got his brains bashed out above and beyond the call of duty.

In his first season, they survived relegation by the skin of their teeth. In his second, they won the League Challenge Cup with a backs-to-the-wall performance in the final against St Johnstone; but in the bread-and-butter they ended up minutes from the drop in the final game before an own-goal saved them.

So come February 1998, Money had just about had enough. He still lived near Paisley, a hundred miles from his office, and was piling up travelling-salesmen miles just to take abuse on a Saturday. After that Stenhousemuir game he could see no way back. Then he picked up the phone to Alex Smith, the man who managed St

Mirren to the Scottish Cup (see, kiddies – I promised it would be mentioned many times in the book) for a shoulder to cry on.

Football people are like that. They turn to each other for solace the way wronged women do. They need to share experiences with a like mind, because things happen in football that don't happen in any other job. Few jobs are as precarious; for a player because of injury and fickle team selection, and for a manager because of chairmen with itchy trigger-fingers. It's all black or white, joy or despair, a new contract or the sack. A manager whose team wins with a last-minute own-goal is a good manager; a manager whose team pound the opposition and *lose* to a last-minute own-goal is a bad one. A player with an injury is a lonely man, so he will seek out another player who has or had the same injury and ask how *he* was treated, how long *he* was out. Footballers may look smart and swaggering, sophisticated young groovers about town, but as far beneath the surface as mud in a cut they are remarkably insecure. When they're together, all for one and one for all, there's a spirit that binds them which I envy so much. To be in a dressing-room every day, on the training pitch, in the treatment room, to share the patter – however banal it might seem when taken out of context – is something I always wanted to do. But when they lose, when it's going wrong and the fans are cat-calling and the press are dropping hints and asking chairmen to give out votes of confidence . . . who'd be in the game then? Especially as a manager?

It is that isolation which makes them turn to like minds. And doing it precisely when Campbell Money did probably not only kept him in his job but set up one of the happiest endings I have ever known in the game.

By the end of his conversation with Alex Smith, Money was bouncing again. Smith told him to get his head up, to work his way through it. Stay strong and the break would come when he least expected it.

And so it came to pass that the following Saturday, on a rain-sodden Boghead pitch, Stranraer got a penalty against the run of play against leaders Clydebank and came away with a 1–0 win. They never looked back and went on the best run of form of any team in Britain bar Arsenal to haul themselves up the table. *Amen.*

Now, 180 minutes from the end of the season, after just two defeats in more than a dozen games, they had a genuine chance of promotion.* Money wandered out of the tunnel, nervous. He gets tense before games, so tense you almost reckon he's thinking the worst so winning will be all the sweeter. It's as though he feels he'd be letting everyone down if he came over all up-for-the-cup if they then didn't get the result – which is ridiculous, because even if they lost their last two games his would have been the performance of a messiah.

Yet, during the week I had phoned to suggest that, whatever happened now, their season had been a success. He nearly bit my head off. 'If we don't make it now, I'll be gutted,' he had snapped. 'We've come too far. It'd kill me.'

I think he might also be as worried about St Mirren as I am, but it's not the right time to ask. I might as well inquire if he'd like to skewer me on a fence-spike. Those last hours before a game are when many managers make caged lions with thorns in their paws look mellow . . .

A TANGENT

Years ago, Walter Smith called me one Saturday lunchtime, raging. He demanded to know if I had sold some story to a Sunday paper about Chris Woods being drunk on the plane home from an England game. I told him I knew nothing about it, which was true. He told me never to phone him again, which I hadn't.

Next time I saw him he acted like an old pal; in my experience that's how he always acts after dishing out a bollocking. Some may call that cowardice or rudeness, but in the complex and ulcer-creating world of the football gaffer, very few man-management rules apply. It is a career I wouldn't take up for Lottery-win wages. It is all but impossible.

All week they work with players, teaching them, training them,

---

*Stenhousemuir, who went second top after that game in February, had slid into the relegation zone and would go down on the final day of the season. I believe the phrase is That's Fitba'.

encouraging them, moulding them; if you're a part-time boss like Money, only twice a week. If the players can get off their work.

They spy on opponents to spot their weaknesses and then pick a team to exploit these. Then injuries wreck the plans, or their main striker spends all Friday trying in vain to remember why God gave him feet. There is so much about which managers can do nothing.

The master of anxiety and paranoia was Jim McLean, manager of Dundee United for twenty-one years. On a European trip to play Dutch side Vitesse Arnhem in 1990, he gave a press conference within earshot of two players having a game of table-tennis, one of whom was Darren Jackson. He told the press Jackson would not play. We filed the story, then took our places at the game in time to see Jackson run out in the No.10 shirt.

We were furious. After the game, which United lost 1–0, I was elected along with another reporter to chin McLean. We asked him why he had told us a lie. He blew up. It was none of our business; who were we to accuse him of lying?

He was last on the bus back to the airport. He took his seat at the front, then bounced back up immediately and headed for me. Ding ding, round two? Wrong. He reached into his jacket pocket, pulled out a scatter of paper – torn beermats, bits of fag packet, scraps from a notebook – and spread it out on an empty seat.

'Look,' he said, 'look at that – I've changed the team so often in the last couple of days. And look, look at that one [he waved a bit of beermat like Chamberlain coming back from Munich] . . . Jackson's in it. And in that one. Then he's out again. Honest, I didn't lie to you. If you want, I'll phone your sports editors tomorrow and tell them.' And he did.

A strange, complex man from what I know of him (which he would say is nothing). Yet his attitude is typical of the football obsessive – convinced that no one else cares as much, that no one else knows as much, that no one has the right to question.

Many successful football people find it hard to express themselves to those on the outside; the ones who talk freely to the media are rarely the ones with cupboards full of silver.

McLean and his brother Tommy, Walter Smith (who learned his trade under Jim at United), Alex Miller, Kenny Dalglish: if they and others like them could spend their working lives without talking to the press they would be the happier for it. They see no purpose in trying to explain their tactics or decisions to reporters, or in telling them who has a hamstring injury.

Then there's your Ron Atkinson. Big Ron. Atko. Mr Beaujangles. Or, as I like to call him, the jammiest sod who ever bulled his way into a job.

The first thing Atkinson did in every job was to get the media on his side. Be open, give out his phone number to anyone who asked, and anyone who didn't. Every after-dinner speaker quotes his quip that 'you can phone me any time as long as it's not during *The Sweeney*'.

Arf arf.

Then he'd pour the drinks and nudge and wink and the media would all go away saying what a great bloke he was. And he would laugh up his sleeve, knowing he had friends for life who would never stitch him up. Because football people collect brownie points from the media, like air miles, and at some point they have to cash them in for an even break. Some take theirs to the counter and don't have enough for a toaster. Others, like jingly-jangly, laugh-a-minute Atko, can buy their way out of the tightest corner since Damon Hill drove a juggernaut in the Monaco Grand Prix. And then start earning all over again.

Does that make my game sound shallow? Maybe it is. Maybe we see too much black and too much white. But a guy like Atko can float from job to job and from pay-off to pay-off, cracking jokes and popping bubbly, and never actually be pinned down on why he keeps getting invited back when his track record stinks.

Atko is also the inventor and copyright-holder of Manager-Speak, a language adapted from the guff politicians spout so they can't be accused of a no-comment but which ensures they never actually say anything.

'*Atko, your team lost 7–0 today, their ninth defeat in a row. The crowd was down to 357 with another 45,789 outside brandishing burning torches and shouting "Death to Atko". How do you feel?*'

'Well, Brian, you know the game – it's all about tickets and lotteries. It's about setting your stall out early bells, chucking your towel on the sunbed and making sure Jerry doesn't get there first.'

'*Yes, but about that defeat . . .*'

'Brian, I said to the lads, I said: "Lads?" and they said: "What?" and I said: "Lads? If you can keep your head when others are losing theirs, you're obviously too thick to realise there's a crisis on."'

'*Meaning?*'

'Meaning I've gone back stick on them, done a blindsider, picked up a beanbag and thrown the other way from me empty hand for the dog to chase.'

'*What?*'

'I've been in, got sacked and had £200,000 compen transferred to me offshore account in Jersey. Funny old game, Brian. Fancy a top-up?'

'*Atko there, dumped by his third club this week. Lovely bloke.*'

I think I prefer the Jim McLean school. I'd rather managers genuinely said nothing than talked for half an hour and *still* said nothing. Then we could go away and write what *we* thought and they would have no comeback.

I also believe journalists should not accept waffle. They should either ask more questions – questions managers can't dance around – or bin bland quotes, ignore them, and write what *they* think. Newspapers have become too reliant on quotes and not enough on saying what needs to be said, reflecting what the fans are thinking. And, in my experience, when you hit the nail on the head, you get far more reaction than if you do the full Atko Linguaphone Tape bit.

Anyway, all of the above is one of the main reasons I love covering games further down the leagues. They actually welcome you to their grounds, and players want to talk to you, to see their names in the papers. Some players at the top end really couldn't give a monkey's whether you wrote about them or not, because the second they signed their contracts it didn't matter what anyone said about them or did to them: they were minted.

In the bottom three divisions, it's different. Guys need to know they're doing well, need the lift of seeing their name in print. These are either full-time boys on no more than factory wages or – far more often – part-timers whose real money comes from a nine-to-five job.

There are players in Scotland getting as little as fifteen pounds a week from the game. To me, these boys *are* football – far more, at least, than the Billy Bigtimes who don't care what colour the strip is as long as the hundred-pound notes are pink.

AND NOW BACK TO THE ACTION

At Stranraer that day there were storemen and students and salesmen, a bloke who works for Asda and another who lugs crates of lemonade round boozers. The only home-town boy, Keith Knox, is a postie. The rest train together twice a week in the Glasgow area and travel on a team bus to home games.

Stranraer are arguably the smallest club in the country. Stair Park holds five thousand at a push. Until a couple of years ago its only stand was that tiny doll's-house across from me, with seating for maybe a hundred people on pigeon-pooed wooden benches. There's still a grass bank behind one goal.

Their players are fifty pounds-a-week part-timers and Campbell Money had long since accepted they would stay so even if they went up. They are run by a committee who take it in turns to be chairman. Graham Rodgers, a bustling little bloke with a hunched back and boundless enthusiasm, has 180 minutes of his reign left. They need drive like his down there, well over an hour's car journey from the nearest opposition. The town's more of a staging-post for the hordes of Old Firm fans who arrive from Ireland on the ferry every week.

They're not demonstrative down here, more like Irish country folk in nature than Scots. They have a lilting accent that swaps 'l' for 'r' in a reverse of the clichéd stand-up comic's Jap. Listen to Colin Calderwood, their most famous son, and you'll know what I mean. It takes a lot to get them excited. But somehow, Money and Rodgers and all the part-timers and the committee men were getting them there. And now came Livingston.

THE STORY SO FAR

Livingston were as far away on the scale as you could get from Stranraer in that season's Second Division. Formed when straight-talking self-made man Bill Hunter dodged endless flak by moving Meadowbank Thistle from Edinburgh's windy Commonwealth Stadium to a site in the nearby new town, they are a club of massive potential. With their shiny, 7,500-seat ground with built-in night-club and full-time players coming out of every orifice, they looked stick-ons for promotion under Jim Leishman; but, just to be sure, ex-Celtic directors Dominic Keane and Willie Haughey had recently stuck a fortune in the kitty to strengthen the team for what looked like the formality of the run-in.

Their cause was helped by long-time leaders Clydebank shooting themselves in the foot and announcing plans to quit Scotland for Dublin. Bankies fans turned on the team because they couldn't get at the owners, most of whom had barely seen a match. For eight games the side could barely put two passes together, never mind get a result. I watched them at home to East Fife one howlingly wet Wednesday night – I say 'home', but they had none; they were sharing rickety Boghead with neighbours Dumbarton – and the abuse aimed at the players was unbelievable. Their own supporters laughed at their every mistake, booed efforts on goal. When East Fife scored, they cheered and enjoyed it so much they cheered twice more as it ended 3–0. Bizarre.

Now the smart money was on them maybe – maybe – hanging on for second place, but on leaders Livingston taking the title. Stranraer were third, still good-priced outsiders.

AND BACK TO THE ACTION AGAIN

At two the teams were still mixing on the park, conspicuous in their suits, carrying rolled-up programmes. Soon they'd wander back in and change for work and reappear to warm up. This is when I really get up for every game. This is where I have to snap out of it today. No matter where you are, no matter the game, World Cup final or a meaningless Third Division fixture they're only playing because they have to, this bit is always the same. Even on public parks, this bit is the same. The build-up never changes, only the prize at the end. This is the bit where you wish you were a player.

I've come down from the back of the stand to wait inside the mouth of the tunnel. I chat to Leish and Bill Hunter, say a few words to Campbell, wish good luck some of the players as they head back to the dressing-rooms.

Then I wandered back up the steps and read the programme and waited for them to come back out and warm up. I love the warm-up, love trying to guess the line-up by seeing who's working up a sweat and who's hanging around the fringes looking disappointed. Subbies never quite look part of it all. When I were a lad there was only one substitute on each team, hanging about like a spare one at a wedding. Now there're three, five or more, so at least they're not Johnny No-Pals. They laugh at their own jokes and look self-conscious as they stretch for possibly no reason.

Does anyone else get the hump with those formation running-and-jumping routines? If teams aren't together by forty-five minutes to kick-off they sure as hell won't be when the whistle blows. They should be left to cross and shoot and pass, to do their own thing, so you could tell more about who's up for it and who's not. Players can hide in the formation routines, do just enough and no more. But miss a cow's backside with a banjo at shooty-in and everyone knows.

Then you watch them disappear a second time, some waving to the growing crowd, others ignoring their personal name-check. Don't you hate it when you shout 'Wullie, Wullie give us a wave' and he doesn't? How much effort would it take?

Then it's that time when everyone in football everywhere is restless. That limbo time from ten minutes to kick-off through to the first whistle. Fans make small talk or stand alone with their thoughts or nip to the loo. Press people check their laptops are plugged in or their pens are working or phone their mothers. (Maybe that last one's just me. I usually phone mine just before the game. But everyone should – phone their mum, that is, not mine; although she's always glad of the chat – because it would reduce crowd tension enormously.)

And down in the dressing-rooms the unease is at its greatest. I spent the day with Ross County when they played their first-ever league game, at Cowdenbeath in 1994. Went on the bus, did lunch, sat in on the team-talk, even broke SFA laws and stood in the dugout with gaffer Bobby Wilson. One of the best afternoons ever. Be honest, it's where we all want to be – mixing with the players, with the roar of the Deep Heat and the smell of the crowd. Few of us are fans by choice; it's a very, very distant second best to being out on the pitch.

I got totally involved with County that day, so pumped for them and so utterly elated when they won 2–0. Yet they had meant nothing to me before I stepped onto the team bus at half past ten that morning.

What a life it must be when you are a footballer and you win. Nothing on earth to touch it – there's being a winner in other sports, I suppose, but none of them matter. Not like football does.

The final few minutes in the dressing-room that day seemed to last forever, and every other player I've asked says it's always the same. They sit and fidget or crouch to stretch muscles, manager pacing like a caged animal, waiting for the bell or the knock on the door that releases a week's worth of energy and planning and waiting and worrying. Some hide in the loo, reading the programme from cover to cover to kill time and get some peace. Some get so nervous they vomit themselves ready. No one but the truly committed fan would understand why it gets to them *that* much. What kind of game is it that makes you chuck your Weetabix in the name of enjoyment?

The subs, as in the warm-up, seem almost embarrassed to be in the dressing-room. They sit huddled together, whispering among themselves, not wanting to draw attention, not really feeling like One Of The Boys. Football teams are like that; if you're in, you're in; and if you're not, an invisible barrier comes down between you and the rest. (It's funny after games, watching the injured or the dropped hanging around outside the dressing-room in their suits, listening for the mood behind the door. There seems to be an official length of time set down in their contracts before they're allowed gingerly to try the handle and risk popping their head round.)

Then, when the moment comes to go out, they all stand and breathe deeply and shake hands and roar and clap their hands. Studs click-clack, the gaffer stands by the door to give them all a personal good-luck message, and out they go, stretching neck muscles and blowing hard like boxers swaggering to the ring.

They leave behind an empty dressing-room, one of the most useless things in the world. A dressing-room without players in it is just an empty space, like a postman who is made redundant is just called Pat.

It's the time players long for and, up in the stands, we share their excitement. Thousands of eyes fix on the tunnel, watching for them coming out of the darkness – or watching the fans *opposite* the tunnel for *them* seeing the team appear.

Then, the tannoy fanfare for the entry of the gladiators (most grounds have their own pet tune; Everton play the theme from *Z-Cars,* while at Love Street, for some reason, they play the music from *The Professionals*) before the music fades away out of respect for the real business.

That roar that comes up, all the different shouts of encouragement from thousands of throats merging into a sort of *whhhhhhoooooo-aaaaarghhhh* noise. Players jogging on the spot, turning to each other and clapping or clenching fists, desperate for the off.

Then the ref blows and waves them forward like a traffic cop and nothing else in the world matters. All the death and misery and crime and flood and scandal, all the worry over bills and kids and women, for ninety minutes they all happen to other people. People who don't have football.

I'm watching more than who's on the ball; I'm trying to track who's running off it. Track who's not. Trying to form a pattern. Trying to second-guess the man on the ball about what he's going to do next. Working out what's coming. Love it when you're right, love it more when you're surprised.

Keep an ear on what's happening elsewhere. Hate it when I hear my team have lost a goal, more so even than when I see it happen. You feel so helpless listening on the tranny – or, worse, hearing it from someone you always reckon is gloating at your misery – and why not – I'd gloat at theirs. As if you could do anything about it even if you were sitting at Love Street or wherever they were playing. Always hate when we lose, wherever I am, whatever I'm doing. Spoils the weekend.

If it's possible, I always stand at the game, find a gangway with nothing to block the view. McDiarmid Park's good for that, on the TV gantry that runs next to the press box. Or in the little passage that divides the press seats at Brockville. And Livingston have a rail you can lean on outside their box.

Most new grounds, Scottish ones at least, included press boxes as an afterthought. You get what was obviously meant as an executive box for eight people, and there's twenty elbowing each other out the way as they try to work. And because these boxes are behind glass and built into the back of the stand, you can't see all the way along the touchline below. I usually go outside at these grounds. The view's better and you get more atmosphere. That and the fact that I can't stand sitting at football, especially when I'm working. You can't follow it properly if you're sitting down, can't move with it. And how can managers watch from the dugout, from so low down? It's no wonder they lose the rag; they're too close, they get too involved. No perspective.

Some try sitting up in the stand, but usually after twenty minutes you see a flash of coat-tail as they come down through the bowels and emerge onto the track to be where the action is. But the manager, the guy who has to make the big calls, should stay upstairs, watching the whole flow.

At half-time you hear the tannoy man – I have never yet heard a tannoy woman – read out the scores, then catch reports on the tranny. Cup of tea. Never Bovril. Back in place before the teams come out again.

Check the watch throughout the second half; wish great games would never end, wish bad ones would explode. Goals, chances, red cards, anything to make it worth while. Curse people who go home early. Why don't they go and live in a cemetery?

Take Rangers fans. They rush to their seats as the teams come out, stream to the God Bless The Queen Mum Sausage-Roll Kiosks ten minutes from half-time, wander back with the second half already started and make for the exits when there's still quarter of an hour to go. It's like they're fidgeting there, going: 'Come on, come on – this game's getting in the way of my busy day's queuing for junk food and sitting in traffic.' What do they do on other special occasions – like their wedding day? Stand outside the church smoking and talking to their mates till they hear the minister start the service? Then wander in, making sure they go along every row to make people stand up? Disappear to Burger King before the end of the first hymn, come back just into the vows and run off as soon as the ring's on to avoid the crowds? You watch them go and you wonder if they do the same at movies – leave ten minutes early. Do they see the rowing-boat disappear over the horizon in *Titanic* and decide: 'Ah well, Leonardo's pan bread and Kate Winslet's not getting rescued – might as well split'? Do they think *Pulp Fiction* ends when John Travolta is shot?

Deep breaths, son. Stay cool.

Ooohhhhhhhhhhmmmmmmm . . .

That's better.

Anyway, long after they've gone, I'm watching the ref check his wrist then look for nods from the linesmen. (Whoever came up with the name 'assistant referee' needs slapped.) Then it's all over.

And I'm drained.

By six on a Saturday I'm fit for nothing. Anti-social. Done in. Even when we've won or there's a night out on, I'll start with great intentions of yeeha-ing then chuck it before the rest have warmed up. Football is all on Saturdays.

Football rules me. Drives me. Makes me mental.

This day, more mental than ever.

ANOTHER TANGENT

Tea. Now there's something that needs sorted at football grounds. What is it with those little brown ready-made cuplets, with their mixed-up brown powder, milk powder and something that looks like sugar but without the sweetening effect?

These little kwik kups (have you noticed how everything which is time-saving but guff is spelled phonetically? It's the law) fit into each other like Russian dolls and come apart to be filled with a sploosh of boiling water into a mush that, no matter how long you stir it, always has a mole of brown gunge left on the surface.

I've stirred these kwik krap kups until the spoon has dissolved in my hand and still that brown bit refuses to disappear. Then you take a sip and before there's any sensation of taste, the sheer *heat* of the thing rasps your tongue. And when you eventually get enough feeling back in the tip to try another sip you realise there *is* no taste.

Some places charge you a quid for this privilege. For that money, they could afford to give you Earl Grey in porcelain mugs personally signed by Sir Cliff Richard. It's the most scandalous mark-up of anything you will ever buy. A teabag costs around 2p, a large polystyrene cup about one-tenth of a penny, and half a pint of hot water the square root of sod all. I'd accept them charging ten bob for a real, handmade poly cupful with real milk and real sugar. So it was a little treat to get exactly that at Stranraer, only for 35p. Magnificent. Five stars in the *Psycho's Good Football Refreshments Guide.*

THANK YOU FOR ALL YOUR ATTENTION

So I've got my real live beverage and I'm leaning on the wall at the entrance to the top row, looking out over the doll's-house stand again to the ferry port and the sea and the hills and the golden sunshine. For a while I even forget about what has made me mental all the way down here. Then I reach into a coat pocket and pull out a tiny radio, plug it into one earphone and tune to Radio Scotland. Just in time.

'. . . *And at Forthbank this afternoon, it's dog-eat-dog as Stirling Albion and St Mirren fight it out at the bottom of the First Division. Defeat for either side means almost certain relegation. Reporting, someone whose voice gives away quite clearly that they'd rather poke their eyes out with a fork than be there . . .'*

There's tea on my boot again. I pull out the phone and dial a Paisley number.

'Kenny? Dad. Okay?'

'*Hmmmm . . .*'

'What you thinking?'

'*We'll win.*'

'Yeah?'

'*Yeah. No problem. Three-nil.*'

'Hope so. Who'll score?'

'*Yardley, McGarry and Mendes . . . no, Yardley'll get two.*'

'You listening to the radio?'

'*Yeah, but I've got Ceefax on as well.*'

'Phone me if you hear anything before I do.'

'*Okay. Bye.*'

'Bye.'

Kenny was eleven then and went to all the home games, but didn't get away yet – maybe next season, if he fancies treks to Alloa and Arbroath. No, trust the boy, he says no problem. We'll still be playing Morton and Falkirk next year. Hibs, too, by the look of it. Maybe even Stranraer.

Their players are out warming up now, in their dark-blue drill tops and white baggy shorts and blue socks with red turnovers. Livvy are in gold and black, like their fans. Stranraer's don't really wear colours. They all seem either to be old blokes or kids; maybe only those too young to know better or too old to care come and see them.

Livvy's fans are swarming in, filling up the doll's-house and milling on the grass verge, sprawling like it was a picnic. Some are even sunbathing. In the doll's-house, someone has unfurled a huge banner with 'Watford' at the top and 'Livvy' at the bottom.

There's maybe a thousand in by ten to three, but the atmosphere's crackling. They all know how big this one is. They all know what might be at quarter to five. Livvy are sitting on 59 points, almost there. Clydebank are on 56, Stranraer on 55. It's hard not to get dragged along with the excitement of it all. But my head's trying.

It's telling me not to enjoy it, to remember there's something far more important to think about. Some far less enjoyable.

Kenny phones me back. '*All right, Dad?*'

'Nope.'

'*Me neither. I'm nervous.*'

'Me too. But it'll be okay.'

'*I know.*'

'We'll win. Three-nil.'

'*I know.*'

'Phone me.'

'*Okay.*'

'The teams are coming out here. [I'm shouting now above the noise] PHONE ME.'

'*Okay.*'

It wasn't much of a first half, here or at Stirling. At least, it can't have been at Stirling because the radio never flashed across to the game there once. Here they fenced with each other, banged it back and forward, probed nervously and cleared the way they were facing. A thousand hands went up to shield eyes time and again as the ball soared into the sun.

I stood at the back of the stand, drinking more tea and chewing more poly, watching it ping left to right to left to right like a game of tennis. A goal was only going to come from a defensive error.

Keith Knox ploughed into Livvy's six-foot six-inch keeper Ian McCaldon as yet another punt hung. Knox stayed down. Yesterday he'd had stitches taken out of a wound from last week's game at Queen of the South. Now it was gaping again. He went off, shirt collar stained red. Came back five minutes later, his head swathed in a huge white bandage with a little bullet-hole circle of blood at the front.

Half-time came with no more mishaps. Nil-nil. The person who would clearly rather be poking his eyes out with a fork was telling me it was nil-nil at Stirling, too. Kenny phoned to confirm it. *What kind of game is it that compels an eleven-year-old to sit in front of a page of Teletext on a blazing Saturday afternoon, willing a 0 to change to a 1?*

Ten minutes after half-time, a ball broke loose to Stranraer midfielder Duncan George and he hammered it first time from the edge of the box, high and wide of McCaldon, bulging the net in front of the Livvy fans on the verge. Of despair.

Old men and wee boys danced and shouted and cheered like in the *Victor*. All they needed were flat caps to wave and rattles to twirl. Campbell Money cavorted on the track, jacket flaps flying and tie hanging over his shoulder like Pete Sampras's tongue.

The phone rang. '*Dad, Dad – it's a goal!*'

'That's right, one-nil Stranraer.'

'*No, Dad – a goal for us!*'

In the excitement here I had missed it on the radio. I closed my eyes and heard the cheers around me fade into the distance.

'*Dad! You there, Dad? Dad!*'

'I'm here, it's just noisy. Who scored?'

'*Hugh Murray. Hit it from twenty-five yards. He's been booked for his celebrations.*'

Booked for his celebrations? They could put him in a Turkish prison for all I cared. *We'd scored.* Half an hour and a bit to go and we were nearly there.

'Brilliant, wee man. Fantastic. Phone me if anything else happens, okay?'

'*Okay!*'

I don't think I'd ever heard him so happy.

Down on the track, Money was yelling above the rising din, making adjustments, telling the players to calm down. The most dangerous time for any team is straight after they've scored, when they're too high to remember how to defend. He leaned forward, hands cupped like a megaphone and screamed something that either no one on the pitch heard or which they ignored. He yelled again, then swung a punch at the air in the frustration of not getting his message across.

I wanted to yell down to him: 'Dib, we've scored! Shug Murray's scored!' I kept waiting for him to look up so I could make a '1' and a '0' with my fingers, but then he might have thought I was talking about Clydebank's game with Queen of the South. That one was also 1–0, to the Bankies.

If it all stayed this way, Stranraer would go into the last day needing one of the top two to drop points. If it all stayed this way, St Mirren would at least go into the last day breathing.

The radio told me nothing more. The phone didn't ring again. Livvy piled forward chasing the goal that would put them up tonight.

On seventy-three minutes, Stranraer broke free, a ball bobbled in the box, and Isaac English, a boy brought up round the corner from me, swung a leg and put it in off the underside of McCaldon's bar.

Bedlam. Money leapt higher than I ever saw him reach as a keeper. Old men hugged wee boys, players danced and punched air and made wild *yaaaafuuuuinbyoooteee* faces. Money turned round and raised both fists to the crowd.

Then the radio said Queen of the South had equalised. The news spread out from those who had trannies to those who didn't and, as mental arithmetic sunk in, a few cheers went up. Then a roar. Then it was bedlam again. If it all stayed *this* way, Stranraer would go second, a point above Clydebank. And then it would all be in their own hands away to Clyde next week.

I phoned Kenny. There was no change on radio or Teletext. I'd call him back at the end. We were two minutes over time at Stair Park when the phone rang. '*We've won, Dad! One-nil!*'

And I noticed the sun and the ferry port and the hills and the beauty all over again. We still had a chance. It was in our hands.

Now it was also in Stranraer's. The whistle had gone and they were dancing and running and punching the air and Money's jacket flaps were flying and the Livvy players were forlornly applauding their fans and the Watford/Livvy banner got rolled up and everyone was gone by the time the bloke who'd rather be poking his eyes out with a fork had told me what I already knew about my team.

All the worrying was over, for a week at least, and now it hit me. *Drained.*

I was slumped against a wall in the tunnel, waiting to speak to the players, when Campbell came out of an all-singing, all-dancing dressing-room. He was chuffed to bits. When he had said his piece to the handful of waiting reporters, he turned to me: 'How did St Mirren get on?'

'We won 1–0. Shug Murray scored. So at least it's in our hands next week.'

'What d'you mean? They're safe.'

'No, we've got to get a result next week,' I said.

'No, they're safe. They're above Ayr and Thistle now – and they play each other next week, so one of them has to drop points.'

I was still grinning when Duncan George came out to talk me

through his goal, the biggest of his life. It was the perfect send-off for a man who now started a six-game ban. Anyway, the ball just came to him and . . .

Sorry, Dunc, but my tape-recorder was listening. I wasn't. I was at Stirling, dancing with my mates and hugging Shug Murray for all I was worth. *What kind of game is it where you celebrate not quite being useless just as heartily as you would winning the damn league?*

A beautiful game – and one which would get even more beautiful for Stranraer the following Saturday. A late, scrambled goal would give them a draw at Clyde. Clydebank would score six at Brechin. Then both would bite their nails for ten minutes until the late kick-off between Livvy and Caley Thistle at Almondvale ended.

When it did, the Inverness side had won 2–1. Livvy, for all their investment, had stayed down, and Clydebank, for all their woes, had gone up. And Stranraer, for all their hick-town naïvety, were champions.

Back in the car on the second-last day, I gave Elvis and his mass-murdering pal time off for bad behaviour. Switched to the radio, caught the end of *Sport on 5* and James Alexander Gordon's second reading of the classified results. (That's a treat in itself every Saturday; not only do you get to play the game of second-guessing the scores by his intonation of the names, but you also get to snigger at him not being able to say 'Wanderers'. He says 'Wandererers'. Check it out. He goes: 'Bolton Wandererers 1, Wolverhampton Wandererers 2.')

Then the news headlines which once again affected the football fan, bite-sized stories of death and tragedy from around the world which still could not wipe the stupid grin from my face. Followed by *6-0-6* with David Mellor. I was so happy I didn't once shout 'FAT TOSSER!' at the radio.

The windows were down, the sunroof open. The evening was shiny and lovely – even stuck behind two geriatric joyriders in a Nissan Micra carrying a bomb programmed to go off if they went over 23mph.

I stopped at Girvan for a fish supper from the chippy whose name I should really have memorised. Sat in the car and pigged out, watching the Rangers buses heading for Cairnryan. Good God, in the excitement of it all I had forgotten. Rangers had lost 1–0 at home to Killie. An injury-time goal from Ally Mitchell. I'd heard it while standing in the Stair Park tunnel but, what with everything else, it had fallen back out my head. It was like finding a fiver in a pair of trousers just back from the dry-cleaners.

Screwed up the chip poke and Jordaned it clean into a bin ten feet from the car. *In my dreams.* I have the throwing arm of the Venus di Milo, which is why I was then walking across the carpark to pick up strewn paper and stray chips.

Should I have been feeling more sorry for those Rangers fans? After all, they've lost and there but for the grace etc etc. *Forget it.* Would they have felt sorry for me if they'd won and St Mirren had lost? Would they even have *known* St Mirren had lost, never mind *cared*? Would they hell.

And, let's be honest, their defeat only stopped them getting to the brink of their tenth league title in a row. Ours would have put us into the Second Division, probably forced us part-time and had JCBs revving for miles around.

Let's get some perspective here. Rangers and Celtic fans really don't know what it is to be miserable. They've never known relegation, they've never gone to games *knowing* they'd slink home again a beaten person. The worst that ever happens to either of the Old Firm is not winning a trophy for a whole season. Big wowee, Gerry.

So what that Rangers hadn't lined up ten-in-a-row? There was always next week, next season, next decade. There's always a next time for them, which is why they don't know real pain, and why – sadder still – they don't know real *joy*.

The foul relationship between the Old Firm means they can't even parade trophies through the streets for fear of riots – but would they want to anyway? It's just another cup . . .

'Hey, Jim, you gonnae put that chip poke in the bin and get out the road?'

What? Sorry, chief. Miles away.

Back in the car, I switched on the CD again. Slid Elvis out, pulled out a pile of others from the boxes in the arm-rest. Realise a sad lack of planning – there's nothing cheerier than The Smiths on board. So The Smiths it was.

Windows down, sunroof open and blast:

Oh, I'm so miserable, and depressed,
I put my head in the oven,
Then realised we're all-electric,
And got even more depressed . . .

Now *that's* what I call music.

When 'Panic' came on and it got to the repeating chorus line 'Hang the DJ', I changed the words to 'Hughie Murray' and wondered if some Stranraer fan was sitting in his car, singing 'Duncan George' to some song on his stereo. Maybe 'Rock'n'Roll Part II' by Gary Glitter:

Duncan George – HEY! – *Duncan George.*

Or if Gregor McKechnie was now writing the words of a sermon that no one would hear in a delirious Alloa fan's Third Division championship-winning version of 'Eleanor Rigby'.

Maybe all over Scotland, happily mental fans were driving home making up songs about the men who had made their lives worth while that afternoon.

But I bet for every one of them there were two others listening to a mass-murderer begging his mama to get up off the kitchen floor . . .

THREE

PENTHOUSE AND PAVEMENT

The car almost went in a ditch just outside Perth when I heard the following statement. I'll never forget the moment; it was 12.58 p.m. on Saturday, 6 March 1999, the closing minutes of Fred McAuley's weekend show on Radio Scotland. His guests were Tony Higgins, top man and PFA gaffer; and Chick Young, a man who, if *Only An Excuse?* hadn't taken him off, would have paid them to do so.

They're talking about chip shops and Chick is saying that one day he'd like to write a book about the best ones near football grounds. I'm just thinking what a good idea this is when he comes close to causing me severe injury in a one-car pile-up.

'My favourite one's in Kirkcaldy,' he says, 'and I was gutted when Raith Rovers got relegated, because now I can't go there.'

The reason I almost crashed is that I took both hands off the steering wheel and clasped them to my head in horror. And if I could have got my feet up that high I'd have clasped them over my hands.

And I'm yelling as other drivers swerve out of the way: 'Why? *Why* can't he go to Kirkcaldy any more?'

Then I'm making and crossing off a mental list of all the possible reasons:

- Did they put a forcefield round the town when Rovers went down?
- Have the council banned baldy people?
- Is there a bye-law forbidding the shouting of *Oh-Ho-Hooooo!* in a built-up area?

Why? Someone tell me why? Of course, once you put your hands back on the wheel and pull yourself back from the edge of that plunge into the Tay and take a long, calming breath, the answer is simple.

Neither Chick nor so many others in the media since Scotland got its – *ahem* – Super League, can go to Kirkcaldy or Greenock or Coatbridge or Montrose because all those places and dozens of others might as well not exist. In many ways a forcefield *has* been put up, but not to keep people out of places like Kirkcaldy; it's to keep the chosen few inside the penthouse that is the top level of our game these days.

Scottish football, 1999-style, is a caste system.

GREED ALL ABOUT IT

Halfway through 1997–98, the chairmen of Rangers, Celtic, Aberdeen, Hearts, Hibs, Dundee United, Motherwell, St Johnstone, Dundee and Kilmarnock voted to break away at the end of the season and form their own Super League.

(*Most of you already know this fine well, of course, but I mention the fact for the benefit of the odd reader who might have picked up the book in the year 2123 in an Oxfam shop for 24 space farthings and knows not of this long-defunct sport called foot-ball. Or for the benefit of those English people to whom the Scottish game is as meaningful as Afghanistanian crop yields. Or for the travel-rug-loving, fleece-wearing, Labrador-walking Volvo drivers of Perth, many of whom have not yet realised that St Johnstone don't actually come from Johnstone and wonder where all those scruffy-looking oiks in blue and white mufflers go of a Saturday. So bear with me . . .*)

These ten clubs set out their intentions to resign their collective membership of the 107-year-old Scottish Football League that summer and insisted they would no longer abide by the rules set up at the start of that season, rules which said two teams would go down from the top division and two would be promoted from the next.

Details of their new set-up were scant; all we were promised was that it would blow us away, that it would revolutionise the game and make the rest of us poor saps wonder why we hadn't handed all the power over to them years ago.

The rest of the SFL opposed this bitterly, of course. They wanted change, yes, but within the existing set-up. Their protests were so much wee-wee in the wind. They were given a simple ultimatum by the Top Ten; change their minds and go along with the breakaway and there would be money in it for them. Continue to argue and they'd be cut adrift without a bean.

They might well have stuck to their guns had they been sure they would have a sponsor come the start of the following season. But Bell's, the whisky firm who had backed the SFL heavily, got nervy at the thought of the game splitting in two and pulled out. Their involvement had been heavily based on the community aspect of the game, not on élitism.

The thirty who would be left in the SFL were now up the creek. Splits began to appear, one or two swithered – among the first, I'm ashamed to say, my own club St Mirren – then a few more, and finally there was no resistance. They would have to go along with the dissection of a body which had existed since before penalty kicks or shinguards or World Cups or substitutes.

What many feared was that we had not seen the last of the splits either. The insistence of the top bananas on allowing just one team to go up from the First Division at the end of each subsequent season would leave too many with nothing to play for. Who could afford to splash out on new players and better facilities in the hope of going up when the chances of doing so had been halved overnight?

The big clubs knew the ten below them, given the choice between festering away with nothing to aim at or picking up crumbs from the master's table, would crack soon enough. For a while in 1998–99 there was talk of a twelve-team top division in the year 2001, but by March those in the First Division who had seen their investments come to nothing were moving towards leaving the two leagues below them behind and forming Breakaway Division Two.

Never mind the grass being greener on the other side. It was the colour of the money that concerned them.

Yet to me there was not a shred of evidence to suggest the so-called élite league they were so desperate to be some small part of was any better than the one the Big Boys wrecked.

PUZZLES FOR BUDDING BUSINESS GENIUSES NO.234

So you're the producer of a long-running TV soap whose popularity has started to wane. The plots are stale, viewers are fed up with the same old characters. It's time for change.

There's your sponsors to think of, however. They're putting buckets of money your way in a joint deal with three other shows. The contract's up for renewal and you can't afford to cheese them off. So, do you:

(a) make the show bigger and better than before, with new plots and more characters?

or

(b) say to hell with the viewers and the sponsors, form your own TV company and relaunch the same show in the same format but with a different name?

You'd think it would have to be (a), because it is bold and innovative and because (b) is clearly a stupid, short-sighted and churlish course of action. Plus, if you go it alone the sponsors will pull the plug on *all* the shows they currently back. Yes, anyone with half a business brain would go for (a).

Sadly, the people who run Scotland's leading football clubs clearly have less than half a brain. Glenn Hoddle would probably say they are paying the price for the sins of past lives. Mind you, quite how the Old Firm could possibly have been any more sinful in the past is hard to imagine. Maybe in the old days they maimed budgies and bunny rabbits as well as condoning religious genocide.

No, the people who run Scotland's leading football clubs went for (b). When confronted with the problems of a league system which had gone stale, they said *pah!* to innovation and boldness and plumped instead for the let's-change-the-name-and-hope-we-fool-everyone option.

And the Greed-Is-Good League was born.

I always fancied getting the contract to decorate their new headquarters. You'd listen to their fantastic plans for the place, take copious notes, nod sagely and tell them to give you a month. Then you'd sit back with a cup of tea and the papers and do . . . *nothing*. Sod all. *Nada.* Not a single bristle of a single brush would dip its tootsies in a single tin of paint. You'd just sit there and twiddle your thumbs and wait for the time to pass.

A month later they'd come back and you'd be waiting for them at a front door masked with polythene, like they do on those telly style programmes. And you'd get them all excited before pulling out your Stanley knife and opening the plastic like a theatre curtain.

They'd step inside, all the Murrays and McCanns and Robinsons, and look round for a second before realising it was all exactly the same as before. They'd round on you and ask what the hell the game was.

And you'd say: 'No, it's not the same. Look at the new nameplate – I've changed the name from SPL Headquarters to SPL Super Headquarters.'

Then they'd all grin and slap you on the back and say well done, that one word made all the difference. Discount for cash? There you go then, worth every penny of £400,000.

Yes, sports fans, the Scottish Premier League was like the Emperor's New Clothes. They fooled enough people into believing they weren't naked long enough to get away with it. They pushed through plans for a breakaway top division which had the same number of teams as in the old Scottish Premier *Division*, playing the same number of games to the same fans who'd been bored by it all after twenty-odd Groundhog Years.

Then they put on their smuggest grins and claimed bare-faced it was something new and fresh and groovy.

The Greed-Is-Good wallahs didn't care about the financial effect this would have on the thirty clubs they'd left behind; they'd soon have a multi-million-pound backer of their own and be bathing in champagne-filled jacuzzis while troughing on huge salvers of mashed potato with giant bangers poking out.

Come August 1998, their league-in-a-bubble was under way. They ordered member clubs to keep hoardings free for their impending sponsor's trackside ads. I am writing this the following March and those hoardings still lie bare.

The news in the past week has been that, at last, a sponsor has been lined up in the shape of the Bank of Scotland. The deal is reportedly £1 million per year.

Yet even if they'd got the bank to stick in £10 million a season it has still meant seven months without backing and the cynic might suggest an organisation with any sort of foresight would not have got itself into that situation.

As I write, the EssPeeEll are also in the middle of a competition for punters to design a trophy for the league winners. All very customer-friendly – but shouldn't they have had the silverware ready on day one to show off to an admiring public? Of course they should.

Sadly, the Greed-Is-Good top bananas have all the foresight of a goldfish whose normal twelve-second memory-span has been reduced by old age.

Sure, they made pompous noises about the breakaway being the way forward and how it would help everyone in the long run and drag the game kicking and screaming into the twenty-first century; but to this day no one has ever explained exactly *how* it would do all these things.

The driving forces behind it all – Old Firm chairmen David Murray and Fergus McCann – certainly never put their own heads above the parapet to tell us what their project was all about. The only time you heard from them was when they made one of their sporadic outbursts about why smaller clubs (hereafter known as the Diddy Teams) were bad for Scottish football, held it back. You put it to them that perhaps the consistent failures of Rangers and Celtic in Europe, which had cost us a UEFA Cup place, might be slightly more detrimental to the game than, say, Albion Rovers simply existing, and they just tutted.

You'd ask them *why* it would be better their way and they'd say: 'They just *will* be, okay?'

But no, it's not okay.

We all know why they've never been able to tell us what the Scottish Premier League will do for football as a whole; it is because all the answers would be negative ones. Fact is, the sole reason this league came about was because Rangers and Celtic in particular were sick of the Diddy Teams having a say in how the game was run. They were also sick of the Diddy Teams getting a cut of TV income despite never being on the box; the fact that the annual amount per club we're talking about wouldn't pay Jonas Thern for a week and a half seemed beside the point.

With the slavering fervour of the truly obscenely greedy, the Top Ten set about hoovering up every last penny to make themselves even more bloated than before. *Greed-Is-Good holed up in a penthouse and left the rest to scramble on the pavement.*

WHITE MAN AT HAMILTON-PARTICK

It's like a castle in the sky, one mile high. Built to shelter the rich and greedy. Rows of eyes, disguised as windows, looking down on the poor and the needy.

Miles of people, marching up the avenue, doing what they've got to do, just to get by. I'm living in a land of plenty and many, but I'm damn sure poor and I don't know why.

Don't applaud me for those words, which sum up so well the divisions in Scottish football today. They come from the lips of pioneering rap guru Grandmaster Flash.

Music critics always assumed those searing words were inspired by Flash's tough upbringing on the iniquitous streets of New York. But no – I can exclusively reveal this gritty look at the canyon between the haves and have nots came from his days watching money tear Scottish football apart.

It's true. He told me himself one day in the pie queue at Palmerston.

I was just having that dilemma over whether to give up when you're four from being served and be back for the teams coming out after half-time or to hang on and miss five minutes in return for getting grease up your sleeve when he tapped me on the shoulder.

'Hey,' I said, 'Flash – ma main man! What can I get you?'

'Chips and curry sauce, bro,' he replied. 'Nobody does chips and curry sauce like Queen of the South.'

And it was then, as we got grease and curry sauce down our jackets and watched the second half of a Scottish Cup replay with Arbroath – Flash is a huge Lichties fan – that he told me how much his music had been affected by watching our game.

Turns out his most famous number of all came to him one horrible wet night when he'd gone all the way to Greenock only to find there was a 6.45 pitch inspection. The ref was ready to call it off because he said he couldn't see the pitch markings, but changed his mind after frantic appeals from players, officials and fans.

That very night, Flash wrote his seminal 'White Lines (Don't Do It)'. Cynical and harrowing, yes, but Greenock does that to a man.

Actually, you'd be amazed at the amount of classic songs which were originally inspired by the side of Scottish football which is more Gory Game than Glory Game. I remember one night walking into a boozer in Renfrew to find Joe Strummer and Mick Jones of The Clash drowning their sorrows.

They'd just had what they thought was a fantastic idea for a single knocked back by their record company on the grounds that it wasn't angry enough, didn't touch the raw nerve of the punk generation.

The boys were sick. It looked like no one would ever get to hear the angst that was their new song 'White Man at Hamilton-Partick'.

But we talked about it over a few beers and I'm pleased to say I suggested a compromise; maybe substituting 'Hammersmith Palais' into the title would scan the same and give it that London scene feel the record execs wanted.

Well, they weren't entirely happy, but they went with it. And made fortunes. Me? I got a pint out of them, so who's the numpty?

Same with Otis Redding when my dad met him at an East Fife-St Mirren game in 1967 and suggested a subtle change to his song 'Sittin' on the Docks at Bayview'. Would Smokie have had such a smash had my Uncle Billy not talked them into rewriting 'Living Next Door to Alloa?'

And how would the course of music history have altered had I not won a ferocious argument with Boy George that a song about Falkirk's most successful junior club just wouldn't sell with the New Romantic set?

'Karma Camelon' my erchie.

All the above is as true as I am riding this bike and I recount it to illustrate the colour and beauty there is to be had at the grass roots level of the Scottish game.

If you believe the élitists around us, of course, you'll be scoffing right now like Billy Bunter drowning in a vat of lasagne. There are those – plenty of them, too – in whose eyes a day at a lower-division match is somewhere further down their list of things to do than a week's half-board in the Black Hole of Calcutta. So it's wonderful when they turn up their noses and come out with dumb statements, only for them to whap straight back in their faces.

It's Radio Scotland, Saturday, 4 November 1995. Fergus McCann is holding forth about how the Diddy Teams must die. 'The trouble is,' he's snorting, 'there's just too many teams in Scottish football. Too many of them are going nowhere and choking the game. Teams like . . . like . . . *Stenhousemuir.*'

Except he said 'Stenhousemuir' to rhyme with 'toxic waste'.

The following day, to the eternal joy of everyone who loves the sport for what it is and not what its competitors have, the part-timers of Toxic Waste FC beat big-earning, full-time, international-packed Dundee United in the final of the League Challenge Cup. God, I love days like that; days when the rich get theirs. No offence meant to Dundee United, a club who built their way up from poverty to be something in Europe, but they're part of it now; they went with Greed-Is-Good. They sing off McCann's hymn-sheet.

The top bananas have tried to put so much distance between themselves and the Diddy Teams that they would never come into contact with them if it could be helped; as well as forming Greed-Is-Good, they have demanded to be excluded from the early rounds of cup competitions and even called for the League Cup to be scrapped.

Yes, outsiders can win promotion to Greed-Is-Good. But only if their stadiums pass the Greed-Is-Good Grooviness Test. Applicants must not only be able to build a team good enough to win the First Division, they must also have enough cash stashed away under the bed to build an all-seated, all-singing, all-dancing ground. The fact that most clubs have the choice of either spending their money on a team good enough to go up and stay up or on new facilities passes them by – even though it's mostly down to the top clubs that this dilemma exists.

The rot started when they stopped clubs sharing league gates. Suddenly all the serious money stayed with the big boys. Then they stopped buying home-based players; for a century we'd produced players who conquered the game, but suddenly Scots weren't good enough for Scottish clubs. It started when Graeme Souness became Rangers manager in 1986 and filled his team with England stars. Next thing, Celtic were on the case, and then those chasing the big two went for the next level down of English talent. Then Rangers moved into Europe for new players. The rest followed. Next thing, wages were spiralling and money was flowing out of the country like poo from a sewage outlet, and the best home-based talent the rest had to offer went nowhere. The drip of transfer cash down through the ranks was cut off. So the investment in more talent dried up. Youngsters wondered if it was worth even trying to get into football when no one was moving on from the lower divisions.

Since David Murray joined the Ibrox revolution on 23 November 1988, Rangers have spent more than £100 million on players in their desperate chase for European glory. They have recouped around one third of that in sales. More than £70 million of their expenditure has gone out of Scotland – and that's only in transfer fees. You can just about double that figure to take in wages and bonuses and pensions and houses and cars and percentages for agents and all the other bits and bobs which go with football deals in the late '90s.

And have they achieved European glory? You know the answer. They almost did it, once, back in 1992–93 when arguably they only missed out on the European Cup final because Marseille were bribing everyone that moved. But that team had a backbone of Scotland men in Goram, Gough, Robertson, Durrant, McCall, Ferguson and McCoist.

Since then, though, they've put their faith in more and more and more foreigners and as each fresh truckload arrives they tell themselves *this* will be the year, *this* is the team to make it all happen; when the rest of us know fine well that nine out of ten new purchases have come for an easy ride towards a rich retirement.

If even one tenth of Rangers' £100 million transfer bill had been spent on Scottish players, the game here would be in a far healthier state and I doubt if they would have done any worse in Europe. If another tenth had been spent on a training ground and youth academy, Rangers might even be going into the twenty-first century with a team of hand-reared stars.

Ajax have done it. Norwegian part-timers Rosenborg have done it. Liverpool did it even before they opened their own academy late in 1998; of their team at that time, Owen, Fowler, McManaman, Matteo, Carragher and Thomson came through the ranks, and Harkness and Redknapp were bought for buttons from Diddy Teams. The only failures at Anfield in recent years have been the big-money foreigners. The club have slipped from the top of the tree since they broke the habit of picking off the best young players from around Britain and making them into superstars.

Why can't big teams learn from experiences like these? Why do they keep throwing their good money after bad? I'll tell you why. Because they're not playing football any more. They're playing a stupid boardroom game of Keeping Up With The Joneses, a non-stop Monopoly marathon with no winners.

Rangers have convinced themselves – and others around them – there is no talent in Scotland, because who'd sponsor a team full of *Scots*, for goodness sake? We'd be the laughing stock of Europe. When, of course, at present the club who won our league nine times in a row from 1989 until 1997 are so widely respected for their brilliant team-building acumen and subsequent domination of top continental competition.

Take then, if you will, the example of Cowdenbeath. They will finish season 1998–99 fortieth out of forty in Scotland, and the very mention of their name sends the Greed-Is-Good people into paroxysms of fury. How many times have I written a piece criticising Rangers or Celtic for their bigotry or their Thatcherite ideals or their transfer policies, and had the same conversation with fan after fan after angry, foam-flecked-mouthed fan.

'See, it's no' us that are the problem in Scottish fitba' – it's the Diddy Teams. It's a' they wans doon the bottom that are haudin' us back, right?'

And how might this be?

'Can you no' see it? They just . . . they . . . they just haud us back, right? They're in the way, nane o' them gie us a challenge and that's how Scottish fitba's crap, right? Right?'

So I try and unravel this and put it back together in some sort of sense, but it's not easy. I point out that the Cowdenbeaths are never in contact with the Old Firm, except when maybe they draw them in the cup, and I ask how then they can hold anyone in the top flight back.

Then I ask what would happen if every single team in the country outside the Old Firm were to amalgamate and Rangers or Celtic *still* won the league? What do we do then?

They get really annoyed when I try to reason that the yardstick for everyone's performances shouldn't be the failure of Rangers and Celtic in Europe, that Cowdenbeath can't be blamed for AEK Athens or Croatia Zagreb beating the champions of Scotland.

Then they explode when I say: 'Scottish football's not just about Rangers and Celtic, you know . . .'

Remove pin. Throw. Stick fingers in ears.

It drives Old Firm people daft, this notion that every fan of every other team feels just as passionately about their lot as do those who follow the big guns. This does not compute in their narrow little minds.

IT'S JUST LIKE WATCHING BRAZIL, BUT WITH BIG TYRES ROUND THE PITCH

Craig Levein tries to explain the same to people who wonder why the hell he went back to Cowdenbeath when he didn't have to. They thought he'd have had enough of Central Park and its stock-car track and its damp and its weeds as a rookie player without coming back as manager once he'd made his name and his fame.

Levein didn't need to spend too long strutting around penalty boxes at Montrose and Berwick for twelve pounds a week before Hearts came and paid £30,000 for him. Within a fortnight he was making his big-time début in a 3–0 defeat at Ibrox. Within a season he was a fixture and in 1986 he was part of the team which came so, so close to the Double but which lost the league one Saturday at

Dundee – when Levein was at home in bed with flu – and the Scottish Cup the next to Aberdeen at Hampden, when he admits he played like he still had the flu.

Early the following season, he damaged his knee so badly that he was out for a year. He came back, but it went again. This time he thought he was finished for real. Yet not only did he play again, but he was called up by Scotland in time to go to the 1990 World Cup in Italy.

'Andy Roxburgh came to see me in hospital, brought me a Scotland shirt and told me I was still in his future plans,' he recalled. 'To be honest, I thought he was just being patronising. It was like he didn't *really* believe I would make it and was trying to keep my spirits up. It was hard to feel positive at the time, to be able to see myself playing at the top again after two serious injuries.

'But by the end of the 1989–90 season I was playing well and realised maybe he hadn't been buttering me up. I was feeling good about football again and then, out of the blue, the chance came to play for Scotland. We had Argentina at Hampden in the run-up to the World Cup and I got my first cap. They were the World Champions and I was up against Claudio Caniggia, but we won 1–0, and from then until Italy I played every game.'

There, he suffered the worst disappointment of his career when he was left out of the opening 1–0 defeat by Costa Rica, before coming in for the win over Sweden and missing the 1–0 defeat by Brazil which sent us home.

'People have said to me it must be wonderful just to be selected for the World Cup, but to be there and not get on the park for the first game was a disaster. It was worse than the injuries and losing the Double put together,' he said.

'Playing against Sweden made it all worth while, though. I'm a council-house boy from Aberdour and to be playing football at that level was unbelievable. The day before the game in Genoa we went to the stadium, and my two brothers, Paul and Gary, were waiting for me, pissed out of their brains. It was superb to see them and know I'd be out there doing what they wanted to do, what all the fans wanted to. But then he left me out of the Brazil game and I was gutted again.'

It was typical of his career: so near and yet so far. Levein, though, is not one for regrets. He always sees the glass as half-full. But when fourteen years with Hearts was ended by the residue of his knee trouble, he could have been excused for deciding enough was enough. Take the pension when it matures at thirty-five and do something less stressful.

Football, though, is a drug for its genuine lovers and he went all the way back to Cowdenbeath for the same reason he joined the first time: because he wanted a start and because they asked him before anyone else did. Loyalty still counts at that level and Levein showed it halfway through 1998–99 when he turned down the chance to step up a division with Alloa, saying his job wasn't done. Mind you, when is the job of managing a club like Cowdenbeath ever done?

He looks around Central Park, the true coalface of Scottish football, and the place could almost have been locked in a time warp since he first saw it at the tail end of 1981. Sure, they've trimmed the weeds on the terraces. They're no longer high enough for Japanese soldiers to hide in, waiting for the war to end. There's a newish pavilion with seats for a couple of hundred punters. And they've put giant tyres round the touchline so the stock cars don't slew off the tracks and carve the corners to bits any more. But it's really still the same ramshackle heap he walked into a cocky seventeen-year-old, a rundown shack where engines scream far louder on Saturday nights than the crowds ever do in the afternoons. On the opening day of last season, the League Cup tie with Livingston was pulled forward to a one o'clock kick-off because the World Stock Car Championships were on there at night. That's where the money is at Cowdenbeath, oily blokes in overalls and their groupies.

'Our chairman, Gordon McDougall, was a stock-car driver,' says Levein. 'He used to drive at Newtongrange, then started promoting meetings here. It's been part of the place ever since I was a player. You used to come to training on Tuesday nights and there would be huge ruts right across the corners of the pitch where cars had lost it and skidded across.

'The tyres Gordon's put round the pitch these days help. The terraces don't have as many weeds either, and the wee stand went up long after I left as well. But it's never really changed, not the feel of the place. There's not the money to do it up.

'I hear people say Gordon's only in it for the stock cars, that Cowdenbeath come a poor second, but that's not true. He loves the football club more and no one should ever forget he saved it from disaster. When he took over they were skint – the wages had gone far too high for the level they were at and Gordon had to sort out the mess. He's done that all right.

'We've still not got much, but we're not going out of business; in fact, when people talk about clubs going down the drain in the current climate I can put my hand on my heart and say Cowdenbeath will not be one of them.

'As well as being more sensible financially, we're also more professional than when I started out. We used to have players who didn't turn up for training because they couldn't be bothered – or, worse, guys turning up for games half-cut. The same problems crop up here as at any big club. The difference is that here you've no time to sort them out. The boys come to training off full-time jobs and the last thing they need is someone shouting and bawling at them to do something they can't do – especially when they're on fifteen pounds a week. If you don't make it enjoyable for them, they could well just turn round and tell you to stuff it. All you can do is get them as fit as you can and as organised as you can and try to get a style of play that works.

'It's the younger guys you can do something with, the next generation. We've started to do well in the Under-18 league. We've got some great kids – and that's the future for us and every other small-town club. We have 160 kids from seven to eleven coming in for training. We have Under-14s. Our Under-18s are going well. We've got a women's team. We've put eleven coaches through SFA badges from E up to B. We're looking after our future. That's where the game has to go, clubs like Cowdenbeath developing players who move up to bigger clubs and on to bigger clubs again, with money seeping down through the divisions.

'People talk about how clubs like ours hold football back, but that's nonsense. We do no one any harm. We live within our means and if we top that up with some Pools money, so what? It's probably as much for a year as a single player with the Old Firm earns in a fortnight.

'We have around three hundred diehards who come here every game, and they would do so whether we won every week or lost every week. Our crowds will never change much and we will never survive on what we make through the turnstiles. We're not like the big clubs, whose gates go through the roof when it's going well – only for the fairweather punters to disappear like snow off a dyke after a few defeats. We have to be self-sufficient and we're good at it; so are an awful lot of other clubs at our level. We're not the ones who'll go out of business.

'They say football's in a state, but it's not. Football to me is no better or worse than when I played. What's in a state is some of the *business* of football. There are clubs whose wage bills have gone up by 400 per cent in a couple of years, but have their gates? No way! Their grounds have actually got *smaller* because of rebuilding, yet they hike the money up to keep players happy. Explain to me how that works.

'If any clubs might die – and I hope none ever do – it'll be those who over-extend themselves, not clubs like ours who try to build with what we have.'

Those Old Firm fans who phone up calling for some kind of football Rentokil to roll up and exterminate the Diddy Teams might give it the big *pssschaw!* at that last statement, but evidence supports it.

Look at Celtic. They conquered Europe and played to 60,000 gates every week for a generation, yet by the early 1990s they had run their affairs so badly they were within hours of the bank pulling the plug before Fergus McCann saved them. Now they're huge again, Charlie Big-Potatoes plc, but they will never be masters of their own financial destiny. One bad season in the old days and they could lick their wounds and start again. But now? Now everyone plays for the City. One bad season now and the share price plummets out of control like Eddie the Eagle and suddenly there's chaos; no one on the football club board (for these outfits are so big they have *two* lots of directors, one for football and one for business) has a say any more.

If the plc board say the manager goes or that there's no money for players or that the star player has to go, that's what happens.

Ask Hearts. In May 1998 they won the Scottish Cup for the first time in forty-two years and all looked rosy. But you can't melt down trophies to pay the bills, and within months it became clear they had next to no dosh.

Why? It's pretty much like Craig Levein said – and after fourteen years as a Jambo, he should know. Millions spent on a ground that ends up smaller than before, so potential crowd income down – but wages through the roof.

I don't know who gets paid what at Tynecastle, but it was well publicised that French striker Stephane Adam was given £10,000 a week to sign a new contract in late March 1999 at a time when the club were not only bottom of Greed-Is-Good but at the very moment they had been forced through debts to sell Scotland defender David Weir to Everton for a measly £250,000 and top scorer Jim Hamilton to relegation rivals Aberdeen for the same money.

Right on the transfer deadline, they then paid £300,000 to Celtic for Darren Jackson and £250,000 to Falkirk for centre-half Kevin James. Jackson and several others at the club are believed to be on – at a conservative estimate – several thousand each a week. Even Carol Vorderman couldn't work out the arithmetic of all *that*; the average Jambo is left to scratch his napper and wonder how one minute they can be so skint that they have to sell top players for a pittance and the next they're giving an import who's well past his thirtieth birthday £1.5 million over three years.

So where does the money come from to pay for deals like that? From the EssPeeEll's deal with Sky? Forget it – at £400,000 per club a year that doesn't even cover Adam's wages. From the EssPeeEll's long-awaited sponsorship deal with the Bank of Scotland? No way – £100,000 per club won't go far these days.

Look at income and look at spending at a club like Hearts and you know the way some so-called top football clubs do business makes no sense. They bring in £500,000 once for two top players yet then give away £500,000 a year to one – and Scottish football's in a mess because we've got too many Cowdenbeaths?

Then there's Clydebank, as mentioned in the previous chapter. Their slump is depressing. Formed in 1965, by 1977 they were in the old Premier League, went back down, came back up for another couple of years and annoyed the rich guys, then settled down as an attractive top-half First Division outfit. Crowds were never great – no, that's an understatement; too often if you followed a crowd down Kilbowie Road at 2 p.m. on the Saturday of a home game you ended up in Safeway – but they produced enough quality players to keep things more than ticking along through transfer cash. They swanned it in a 10,000-capacity all-seated stadium when Ibrox and Parkhead still had cavernous terracings; they were the model small club.

Then their owners, the Steedman family, decided to get out. But instead of letting someone buy them out lock, stock and barrel, they sold the ground separately. The Bankies were moved to share with Dumbarton at Boghead – further reducing their fan base – before a buyer was found.

They were on the floor by then and those who took over put the boot in even harder. Marshalled by a financial adviser called David Low, the new board hatched a plan to move Clydebank to Dublin, change their name and apply to join what was then the proposed EssPeeEll. The protests which followed are detailed in the previous chapter – and I'm glad to say this scandalous hijacking was blocked at every turn.

But what happened next was that the owners, their scheme in ruins, saw no further need for a club which had only been a flag of convenience in the first place. And they left it to rot. Players started the 1998–99 season on month-to-month contracts and stayed that way; except that with each passing month, one player after another had to be jettisoned to cut costs.

Clydebank ceased to be a football club. Instead, they were a bunch of mates who got together to train and play, watched by a knot of diehards who kept coming because they had nothing better to do. All that bound them were the red-and-white colours, a fighting spirit and the faint hope that they might still be trundling along haphazardly the same time a year on.

I've always thought Clydebank would survive because enough

people want them to and usually in football that's sufficient to galvanise some kind of recovery. The dream is to get some land and a few bob in grants and loans and build a trim little ground from where they can start all over again, just like they did when the Steedmans took over a junior stadium in 1965.

What was allowed to happen to Clydebank in the recent past is a blight on football, and those who run the game should be ashamed. They did nothing to stop a bunch of charlatans wrecking something which meant so much to its workers and its followers; in business they call it asset-stripping and there are laws against it. In football it's called Who Cares, It's Only A Diddy Team.

But just you wait for the day when some industrial conglomerate tries to take over Rangers with the intention of moving them to Dallas. Just wait for the uproar then, when the fans plead for mercy and the Acme Money-Laundering Company Inc swats them with a copy of the *Wall Street Journal* and says who cares about 50,000 angry Scots when there's 5,000,000 ready to buy souvenirs of the all-singing, all-dancing Texas Rangers Soccer Team.

Those who come to people like me and complain about the small causing them a problem will have to realise that in the money markets to which their clubs have remortgaged their souls, *they* are so tiny as to be flecks of dust on the end of the leg of a chair in the middle of deepest space. Maybe one day, if they do get their way and there's only Rangers and Celtic left and they go off to join a European League, they will know what it is like to be Cowdenbeath. And they might wish then they had stuck to buying their own country's players so the game here could prosper and they had some pals left, instead of throwing their lot in with foreigners who saw them solely as a meal ticket to the best restaurant in town.

Anyway, despite the prudence of those trying to manage like proper businesses – that is, within their means – and despite all the momumental waste of money and lack of direction at the top that makes Mark Thatcher look like an Apache tracker, the SPL clubs believe they know best about who is and isn't good enough to play with them.

A PRESS BOX BUILT FOR TWO

So all us scumbags on the outside can do is long for the odd, wonderful occasion when the Diddy Teams get to kick the shins of Greed-Is-Good in cup-ties and pray we bring them down once in a blue moon.

Take the day Stenhousemuir went to Ibrox in the Scottish Cup. If I could have changed one thing about that day, it would have been that the game wasn't played at Ibrox.

Stenny's committee would have had nine synchronised heart attacks, of course. They were on £150,000 from the gate, just for turning up. But, God, I'd have loved to have seen Rangers at Ochilview that January day when they were just back from two weeks swanning in Florida. I'd love to have seen their millionaires squeezing through the corridor to the little away dressing-room, then squelching through the bog of a pitch. I'd love to have seen the faces of their fans as they realised there was only one pie stall in the whole place and no banks of TV screens under the stand so they could catch the highlights at half-time.

And call me a sadist, but I *always* love watching my own lot, the press, suffer when the Big Boys go to face the Diddy Teams. It had been funny enough at the second-round replay when Stenny played Whitehill Welfare. There were about a dozen reporters there, the top level of those who hadn't been sent to cover the Premier League teams on the winter holidays. The odd one, like David McCarthy from the *Daily Record*, knew the score at grounds like these. The rest gathered at the mouth of the tunnel, baffled, wondering where the press facilities were. I told them there weren't any on this side, in the new stand. But if they cared to follow me round the pitch . . .

So we trudged round to the other side, to the stand built seventy-odd years ago but now disused. (A stand, by the way, which was planned and approved and built and ready for action before they realised there were no stairs in or out. They hurriedly put up a flight which looks like it should lead to a granny flat.) The dugouts were still there and the first-aid room was open, but no punters got in.

And then I showed them it. A press box built for two.

It was a little rabbit hutch with a window and a side door.

Already in it were the guy doing BBC Radio and the local paper's reporter. The rest asked where they could go. I said I was going to stand behind the dugouts because you get all the crack from the managers, and they looked at me like I was daft. They said they were going up into the disused stand. They'd hardly settled down, still mumping and moaning, when a steward came and ordered them out: 'It's condemned . . . come doon before it fa's doon.'

So they stomped back down the steps with much harumphing and stood in a miserable little knot to the right of Terry Christie and his Stenny bench. 'Jesus Christ,' mumbled one of them as he came past me, 'no wonder no one comes to cover these bloody games.'

Er . . . no. What he couldn't get was that the facilities are the way they are *because* no one comes to cover these bloody games. For decades the reporting pack would rather have put their heads in a lion's mouth while flicking its wedding tackle with a wet towel than go to Ochilview or Cliftonhill or Glebe Park or Shielfield.

They leave it to the local stringer – little middle-aged blokes with Middle Ages names like Hutchinson of Cowdenbeath or Simpson of Alloa or Neil of Stranraer (*they sound like medieval knights; 'Ah, 'tis Neil of Stranraer.'*

'Forsooth – my liege Hutchison of Cowdenbeath. Shall we fight to the death?'

'No, let's gang up and chib seven colours out of Forsyth of Arbroath.'

'Hurrah!') to supply match reports year in, year out. And club officials see this and assess their needs and build press boxes for two – the stringer and a Hospital Radio commentator.

Then, once in a blue moon, one of the Old Firm get drawn to go there and the Big Boys of the press are forced to lower themselves to attend and wonder why they don't get welcome mats and heated seats and dancing girls and lobster thermidore at half-time.

And the local stringers and the Hospital Radio guys are shoved to one side and treated like the poo on the superstars' shoes.

In my second season as a reporter, working for the *Clydebank Press*, the Bankies drew Celtic at home in the third round of the Scottish Cup. The wee glass box we worked from, upstairs in the social club behind the Kilbowie Road goal, was heaving with Big Boys. They were already miffed that these were licensed premises and yet they were not allowed to bring bevvy into the press box. Add this to their grumpiness at actually having to be there, and they were not in good humour.

Halfway through the first half, the Bankies nearly scored at the far end. One of the Big Boys asked who hit the shot.

'Jimmy Given,' I said timidly.

'I think it was Gerry McCabe,' one of them said.

'Er no,' I tried again, 'it was Jimmy Given.'

'Gerry McCabe? You sure?'

'Er . . . chaps . . . it was Jimmy G –'

'Okay, so we're agreed – it was Gerry McCabe.'

They weren't going to listen to me; they never even heard me. I could have stripped naked and danced along with windowsill carrying a placard reading IT WAS JIMMY GIVEN on it and they wouldn't have taken my word. They didn't even know who I was, so how could I be right? So I thought, sod them. If they go by consensus instead of knowledge, let them be wrong.

Sadly, that is still the way with older members of the media pack. Even if they're wrong, they'll stick together on decisions because that way none of them will be out on a limb. For me, it's no way to work, but then I'm not in their gang.

It is amazing to think there are people hired as experts by the national media who are experts in maybe 5 *per cent* of their field. But that is how it is with some of our top writers and commentators. They spend their life following Rangers one week, Celtic the next and only break the cycle to go with Scotland. Yet they can write that the rest of the game stinks. Hmm? Anyone else spot an anomaly here?

I probably know about three guys in national newspapers who would go to a Second or Third Division ground simply because they fancied the game. No, that's a lie. It's more like two. And I'm one of them.

For a while when I was sports editor at the *Daily Record* I tried rotating the writers between the divisions to give them a better view of the game as a whole and some really enjoyed it in a kind of Princess-Di-visiting-the-sick-and-the-needy way, but with some you knew it was like being asked to clean the toilets.

Some football writers have this idea that the only real football is played at Ibrox and Parkhead and the other Premier grounds; yet week after week you read their reports and they slaughter what they've seen. But from this narrow perspective they deduce that Scottish football is guff, their argument being that if they don't like what they see in Old Firm country, what chance is there of a decent game at Cliftonhill or Shielfield?

This, of course, is cobblers. A good game of football is a good game of football and a bad one is a bad one, whether it is in the Bernabau or a blaes pitch on Benbecula. What too many football writers *really* object to is being asked to watch football in conditions where they are not pampered – although even when their every whim is catered for, some wouldn't be happy as long as their bums pointed at the floor.

Would you believe there were reporters at the World Cup moaning about how much work they had to do and the travelling and the hanging around? At the World Cup! Not only were we there for free, but we were being paid as well. And they were moaning!

ANOTHER ONE OF THOSE TANGENT THINGS

I'm in the queue for pies at Glebe Park, last day of the 1982–83 season. Brechin *v* Clydebank. Bankies fans, as was their tradition for the final away game, have come in fancy dress. There are guys done up as schoolgirls, guys done up as nuns. There's a boy in full Highland kit, another dressed as a wasp. There's Dennis the Menace and a full-on punk. And they're all waiting patiently in a line snaking up to the little wooden hut with all the good smells.

These, to paint a clearer picture of this sun-drenched May afternoon, were still the days before City had built their smart stand behind one goal. Some things, though, never change. Now, as then, the boundary wall down the pie-stall touchline was a neatly trimmed hedge and the half-time draw prize was a large cream cake.

So I'm getting nearer the front as the schoolies get served, then the nuns, then the kiltie, then Dennis, then the punk. I'm two from the front when a gorilla appears round the side of the hut, pops his head in the hatch and says: 'Any bananas?'

Try that one when your team's playing at Ibrox and see how long it is before the stewards get you by the scruff of the fur and bounce you out onto Broomloan Road.

In fact, go to most big grounds these days and try anything that doesn't involve sitting down and shutting up and you're liable to be chucked out. Big money, big business and big attitudes have taken the fun out of big-time football.

A few years ago the game I was going to was postponed, so I went with some Arab pals to see Dundee United at Ibrox. There were five of us and as we went into the Broomloan Lower the steward asked to see our tickets. We showed them to him, he told us where our row was and we sat down.

Five minutes later he came down and asked to see our tickets again. We could hear the bits of his brain grinding as he scanned them, lips moving. Then he told us we were sitting in the wrong seats. We checked the numbers on the ticket against the letters on the steps at the end of the row and the numbers on the seats and told him he was mistaken.

But he said no, we *were* in the wrong seats. We were in *each other's* seats. We were sitting in *the wrong order* and not only were we required to sort it out but if we didn't do it pretty damn quick we would be cordially invited to leave the stadium.

We thought about just swapping tickets with each other but reckoned there was too much risk of him whistling for armed back-up, so we grudgingly switched around until he was happy. The jumped-up, yellow-kagouled git.

Little cameos like that stick with you, put you off people. I mean, I'm sure nine out of ten football ground stewards are lovely folk who are kind to animals, love their mothers and hardly ever throw their weans out the house for putting their feet up on the couch. It's just that ever since that day at Ibrox I seem to have had nothing but grief from them. Every one I come into contact with seems to jump into a phone box when he sees me coming and reappears as . . . Super Jobsworth! Willing to give you guff directions with a single brain-cell! Able to block your view throughout the game! Desperate to move you along if you stand still in a gangway for more than half a second!

These are the only people in Britain who watched that miserable docu-soap about wheel-clampers and sighed: 'I wish that was *me* ruining everyone's day.'

A MINI-TANGENT

By the way, is it just me or are all those docu-soaps just the worst pieces of televisual vomit ever to be thought up by pony-tailed coke-sniffers with Oxbridge degrees in patronising the oiks?

I mean, you spend your days swiping tin after mindnumbing tin of baked beans across the barcode-thingy in Safeway; the last thing you need is to come home, flop on the couch and find that peak-time entertainment on the box is half an hour about a day in the life of someone who spends *their* life swiping tin after mind-numbing tin of beans across the barcode-thingy in Safeway.

And why do they *all* have to star a camp twat with a goatee beard?

THANK YOU FOR YOUR PATIENCE.
BACK TO THE ORIGINAL TANGENT . . .

Sadly, too many stewards failed the personality test to become traffic Nazis – that is, they were found to have a trace of personality – and thus they spend their lives taking out their frustrations on football fans.

But, for all that I cannot excuse the sadism of someone who can be bothered making five paying customers play musical chairs just to satisfy his petty mind, I can understand it. The over-inflated sense of importance given to stewards at Scotland's big grounds is merely a by-product of the way the game at that level has been taken away from the people for whom it was invented.

And the reason that has happened is that in the eyes of those who run our top clubs, the fan is no longer the reason their businesses stay afloat.

The higher you go up the football food chain, the smaller the percentage of income that comes from the turnstiles. Commercial income is taking over. TV cash dictates when games will be played.

When I was growing up, season-ticket-holders were toffs. They had enough dough to pay for a whole campaign of home games all at once. Wow. They nearly all had shiny Triumph Heralds and string-backed leather driving gloves.

(*There's another thing; why were driving gloves string-backed? What possible purpose is there for having a bit of vest on the back of your hands? Is it like, cars have a glove compartment, so gloves have a very-small-items-of-shopping compartment?*)

Nowadays, however, nearly everyone who goes regularly to top-division games in Scotland has a season-ticket and clubs use this as evidence that football is booming. Nearer the truth is that more people are buying season-tickets because more grounds are all-seated and having your own seat is the only way to be sure of being beside your mates or your family.

Thus the season-ticket has ceased to be a status symbol for the better-off; it is now a necessity for many who had always budgeted their football week-to-week and who can ill afford nine months' outlay all at once. And they soon find that going into debt – for many do – does not guarantee you any privileges as a customer.

Say you support Rangers; you pay, let's say, £300 for a season-ticket which tells you on what days and at what times the matches you have paid to see will be played. Yet at least eight times during that season, fixtures may be changed to suit the demands of television. This will usually mean Saturday games moving to Sundays. But say you work on Sundays? What can you do about it? The square root of sod-all, mate. Your club already has your dosh gathering interest in the bank or helping pay for the latest superstar who earns more in an hour than you scraped together for your little book of briefs. If you can't actually use those briefs, tough. No longer is an empty seat a loss-maker.

Hey-ho, though, it's the price you pay for your club 'modernising' the game. The price you pay for your board dragging football 'out of the dark ages'. Because the new age of the people's game does not include people like you.

A football match without fans? Surely not, surely it would be impossible! Oh yeah? Tell that to some whizzo commercial director who's sold the TV rights, filled every advertising hoarding, packed out the restaurants with big-spending corporate guests and made his club a million quid before a ball is kicked. All without that old-fashioned lottery over whether money will roll in at the gate. No more worries over what to do with unsold pies that are costing you money just to go mouldy; now all the smoked salmon and sirloin steaks are paid for – well over restaurant prices – before they even reach the kitchen. Who cares how many pounds of leftovers they have to toss out at the end of the night?

It's an obscene business of people with more money than sense jumping on a tax-deductible bandwagon which has nothing to do with football and everything to do with image, with impressing clients, with pressing flesh. These are the guys the top clubs care about now, not the working punter spending a mighty wedge of his or her wages to take the kids to the game. But, as I say, if you follow one of the big boys it's the price you pay for being part of New Football.

When Aberdeen, as another example, went out of the Scottish Cup to Livingston on 23 January 1999, it was their last Saturday home game until early April. If that is good for football then I am Gloria Hunniford. Yet even then my sympathy for Dons punters is diluted by the memory that their board wanted it this way and no one did anything to stop them.

The fans I feel sorry for are the ones who have no choice, no say in the matter. If you were, for example, a Falkirk fan who bought a season-ticket in August 1997, you did so in the fervent hope that come May your team would be one of the top two who went up to the Premier League. Come Christmas this looked a distinct possibility. Sure, Dundee were running away with it – but runners-up spot seemed yours for the taking. *Until some suits who didn't give a toss for a manky little team from a manky little ground decided you weren't getting in.*

END OF TANGENT. BACK TO THE MAIN REASON FOR ALL THIS BITTERNESS

So you see why I'd have had more twisted pleasure out of Stenhousemuir being drawn at home to Rangers in the third round of the 1999 Tennent's Scottish Cup than at Ibrox. Mind you, they probably wouldn't have let them play it at Ochilview, would they? We can't have the big teams slumming it, can we? They'd have come up with . . . um . . . *safety reasons* and switched it to Broadwood or Tynecastle or somewhere that didn't have the stench of poverty about it.

But they did go to Ibrox and they did get the fat cheque and they did have a brilliant day and arguably they gave Rangers an even bigger showing up than they might have at home. More people got to see the laziness and arrogance of the football rich this way.

Rangers won 2–0, but some of their players were a disgrace. I watched Andrei Kanchelskis, the most expensive player in Scottish football history at £5.5 million, saunter around and I wondered what the hell they were paying him £40,000 a week for. Think of that for a moment. Forty grand a week. That's £160,000 a month. Which is just about as much as Stenny took from that game and used to pay off their entire debt, knock down their derelict stand and put a business plan in place for the next three years.

Yet the deal with Kanchelskis seemed to be that *because* he was getting so much money, *because* he was so valuable, he didn't have to graft. Surely that's all the wrong way round? Surely the more you earn, the more they rate you, the more effort you should be putting in to justify yourself?

He was up against Adrian Sprott that day, a thirty-six-year-old civil servant who plays part-time for fifty quid a week and doesn't really enjoy being a left-back. He wants to get the ball and run forward. He plays for fun. Kanchelskis should have got the ball in the first minute, run past him and stuck in the first of a million crosses for his £30 million worth of mates to bullet past a shower of part-time defenders whose total wage demands for a year match Colin Hendry's for a week. Then he should have demanded the ball and skinned him again and again and lots more agains until Sprott got down on his knees and wept as he begged for mercy.

But no. Instead, Kanchelskis spent his afternoon shuffling up to the full-back and if there was the slightest resistance he'd check inside, or turn and pass back the way. Or run straight into him. At one point in the second half, Sprott took the ball off him and started one of his runs forward. Kanchelskis pulled him back by the shirt and got booked. How much effort would it have taken him to chase back, tackle and start another move? Plainly too much.

And he wasn't alone. Rangers scored in five minutes, a Stephane Guivarc'h shot which looped off thirty-nine-year-old centre-half Crawford Baptie's toe and over thirty-five-year-old keeper Lindsay Hamilton. Then they scored again when a Jorg Albertz shot zipped off the turf, hit Hamilton in the face and dropped for Rod Wallace to score.

Before and between and after those goals, though, Stenny did superbly. Every man played above himself, the only chance they had of keeping the score down. But even then, all the Rangers players had to do was raise their game by 10 per cent and they could have walked it. But they couldn't. Or, rather, they didn't.

They played like a team who knew they would win – and so why bust a gut? As they did win in the end, they'd probably say they were justified. They'd only have been kidding themselves.

I have a theory about these clashes of Diddy and Goliath. I've never seen one yet which didn't turn on the Diddy Team getting a golden chance to score. Sadly, nine times out of ten the excitement of the moment every one of them has dreamed of turns their legs to jelly.

So it was with Stenny at Ibrox. Twelve years before, Adrian Sprott had scored the winner when Hamilton won there in the Scottish Cup and inside three minutes he could have done so again. Alan Lawrence slung in a cross that keeper Stefan Klos and Colin Hendry both left to each other and Sprott came galloping in at the post. He threw himself into a ruck of bodies, got his toe to the ball and stuck it past Klos but against the near post. It was right in front of the Copland Road end. The sound of jaws on concrete was deafening. Within a minute, Guivarc'h had scored his jammy goal and the chance was gone.

My other theory about these games is that the Big Team will always, *always* get a break from the ref they don't deserve. If there's a tight offside at either end, it'll go against the Diddy Team. If there's a foul on the edge of each box, the Big Team will get theirs and the Diddy Team won't. And the Big Team will always, *always* get a penalty if they need one.

Two nights after the Stenhousemuir match I watched Oxford *v* Chelsea in the FA Cup on Sky. A club £14 million in debt, where the public send food parcels in because the staff went ten weeks without pay, against the swaggering multi-millionaires from the top of the Premiership. Diddy *v* Goliath to the power".

Oxford played superbly, far above themselves. Chelsea evened the scales further by performing below their best. By the fifty-fourth minute the balance tipped the way of the Diddies. A corner found Dean Windass, once of Aberdeen, and he headed them in front.

Then both Diddy *v* Goliath theories came into play. First, Oxford split the Chelsea defence apart and a cross found two men unmarked in the box. The first, six-foot seven-inch sub Kevin Francis, tried to hit it with his standing foot and fell over. The ball spun to teenager Jamie Cook, who was so surprised it hit his shins and went wide.

Still, Oxford led into the second of four minutes' injury time – until Theory No.2 reared its ugly head. Francis, back defending a corner, slid in and won the ball clean as a whistle from Luca Vialli. But ref Mike Reed pointed to the spot. It was so cruel you could have wept.

They asked Oxford boss Malcolm Shotton afterwards if he thought his side would have got a penalty in the same circum-stances and he just laughed. Studio guest Jim Smith, the Derby manager who used to boss Oxford, was beside himself with anger. He said they had been cheated. The ref claimed he'd had a perfect view and, even after seeing video replay of it in the tunnel, insisted it was a foul. But the whole country knew it wasn't.

Yes, Oxford were cheated, just as all our teams have been against the big guns. But no matter how angry it makes us, it doesn't mean the refs who cheat us are cheats. Does that make sense? No? Well, neither does football.

What I mean is that so many people who sit in judgement over the game – be they referees or linesmen or administrators or journalists – have been brought up supporting the big clubs. That stands to reason, as more people support the big clubs than support the wee clubs. And because they were brought up that way and are used to things going their way, following what they believe to be the natural order, they automatically see things from the viewpoint of the big clubs.

Take my own area, the press. If Dunfermline go to Parkhead and win, they will get little credit; nine out of ten headlines will scream that Celtic lost and the inquest will begin. If Motherwell go to Ibrox and put eleven men behind the ball to scrape a draw, they get slaughtered for killing the game. But if Rangers then go to Milan the following Wednesday and defend in depth for a draw against Inter, they would be hailed as heroes.

Or take red cards; the sending-off of an Old Firm player is *always* controversial. The sending-off of a player *against* the Old Firm is just the way it goes. I even once read a guy in a Sunday paper claim, after Colin Hendry was sent off for handball on the line against St Johnstone, that he had 'bravely sacrificed himself for the cause'. Send that man the Queen's Award For Guff.

Then take bigotry. *Please.* People will tell you – and this one really bugs me – that nothing can be done about the obnoxious bile of Old Firm fans because *it's just part of life*. But that's only true if it has been part of *your* life, if you're one of those people who believes we're all on one side or the other of The Divide. The rest of us would happily do something about it. Like banning all sectarian songs, scarfs, flags and badges from football grounds and jailing the creeps who flog all the paraphernalia from their nasty little stalls outside. But we go unheard, because for the clubs involved it's not only part of life but a damn profitable part, too.

And into this blinkered world of institutionalised division come referees. It stands to reason that if there are thirty on the grade one books, then maybe twenty will have a leaning towards one of the Old Firm – and will have the same inbuilt attitudes as everyone else in the same boat. That's not a criticism; that is a fact of human nature.

They maybe won't go out of their way to favour the team they support or supported, but they will naturally see things from their perspective. Therefore if Rangers are all over Stenny in the last five minutes, chasing a winner, and tackles are flying and a Rangers player goes down in the box, they may automatically assume the defender has made the desperate tackle of one who knows the game is up. They may also be swayed by 40,000 people shouting PENALTY! all at the same time. After all, which of us does not react with the mob in a mob situation? They may also have millions of pounds' worth of internationals turning to them at once screaming for the decision and be swayed by this pressure.

I say this as someone brought up to react against what the Old Firm are all about and against the favours they get and I admit I probably go into every game of theirs that I cover with an inbuilt cynicism. But I'd contend that's healthier than turning up believing it is their right to win.

Think how much more dissent the captains of the Old Firm get away with compared to any other player in the game. How many times have you watched TV and lip-read as Terry Butcher or Roy Aitken, Richard Gough or Tom Boyd scream in the faces of officials and get away with it? And how many times have you then seen a Diddy Team player question a decision half as vehemently and go in the book? Benny from *Crossroads* could do the maths.

When Dunfermline played Celtic at home, the TV cameras showed Craig Burley waging a non-stop war of words with referee Hugh Dallas, querying every foul, yelling in his ear, cursing and swearing the air blue. Was he booked? Of course not. But then Dunfermline defender Jamie Squires got a four-inch gash in his shin, and when the ref wouldn't stop the game, he yelled for help and got a yellow card.

Multiply that injustice by a thousand every season and the frustration of the Diddy Teams is hard to ignore. How many times did Paul Gascoigne get away with elbowing opponents when he was with Rangers? But how often would opponents get away with elbowing Old Firm players? Get those shoes and socks off again, Benny . . .

All of us who don't follow the Old Firm nurse our wrath over one particular injustice which ranks above all others. Me? I'm driven to this day by the memory of St Mirren's Scottish Cup semi-final defeat by Rangers in 1983. It was nil-nil in injury time in extra time in a replay at Hampden. Then they got a corner at the Rangers End. In it swung, up went Sandy Clark, down went the header. Lex Richardson, defending on the line, chested it down and hoofed it clear.

Brian McGinlay whistled for a goal.

No photograph or TV replay has ever convinced me the whole of the ball crossed the line. Yet worse than all the anger and frustration and despair we were left feeling then and since was the most painful emotion of all when you take on the Old Firm: helplessness. We felt helpless because we knew no one would kick up a fuss or demand TV evidence be used to reinstate us or call for the ref's head. Or give a monkey's, in truth.

Malcolm Shotton's right. Had it been the other way round there's no way the ref would have put Rangers – or Celtic, just so I don't get firebombed for being biased – out of the cup in the last seconds of injury time in extra time of a replay. It doesn't happen that way. Check your record books.

It makes me laugh – but only that kind of humourless laugh where you hear your throat go *ha!* – when the Old Firm argue over which gets the worse from refs when they meet. Who *gives* a toss? It's only four games a season. They get everything else that's going the rest of the time.

Rangers, by the way, got their regulation penalty that day against Stenny. Neil McCann turned Alan Lawrence and folded like a deckchair. Lawrence was booked for protesting, then Lindsay Hamilton dived and tipped away Jorg Albertz's kick. Hamilton now goes by the assumed name Joey Joe-Joe Junior Shabadoo and lives under MI6 protection on Orkney.

It was then the Rangers fans started heading home. By full-time the three thousand Stenny fans almost outnumbered them. It is the way of things. As I said in Chapter One, football is a seventy-minute game for many big-time fans; nothing more than an exercise in seeing their team go through the mechanics of winning so they can remind themselves they're best.

That's not what the game is about for me. It *has* to be about more than turning up just in time to get what you expect and then heading off again to beat the crowds. It has to be about travelling as much as arriving, about anticipation and rollercoaster emotions and about meeting new people and seeing new places.

It's about coming over the bridge by Perth on the way to Dundee and seeing the scenery open up in front of you like a giant curtain rising on the greatest theatre set ever built. It's about talking the hind legs off the game as your train goes over the Forth Bridge by night and the lights of the boats dance on the water.

Or coming back from Dundee via the multicoloured Perthshire countryside just as dusk hits, and watching the sun bleed onto snow-capped hills like strawberry sauce onto a cone when you were a kid. Or going to Dingwall for a midweek game and crossing the Kessock Bridge in Inverness just as the sun goes down over the Black Isle.

It's about standing in a deserted Forthbank an hour before a cup replay between Stirling Albion and Montrose when *Carnival de Paris* comes on the tannoy and you wonder who the hell they're playing it for. Then you think: It's me. They're playing it for me, because I'm the only person in the whole damn place and if I didn't think I might get caught on police CCTV I might have a bit of a dance right now.

It's about a pint of Guinness and a pie and beans with your mates in the pub beforehand, about watching the previews on the telly and wondering why only dogs can hear Mark Lawrenson. It's about that moment when the consciencious one in the company clocks the time and nudges you to drain your glasses and you button up tight and go out into the cold to join the march to the turnstiles.

It's about being able to laugh when you've lost and feel sorry for the losers when you've won. It's about diving for the Sunday papers to read all about it all over again.

All these things and so many more are a huge part of a day or a night at the game; it doesn't start when the whistle blows or as soon after the whistle blows as you can be bothered to dawdle into your place. It's always been a *day* for me and I have my dad to thank again for that.

It shouldn't be about routine, about getting no more and no less than you think is your due.

Fans of Big Teams aren't the ones who give me a buzz; not like the ones at grounds where they turn up with smiles on their faces. Funny, that; the less chance there is of actually winning anything, the more fun the punters seem to have. It's as if winning is stressful.

Watch Man U fans on telly or listen to them on radio phone-ins. Check how joyless they are. See their reactions when their team scores; it's not the release the rest of us get, that moment of football orgasm. No, they're looking for the other lot's fans, to taunt them, to give them the V, to get right in their faces and scream: 'How d'you like *that* then? How does it *feel*, loser?'

Then they tell them to rearrange the words *right up it get you* into a well-known phrase or saying and mull it over.

Listen to them when they phone in to David Mellor, even after watching their team score six or seven. They can't be satisfied with glorying in the brilliance of the team Fergie built. No, they call up to tell the rest to forget it, that they're all going to be ground into the dirt where they belong.

Where is the *fun* in these people? Is that what constant success does to you, turns you into a bad winner? Because if so I'm happy to take defeat.

They're like the kids in school who loved nothing better than to get in a circle and shout *fight, fight, fight* when there was no fight, just some poor wee geek in the foetal position on the playground concrete, wishing he was an octopus so he could protect all his bits from Headbanger Henderson's flailing boots.

You wonder how many of them could have found their way to Old Trafford with Sherpa Tensing for company before Fergie made them great; just as you laugh at the 200,000 Rangers fans who claim to have been there when crowds went down to 2,000.

You've also got to laugh when Celtic fans tell you they're the greatest in the world because they stay behind and cheer when their team lose the odd game and who thought slumping from European Cup-holders to only being third or fourth best in Scotland was a crisis.

It's easy to support Man U or Rangers or Celtic or any of the Big

Boys, because the worst that's ever going to happen from season to season is that you might not win a trophy. Pass the cyanide.

But it's hard to follow Albion Rovers or Berwick or Montrose because the *best* you can ever hope for is that one year a squadron of pigs might fly past your bedroom window and herald a once-in-a-generation promotion run.

I followed the Rovers in the run-in to them winning the Second Division title in 1989 and, just like Stranraer in 1998, it was wonderful – far more rewarding than covering every game as one of the Old Firm put yet another league flag in their bottom drawer with a barely stifled yawn.

In Stranraer's title season, I watched more than eighty games in all four Scottish divisions, all four English divisions, the Scottish Cup, the FA Cup, both Coca-Cola Cups, the League Challenge Cup, friendlies, the UEFA Cup, Cup-Winners' Cup, World Cup qualifiers and finally France '98 itself. I tell guys in my own game this and they look at me like I'm a pitied cousin who's one abdominal muscle short of a six-pack. They can't work out why anyone would want to go to Dumbarton on a miserable Tuesday night, why you'd go out of your way to watch Stenhousemuir training in the middle of winter when there's McTague of Larbert to do chores like that for you. It seems almost stupid to tell them it's about actually loving the game we're paid to watch, so I usually shrug and say the expenses for the mileage is good and they nod sagely and tap their noses. Hiking up your money they can understand perfectly.

Anyway, if I hadn't gone to Stenny on a freezing Tuesday night in January I wouldn't have had all the fun with the dufflecoats, would I?

Ewan Smith, a young reporter at *The Sun*, came up with the idea before the Rangers game of getting all the players in Gloveralls like the one famously worn by their gaffer, Terry Christie. The picture desk phoned the duffle-makers and asked for a loan of sixteen. Gloverall said okay, if we picked them up from their factory in Northampton they'd let us keep them. So we sent a boy down to get them. Mike Schofield, one of our photographers, then humped them all in the back of the car and we put one up on each peg in the away dressing-room before the players turned up for training. When Graeme Armstrong, Christie's No.2, told them about the picture we wanted they thought he was winding them up.

But in they trooped to the away dressing-room and saw all the coats hanging up and dutifully they grabbed one each and put them on over their training kit. And for the next hour we had a hoot taking snaps of The Boys In The Hoods.

We had this brilliant idea of winding Rangers up by mimicking Celtic's famous pre-match Huddle – only we'd do the Hoodle. Sadly, the pic never worked out, but it was still a top night.

And best of all was the collective look on their faces when we told them they could keep the coats. They were thrilled to bits, more so than if we'd thrown them the equivalent in dosh. Mike asked me what I thought would have happened had we tried to get the Rangers players to do a pic in daft coats and then told them they could keep them. The question didn't need answering.

Come the Saturday, Stenny sub Alan Lawnsdowne went up to £5.25 million Rangers midfielder Giovanni van Bronckhorst and asked to swap shirts. The Dutchman turned up his nose and said no. I found this out back on the team bus – I'd spent the day with the players – by which time I was already fuming at Rangers coach Dick Advocaat. He'd been asked in the press conference what he thought of Stenny's performance. It would have taken nothing for him to say that they should be proud of themselves, that they were a tribute to their division, that all the credit should be theirs. Instead, he shrugged and sighed: 'They did as well as they could have.'

Meanwhile, up in one of the stadium's labyrinth of suites, Graeme Armstrong was receiving an award from the SFA for playing his 1000th competitive game. It was his third such presentation of the day after picking up a Viking horn from the club's Norwegian fans and a decanter and glasses from Rangers. He accepted them all in the quiet grace of the kind of gentleman he is. He charmed all around him – and, at forty-two and a half, he also played so immaculately the sponsors gave him a bottle of champagne as their Man of the Match. On the way out, he shook hands with old Stan the commissionaire and said thanks for having him.

On the Monday morning, Terry Christie resigned to become manager of Alloa – the job Craig Levein had turned down – and that night Armstrong was appointed manager of Stenhousemuir. He would have to juggle a busy job with a whisky firm with managing *and* playing for a team going for promotion to the Second Division. But he would do it with a smile, even when his first game ended in a 4–1 tanking away to Queen's Park and his second in a 2–1 home defeat by Albion Rovers, and their dreams looked to be dying. He would work away quietly and turn the team around and put them back up there in pole position to go up.

No one would deny him his success, on the pitch or off it. Scores of people would phone and fax and write to congratulate him. He would reply to them all, graciously and modestly, because he knew that it was right and because if you don't show people respect when things are going well they will not be there for you when things are going badly.

Sadly, too many of those in Scottish football's so-called élite, the Greed-Is-Good merchants, have forgotten about simple courtesy, about customer service, about humility. They've got their power and their TV deal and their sponsorship and their smart talk and they're sorted.

What they don't have, unlike those who live simply for football and do so within their means, is friends. But then that, sports fans, is the real difference between rich and poor. *Class.*

FOUR

I DON'T WANT
TO GO TO CHELSEA

I believe it was Dr Johnson who said that he who is tired of London is tired of life. Which only goes to prove what a lard-arsed olde planke *he* must have been.

It is not the person who is tired of London who has the problem. It is the place. I know, I lived there for approximately 20,822,400 seconds and each tick of the clock felt like one of Doug Rougvie's size 11s in the danglies.

People say it must be a wonderful place to stay; all those clubs and restaurants and theatres and tourist attractions on tap 24/7. What they don't click is that that stuff is *for* tourists. Stay for a weekend and you never see the rest of it, the traffic-jammed artery roads leading out to grey boroughs, the rows of houses repossessed and boarded up, the unhappiness of the drones.

Those who stay there longer than the time it takes to eat a couple of overpriced hamburgers, take in a show and ask if that really *was* Vic Reeves you saw on the other side of Piccadilly are the most miserable creatures on earth.

As Rab C said far more accurately than Doc Wobblebottom ever could have: 'The London's awright for a fracture, but ah widnae like to be terminal wae it.'

Amen, bandage boy.

However, I will be putting it to the new Scottish Parliament that every football fan of every club in this great country of ours should be forced to spend time in London. Call it a sort of national service. Then maybe they'd stop whingeing so much about their lot and realise what a wonderful place we live in and what a happy and relaxed number our game is.

I know, I was that conscripted soldier – and the place burst my head in six dispiriting months. London drains your spirit like a leech drains blood. Anyone who tells you they've lived there and had a non-stop yeehah undoubtedly did so with the aid of chemicals.

I went down there in March 1997. Packed in the job I had always wanted, sports editor of the *Daily Record*, and gone sarf with no future sorted out. Luckily, *The Sun* took me back. I worked on the desk in Wapping and wrote two columns a week for the Scottish edition. Then *Scotland on Sunday* asked me to cover English games for them.

Work was great. London was guff. The only positive function the place had was to make me realise how lucky we all are to have Scotland as our homes.

Before I went, I had got so cheesed off with the forty-minute, twenty-five-mile rush-hour drive from Falkirk to Glasgow every morning. Once I got back home again it seemed like nipping round the corner to the shops. In London, every day is one of the Great Railway Journeys of the World. Everything in London is a slog. You'd go crackers if you lived in Dundee and travelled to Glasgow and back for work every day – but that was the equivalent of me going from west London to the *Currant Bun*. A two-and-a-half-hour round trip – and that's without delays.

Forget even *trying* to drive to places. On my first weekend I took the car eight miles south-east to watch Newcastle play Wimbledon at Selhurst Park on a Sunday afternoon and it took just over two hours.

From then on the Tube won. And I lost the will to live. From then on the deal was:

A five-minute walk to the bus stop, a ten-minute wait (don't ask why I didn't leave the house ten minutes later; no matter *when* you went it was *always* a ten-minute wait. And it's true – three *do* come together after that).

Twenty minutes to Ealing Broadway Tube station.

Ten minutes minimum fidgeting on a train waiting for it to move (and very often seeing the one on the next platform go first, even though the board said the opposite).

Forty-five minutes to Tower Hill – if the rattling, smoky train didn't break down.

A final ten-minute hike to Chez Rupe.

The last leg was the only bit when you felt human.

The first thing you see when you come up from the bowels of Tower Hill station is the Tower of London. You walk down through its tourist-heaving gardens, through the only underpass in London which doesn't stink of stale pee (and when you live in London long enough, you get to know the difference between stale and fresh pee; you smell so much of it in phone boxes you know what vintage of Thunderbird the peeist had been drinking) and emerge into St Katherine's Dock.

It's beautiful there, an oasis of class and calm in a Sahara of fumes and noise and ignorant, arrogant doofwits. One hundred square yards of boats big and small, moored by the rich and even richer, all surrounded by picturesque shops and cafés and pubs and restaurants.

In the middle, there's a little bridge which slides open on chains to let pleasure boats come and go. It was the only place in London I saw people standing waiting and didn't feel they were one tut-tut away from a riot.

I loved that walk, because it was the only time in London I didn't feel threatened. Not physically threatened – I come from Paisley and after thirty years there everywhere else is bufty country – so maybe *oppressed* is the word. The atmosphere smothered you.

London choked you. The air was stuffy and smoggy and clung to your clothes like smoke in a boozer. The traffic was like constantly being pushed along by a baying mob which had lost all reason. The people were suspicious and unfriendly at best and hostile at worst. You could feel ill-will coming up through the pavements like the goo in *Ghostbusters*.

In St Katherine's Dock, you were somewhere else. You could have an overpriced beer or an overpriced takeaway sandwich or windowshop for overpriced shoes that London's manky pavements would ruin in a week and for once not feel resentful about being ripped off or begrudge every particle of air that, outside, you were forced to swap for black gunk.

But then you were out the other side, into the building site of another block of £250,000 penthouses just big enough to swing an undernourished gerbil in, across the road to a Godzilla-sized office block with about 20 square feet of prime-rate space actually in use, past a giant Safeway side by side with a plastic chainstore pub called the Old Monk, through the high-security turnstile and into Chez Rupe.

The Old Monk is an odd boozer, a huge, soulless barn with piped music and bland, dark-wood tables. It's like a giant hotel lobby. There are loads of them in London, these chainstore boozers; all with zillions of staff, 99 per cent of whom are Aussie backpackers with more body piercing than IQ points, yet hardly any punters.

You could hear the beeping and pinging of half a dozen slot machines hanging round the walls like barrel-chested geeks with loud shirts and no pals. Eerie.

Pass by any time in daylight and you'll see maybe twenty or thirty drinking at a time. Some nights when I was finishing work, around ten, they had more guest real ales than customers. It was like Hampden at a particularly unappealing Queen's Park home game in the middle of the Glasgow Fair.

Then, if you were there at about quarter to six, you clicked why they had all those backpackers on standby, all those slot machines, all those treacly guest ales like Olde Toenail and Dead Dog's Scrotum. At quarter to six, every office within a mile emptied to fill every square inch of the Monk.

From then till about eight, it was pandemonium. Happy Hour Again. Ties got loosened and hair shaken free and inhibitions left in a heap with the briefcases and handbags. I've seen women whip their tops off, grey-suited blokes pour pints over each other's heads. Even saw one of the Aussies serve someone in turn. Once.

Then, as quickly as the place had filled, it was over; as suddenly as a Caribbean rainstorm or a mother-in-law's good mood. Empty. You could hear the beeping of the machines and the clanking of the Aussies' faces. From then until closing it was like the grave, so quiet you could hear the manager laughing in his office as he counted the piles and piles of tenners and twenties. Who needs all-day opening? The Old Monk could operate from teatime till the end of *Coronation Street* and turn over a million a year. And when it closed every evening, all the beer-pourers and top-whipper-offers could straighten their ties and pile up their hair again and pick up their briefcases and handbags and scurry off to catch trains and the Tube to all points dull and sit there never looking at or talking to another living soul. *For that, sports fans, is London.*

All the glitz and the glamour and the anyone-who-doesn't-party-all-night-is-a-wuss stuff is a front, it's all false. Yes, thousands and thousands crawl home at six in the morning and sleep and get up and start all over again, but they don't do it because they enjoy it. They do it because they think they *should*, because magazines and the telly and adverts *tell* them to. Baaaaa.

Rab C's right. The London's fine for a visit; restaurants, theatres, Buck House and all the other rope-a-dope tourist traps. But to live in? To live in it is a God-awful, soul-sucking, mind-rotting, lonely, miserable, bloody hellhole. And not just for the thousands sleeping rough or the runaways who end up selling their bodies and their souls for a roof and a fix.

All over London, from the Irish communes of the north to the barra-boy wideness of the south and east, to the west with its uneasy mix of the professional, the artistic and the ethnic, there are hundreds of thousands of unhappy people who pretend they're having the time of their lives.

Nowhere is it more lonely or miserable than on the Tube. How many hours did I spend on it? How long did I waste waiting for trains to shake into rattling action, counting the twenty-two stops from Ealing Broadway to Tower Hill and back again?

Getting off because the engine was knackered, squeezing on to the already-heaving next one. Seeing resentment burn in the faces of your fellow passengers because you dared bid for more than your allocated eighth of an inch of standing space.

How many times did I finish my paper or the chapter of a book and look up to find myself in eye contact with a stranger, only for them to look away like they had caught me doing something rude with the Queen Mother?

How often did I see them eye my discarded *Evening Standard* like it was a T-bone and they were an alsatian, knowing all the while their buttocks were clenching and unclenching with embarrassment at the thought of actually asking someone they didn't know for a swatch at the telly page? Because, of course, by asking for a look at my paper they would have to communicate with a stranger and that might – *nightmare scenario* – lead to a conversation and after that it would only be a short step to me chopping them into tiny pieces and feeding them to *my* alsatian for want of a T-bone. So they'd glance at the paper and then at me and then back at the paper and then at the person next to me and take their eyes straight back off *them* because they *also* had a paper they were finished with.

Then I'd cross my legs and brush the leg of the person opposite with the toe of my shoe and they'd look at me like I just exposed myself, which I very rarely did. Bodily contact on the Tube is even more offensive than eye contact. Saying sorry only makes it worse, because then you leave them in the dilemma over whether to say sorry back – Londoners always reply to apologies with one of their own – or to ignore you.

If they say sorry back it opens the door once more to dreaded conversation and the probability of the chopping up/hungry alsatian option. But if they ignore me and I turn out to be a psycho (because everyone in London who is not you is a psycho; it says so in the *Standard*) I might chop them up and feed them to Sabre as punishment for their ignorance.

So generally they compromise and mumble something that sounds like *Wuh-hurghle* and that's as good as you get. *Wuh-hurgle* is the Tube traveller's equivalent of three hours' witty banter round the dinner table with Oscar Wilde and Chandler from *Friends*.

Worse still is travelling on the Tube with football fans, because then you have *actual* menace to cope with and that's even more distressing. Catch a knuckle-scraper's eye and he'd pull a rottweiler out of his back pocket like a sharpened comb and have your gizzard out. But catch a normal Londoner's eye when there's knuckle-scrapers on board and they'll freeze with horror at the thought that you might be a knuckle-scraper's lookout, ready to alert the rottweiler-carrier-in-chief that someone was looking at you for fear of looking at *them*. You can see them fingering their gizzards in fear.

You know the drill with thugs on a train. You pretend they *are* alsatians. Ignore them, show no fear and they'll ignore you. They want confrontation, it brightens up their grunty little lives. But Londoners, despite years of practice, have never mastered this stand-off.

You see them wanting to get off, even though it's not their stop; but that would mean not only the prospect of saying 'Excuse me' to a *normal* fellow passenger/potential psycho and all the perils that entails, but also the possibility of brushing past a knuckle-scraper, who would without fail take that as a challenge to fight.

And by fight, of course, I mean pummel.

So they sit there and try not to look at anything; me, the knuckle-scrapers, the air, the adverts, the outside world. They can't think of anything happy in case they smile involuntarily and the knuckle-scraper grunts: '*You laaaarfin' at me?*'

Yet they can't close their eyes and pretend to sleep, because someone might steal their paper or their wallet or their trousers. And they can't get off and catch another train, because they might get rottweilered on the way past – and, anyway, why should someone else get *their* seat? So they sit tight and try to fix on some point in the atmosphere that magically vaporises them.

Some Londoners stay on the Tube forever, they die in their seats, rather than say 'Excuse me' to someone blocking their way at the best of times. So they'd rather eat glass than manoeuvre round a bloke with a sharpened dog in the back of his fainty-arsed 501s.

When knuckle-scrapers are aboard the Tube, some Londoners get so fazed they end up getting off *with* them, being herded along with them to the ground, pickpocketing a coupla geezers at souvenir stalls, breaking the police cordon to ambush rival fans in a boozer and stabbin' a copper.

'*Well, 'ee looked at me, din'nee?*' *Mr Arnold Normal, 43, a chartered surveyor from Crouch End told the Old Bill.*

Middle-aged women in twinsets and cashmere carcoats who set out to buy trout at Harrods end up at the New Den, booing black players and Yiddos and organising after-match rucks on their mobiles.

Well, it's easier than asking for a look at someone's paper.

The New Den. Gor blimey, guv'nor. The scariest place I've ever been and I've been to Greenock. Went to cover a midweek Second

Division game against Bristol City for the *Currant* and never once felt comfortable. As Dr Johnson might have said, he who isn't careful at Millwall games is tired of living.

The New Den is a big version of St Johnstone's McDiarmid Park; four separate, grey, concrete stands and about as much life as a morgue. Especially on a misty, damp Tuesday night in October when it's two-thirds deserted. It was built to hold 20,000, frighteningly optimistic for a club with a hard core of less than half that in their old Den days. Maybe they elected a couple of knuckle-scrapers to the planning committee as fan reps and the architects did wot they woz taaaaawld, know wot ah mean?

The old Den was a horror story, a cramped nineteenth-century hole down a street called – no kidding – Cold Blow Lane. How attractive did *that* make it sound? In the '70s a manager of theirs called Gordon Jago tried to get the council to change its name to Montego Bay Avenue, but he was larfed out of court, wunnee.

Since the dawn of time, at which point in history the evolution of their fans ended, the Den had a record of regular pitch invasions, FA-imposed shutdowns and attacks on refs and rival players. The punters were hard-bitten Saarf Laaahndahn wideboys (that is to say their heads were narrower than their necks) with no time nor respect nor nuffink for anyone from ahtside their manor.

I think the deal was meant to be that when the New Den – or Senegal Fields as it is also bizarrely known – opened, Millwall would reinvent themselves as a family club and thus double attendances figures overnight. This worked at other clubs, where mums and kids had only been put off by the previously prehistoric facilities – but here they still stayed away because of the prehistoric company they were still forced to keep. And thus all that happened was that the knuckle-scrapers had more room to spread out and their abuse of blacks and Yiddos gained an eerie echo, like someone shouting threats at you down an alleyway.

To get there meant a fun-filled twenty-five minutes on the Tube to Charing Cross, just behind Trafalgar Square, a hop upstairs to the overland platforms and a train to South Bermondsey. It was chocca with Millwall punters.

Funny, I'd never been bothered about people hearing my accent in London's melting pot of cultures. But now I found myself keeping schtum.

Luckily the first-time traveller to any ground need never ask which station to get off at. You just follow the scarves and they lead you all the way to the stadium. Plenty were getting off and I was damn glad of it, because South Bermondsey station was not the kind of place where you wanted to be alone at night. It's high up off the street, one of those where you access both directions from a central platform, with a ticket office at the entrance end and then a winding, fenced-off path down towards ground level. But halfway down the fence has been cut and the gash reveals an unlit slope of wasteground from which you can hear the sound of rottweilers being sharpened. Turn left and down and you hit the road.

It's all houses round there, pretty modern, though in the dark it was hard to tell who'd live there. In London, new brick-built estates for yuppies stand cheek-to-cheek with identikit council schemes, and the inhabitants of each keep an uneasy distance. The yuppies live in fear that the council punters will ransack their homes and strangle their cats; the council punters resent the yuppies for gatecrashing their manors.

All I could sense here was that it was the kind of place where if you were on fire they wouldn't run out with a glass of water. I stayed close to the group of fans who looked least likely to be carrying cans of petrol.

It was to be the way of that evening; always had you on edge. The New Den is the kind of place where you pray for the home team to win – but where even if they do they might still give you a kicking to make sure you respect them.

If Bristol City knew this, they obviously didn't care for the welfare of their few hundred followers. They cantered to 2–0 up before half-time and were worth more. Millwall were woeful, all eleven of them. But ten got off the hook. All the stick was piled on their pint-sized midfielder Bobby Barnes.

Well, 'ee wuz a nigga, wunnee?

A local reporter told me the boy could score a hat-trick, perform open-heart surgery and invent an individual potlet of milk that didn't splash your tie when you tore it open, and still get slaughtered. All because he's black. You had to admire his guts for even turning up to work.

Afterwards, I asked the press steward to get me City's right-back, Adam Locke, for an interview. He'd scored to cap an excellent performance. It was just my luck he was a local boy and half of Saaarf Laaahndahn had come to see him. He took ages with them in the Players Lounge before coming through.

I just made the deadline with a rewritten match report including his quotes, which meant I didn't get away from the ground until well after ten. The carpark was close to deserted.

It was about a mile back to the station; out of the stadium, under a railway bridge, turn right opposite a boozer called the Severed Head or the Tattooed Arms or something equally black, and straight on past red-brick houses with their deaf, dumb and blind occupants.

I hate railway bridges. When I was a kid I had a phobia about walking under the one at the bottom of the Chain Road that separated Foxbar from Ferguslie Park. Dad and I used to go down that way to get the bus out to watch his work's team sometimes, and every time we went under the bridge I cringed at the thought of a train crashing through and crushing us. That and the fear of pigeons pooing on my head.

I've not changed, still hate railway bridges. And especially railway bridges where Millwall fans could be hiding round the corner brandishing sharpened rottweilers. The 10.45 to Charing Cross coming down on my head would have been a blessed relief.

I walked with that sense of tension in every muscle that you get in scary places, shivering and not just with the biting cold. Every few paces I'd spin round, sensing a huge fudwit was standing there holding a big stick with a nail in it. It was horrible.

And the nearer I got to South Bermondsey station, the more I could see in my mind's eye that hole in the fence and the gang of grunting neanderthals who lurked on the wasteground behind it, ready to jump out and ask 'oo I wuz lookin' at. If they heard a Jock accent, they'd be in their element and I'd be in handy bite-sized cubes.

Had I seen a cab there and then I'd have flagged it down and taken it all the way back to Ealing, thirty-five quid away. Your money or your life. But none came and, hard as I tried to walk on the spot, I was at the path and climbing with ever-heavier legs towards the hole in the fence.

Scared? Only Pullars of Perth will ever know *just* how terrifying that walk was.

It's fear of the unknown that gets me. Mum always told me to watch it in That Glasgow when I went out with my mates, but you knew where to go and where not to. Anyway, I was eleven. I could handle myself. Paisley itself is as mental as you can get, but you savvy how to steer clear of trouble.

But here? I knew no one and nothing except that I wanted to be at home, in Falkirk, with a cup of tea and a fresh pair of boxer shorts. Suddenly I was at the fence. No one jumped out. On and up I walked, but with that sort of half-run people do when they're being followed, which I wasn't but might well have been.

There were maybe a dozen others on the platform, waiting for the next train towards The London. Among them was a press boy from one of the Bristol papers and he looked just as unsettled as me. We didn't speak, me hiding my Jockness and him his Carrot-Crunching drawl.

Then I spotted them, staring across at us. Three geezers so neanderthal the wheel would have been unimaginable science fiction to them. Their scars had scars. Their hair was so cropped they must have clippered it from the inside. The arms of their chairs had tattoos.

I made eye contact with the biggest one and heard his back pocket go 'Woof'.

'Oi, mayte,' he called, 'wossatoime?'

I made a *what-was-that-chief?* shruggy face at him. He walked towards me. I fumbled in my coat for something to defend myself with. I would either be done for assault with a deadly Refresher Bar or GBH by spiral notebook.

Ug – he looked like an Ug – was two steps away from me. 'Oi said – wossatoime, mayte.' He pointed at his wrist. I was a dead man.

Now, sports fans, I didn't choose to do what I did next. It just happened. I looked the most frightening person I have ever encountered straight in the eye and said: 'Cor, sowwy mayte – didn't 'ear ya, did oi? It's Bill and Ben t'Somerset an' Devon, innit?'

'Cheers, mayte.'

'No problem, me awld foive-speed gearbox. Do wot, knock it on the 'ead.'

Either it was the most convincing Cockney accent of all time or he was more frightened of this gabbling halfwit than I was of him. The Carrot Cruncher just gawped. I'm pretty sure he was about to say: 'But aren't you a Scotsman . . .' and get us both mutilated, but just then the train pulled in. I held him back by the arm until the knuckle-scrapers had lurched into one carriage and then led him to the other.

And all that for a £53 match fee.

This air of intimidation hangs heavy around much of English football, but more than anywhere else in The London, where the people carry the added weaponry of all that bitterness and bigotry and pent-up anger.

Londoners – and by that I mean people who live in London, not just those who actually *belong* to it – are mean-spirited, insular, suspicious and selfish. Not that I want to make any sweeping generalisations here. Or get personal. But they are.

Go into a pub with five Londoners and see the reaction you get when you offer to buy a round. Their faces all read: Does not compute. Then they all start making *naah, Gawd bless ya* noises and saying they'll get their own. So you're insisting and eventually you wear them down and get them in – then when they're done they split into twos or threes for the next round.

And they say *we're* tight.

That attitude spreads right through their lives. They'll get their own, what's theirs is theirs, don't invade their space. I'm All Right Jack, Pull The Ladder Up. It all makes the idea of home and away fans mixing easily at their football games a non-starter.

Go to a London ground with away supporters and you'll know what it's like to live in a Police State, which is no slight on the police. They simply intimidate the punter because it's the only way to be as sure as anyone can be that it won't All Go Off.

That's what they call trouble down there: '*It all wen' off, dinnit?*' The whole atmosphere about London is that they're all just waiting for the day when it all goes off, and every football match is a microcosm of that feeling of doom.

The cops wear visors and carry big sticks and shields and wear protective body-armour; the *horses* wear visors, for God's sake, because knuckle-scrapers have been known to scoosh ammonia in their eyes to cause a panic.

The orders from the officers with scrambled egg on their shoulder is clear: keep the lid on. Nothing more, nothing less. If that means putting a cramp on the enjoyment of the many to keep a grip on the doofwit few, so be it.

You constantly feel you're being watched. By the police, by locals, by shopkeepers. You know that scene at the tail-end of *Reservoir Dogs*, when they've all got their guns trained on each other and the eyes are darting back and forward waiting for someone to make the first move? That's the atmosphere in which London football is played.

I hate all those novels that have made hooliganism cool; *Steaming In, Headhunters, Stab 'Im Stan* and the particularly chilling *I Set Out to Buy Trout at Harrods and Ended Up Organising a Fatal Ruck on My Mobile*. They're football porn for the middle classes, shock-fodder for the New Fan to read and shriek about over the *boeuf en croute* at their next dinner party.

Nick Hornby started it. Him and *Fever Pitch*. If you haven't read it, it's about him growing up as so much of an Arsenal fan that when he went to Cambridge – as all mad mental Gooners do, of course – he couldn't be bothered getting the train back into London on a Saturday, so he patronised the local Diddy Team instead. Not quite how the *Sunday Telegraph* reviewed it, but there you go.

Fever Pitch made football screamingly fashionable for the Cabernet Sauvignon set, for graduate types who had previously seen all fans as . . . well, as the sort I've spent most of this chapter describing. Now it was cool to be seen at the footy. Suddenly there were hordes of yuppies buying season-tickets for Highbury and Old Trafford and Stamford Bridge, even though some of them had never seen a football match before. Others would claim they *used* to support Orient or Bury or Colchester. Or at least those were the teams closest to Mummy and Daddy's house when they were little and they went once for a *scream* with their chums and asked loudly why the little umpire in the tight shorts kept raising a funny flag.

I said earlier in this book that people who claim to know nothing about football do my head in. But not as much as people who know nothing about football but go anyway and make it clear they know nothing about football.

About ten years ago some mates of mine who are Celtic fans took a lad from London they'd met in the pub to an Old Firm game at Parkhead. The things drink make you do, eh? Now, the boy *claimed* to be a football fan – but once he got there he almost got them killed.

They're behind the goals and Rangers are kicking away from them. Ten minutes in, Rangers man goes down in the far box. Penalty. Celtic End goes mental.

'*That's never a ******* penalty, ya masonic orange Billy Boy royalist Queen Mother-lovin'* ******* **** ****** *******'

'That's right, Father Fitzgerald, you tell the ********!'

'*Thanks, Bish.*'

Chaos, bedlam, madness, pandemonium at their end. Eighteen thousand red, white and blue scarves going up in the air at the other.

And the London boy says: 'Well, to be fair, we're quite far away from it here – but it did *look* like he caught his ankle.'

Ever heard 40,000 people go quiet at once?

So my mates are putting their arm round him and saying loudly what a josher he is and how he really, really hates they Huns, and he's an alternative comedian and he's been sarcastic; all the while praying the boy gets the message.

But up steps Mark Walters, puts Bonner the wrong way and he goes: 'Oh, well taken – wasn't that well taken? That's a perfect penalty . . .'

Today that man is Tony Blair.

And even worse than the Know-Nothings at the football are the Turncoats. They ones who say they grew up supporting Ayr United, but now never miss a Rangers game – except when they're playing a wee team, of course. No point taking it to fanatical extremes.

By that reckoning, if fundamentalism continues to rise in the Middle East these people will soon be saying: '*Well, I grew up Church of Scotland. But I'm Islam now, because they've got more chance of winning a big war. Never miss a call to prayer – except when it clashes with* Style Challenge, *natch.*'

Sadly, the next post-Hornby spin-offs were those trendified accounts of life among the knuckle-scrapers. A never-ending spew of books that make hooliganism sound like such a buzz. Suppose they must appeal to the knuckle-scraping element themselves, as long as there are plenty of pictures of coppers getting their heads panned in, and to the weedy ones who hang about the fringes shouting then running like hell when it All Goes Off.

But I reckon they also went down a bomb with thrusting London stockbroker types, the post-Thatcherite stormtroopers who'd tread on grannies to get to a fast buck. Let's face it, they're just thugs in stripey suits anyway. So for corporate raids read pub ambushes and for the aggro of the stock market floor read running wiv the lads.

The *Steamin' In* genre portrays football violence as cocaine without the impotence and the collapsed nostrils. A massive high. But anyone whose knuckles don't scrape and who's been caught up in crowd trouble at the match knows that it doesn't leave you with a buzz. It leaves you in shock.

Sure, being on the outside of it – that is, the bit beyond where even the weediest fearties hang about – can be exciting, when you're shouting across a police cordon or through a fence at the other lot, taunting and making come-ahead signals when coming-ahead is not an option. When it *does* All Go Off, though, you need to be some kind of animal to get a kick, physically or mentally. I've never been anywhere near aggro in or around a game where I didn't wish I was safe at home.

Yet they peddle this guff about it being cool, make TV dramas and movies about it, dish out cheap thrills and turn it into this folk opera where no one gets hurt but the bad guy who deserves it. Tell that to some poor kid who gets stabbed in a mêlée outside a ground, just for being in the wrong place at the wrong time.

I never once went to a game in London without at some point

entertaining the thought that it might be me this time, the lost boy who turned the wrong corner straight into Mrs Twinset with the Harrods swordfish and the cold, killer eyes.

And you know what? It strikes me now that to add to all the other drawbacks of football in the Smoke, all the menace and the tension and the travel hassles, I never saw a Premiership game worth a monkey's anyway. Arsenal 0 Spurs 0; Spurs 1 Wednesday 1; Spurs 1 Boro 0; Arsenal 1 Liverpool 2; Chelsea 1 Newcastle 0; West Ham 0 Newcastle 0. Not a classic among them.

Yet I don't remember fans being either up or down at home-time, which always made me wonder how many of them really *were* fans and how many had just read some Nick Hornby and thought what a *hoot* being a footy fan would be.

Big-time London – and all of big-time England – gets away with mediocre games because of the *experience*. The marketing men behind the Premiership are geniuses. They have reinvented football for a whole new audience.

The New Fan wouldn't know the difference between a duff game and a Waldorf salad. All that matters is having a Good Day Out. And the Premiership guarantees that. Watch Sky Sports, watch the cruddiest Wimbledon *v* Southampton Monday-Night Stinker, all howling rain and Marcus Gayle. Do you turn off halfway through? No, because the Sky guys *promise* it's going to get better, any minute now.

Which means in The London you stand outside games worrying that any minute now it's All Going To Go Off – then once you're inside you believe that it's All Going To Go On.

They never wander away with ten minutes to go, Premiership fans, because they're on a Good Day Out and by God they're going to wring every minute's worth out of it. Good on them, too. Why go if you're not going to stay?

But the only place I saw a real, knock-'em-dead game of football in all the time I was in London was at the Valley, Charlton 4 Bradford 1, on a sunny September Sunday in the Nationwide First Division. But even then it All Went Off beforehand.

Me and a baldy old taxi driver, square go.

It was a one o'clock start, for Sky. I was covering for the *Currant*

Bun, thinking, Sunday, easy-peasy, plenty of time to read the papers, have some brekky, then head off. Get there in bags of time.

Wrong.

At half ten I was standing at the bus stop, two and a half hours from kick-off. Five to eleven the first bus came. Dropped me at Ealing Broadway at quarter past. Cones on the Hanwell Road. Now I need a Tube to Charing Cross and a train out past the Greenwich Observatory and the *Cutty Sark* to the game. Loadsa time.

Wrong again.

District Line services were terminating at South Kensington for engineering works, but a bus service was running to Embankment, one stop past Charing Cross. I'd never make it unless I bit the bullet, sold a kidney and took a cab.

There was a rank across the road. A rank without taxis. Well, there was one – but he said he had got to go home for his lunch and there was no way he'd get into Charing Cross and back by then. And here was me thinking they did this for a living. Obviously, I was wrong. London cabbies are, in fact, actually eccentric million-aires cruising the city for no other purpose than the chance to meet interesting people. He said he'd radio in for someone who wasn't about to tuck into his pâté de fois gras and roast beef, which was nice of him, and ten minutes later – by now it was twenty to twelve – an old geezer in a cardy and bifocals rolled up and asked where I was going.

'Charing Cross please – in a hurry.'

'*Oooooooooooooohhhhhhh . . . naaaaaaaaaahhhhhh.*'

'Oooooooooooooohhhhhhh . . . naaaaaaaaaahhhhhh what?'

'*Oooooooooooooohhhhhhh . . . naaaaaaaaaahhhhhh twaffic, mayte.*'

'What about it?'

'*Woadworks all over the shop. Cones, contwas, diversions. When you gotta be there?*'

'Ten minutes ago.'

'*Cor, you shoulda left eawlier, shouldnya?*'

Check out the big brain on No.3467 . . .

Now, you can drive from Ealing Broadway to Trafalgar Square any one of three ways. Through the leafy avenues to the A4 and all the way in through Knightsbridge and Piccadilly; down the A4 before cutting off for Chelsea and the Embankment and up past the Houses of Parliament; or onto the A40, past Madame Tussaud's and down Regent Street.

I now discovered a fourth, as No.3467 headed through Chiswick, up to Holland Park, down by Bayswater, past Alton Towers, onto the ringroad around Newcastle-upon-Tyne, along the seafront at Kirkcaldy, stopping off for twenty fags and a 99 at a pavement café in Naples and then taking all points towards early retirement on the Costa del Sol the minute the meter stopped whirring.

But I let him go, because he's got The Knowledge, innee? He knows the streets. He knows there's roadworks, so he's doing me a turn, yeah?

Wrong yet again.

By the time I raise my head from the *Sunday Mail* and see the sign for Barcelona Zoo I'm starting to think he was at it.

'Excuse me, chief, where we going?'

'*Chawing Cwoss, wunnit?*'

'Yes, that's where I *want* to go – I was just wondering where you're *actually* going.'

'*Jast gettin' you there, mayte, jast beatin' the twaffic, narmean?*'

Okay, I gave him the benefit. Then a couple of minutes later I glanced up at the meter and do one of those *Wha-at?!?* comedy double-take things. It's sitting at £32-and-a-bit and we were still at least ten minutes away from Charing Cross. The whole journey should have been about a score.

Then it clicked. The accent, the newspaper. Might as well have had a red beard and carried a catering pack of Scott's Porage Oats. He was touristing me.

So I sat tight, said nothing, until he pulled up opposite the side entrance to the station, outside the theatre where they do the *Jack Docherty Show* on Channel 5 (the only programme filmed before a live audience bigger than the one watching at home) and clicked the meter off at £38.60.

Then I said: 'I assume you're kidding. Like, this is Comic Relief. Red Nose Day.'

'*Sowwy, mayte?*'

'The fare. Double what it should be, thanks to a route twice as long as it should be. Surely it's the kind of witty jest you wacky Londoners are so fond of?'

'*Wot?*'

'Or maybe you thought, do wot, I've got a Sweaty Sock dahn in the Smoke for the weekend, reading his Sweaty Sock newspaper, who don't know where 'ee's goin', so Magical Mystery Tour time and make enough to take the afternoon off? Eh? EH?'

'*Dunno wotcha mean, guv.*'

'What I mean, guv, is I'm *not* a tourist. I live here. I know the fares. I'm actually going to work and I only got a cab because the Tube's knackered and I'm late. And now, because of the maze you've led me through to rip me off, not only am I even later, but I'm now faced with a £38.60 fare that I am *not* paying.'

'*Then I'll have to call the police.*'

'Fine – and I'll remind them you're meant to take me the quickest way possible. And then I'll call my consumer editor at *The Sun* and . . .'

'*The Sahn?*'

'Yes. Sorry, didn't I say? I'm going to Charlton to cover the game for *The Sun*. Why do you ask?'

'*Well, I didn't reawise . . . I mean . . . well . . . how much did you say you'd usuawy pay?*'

'Twenty, tops.'

'*Well, let's call it . . . er . . . nah, tellya wot, mayte – 'ave it on me. Don't wanna cause no trouble nor nuffink, so onya go.*'

And suddenly I felt guilty. 'No, no – here, take the twenty and we'll forget all about it. Put it down to an honest mistake. Here, take it.'

'*No, no – put it away, mayte. I don't need no 'assle nor nuffink, so you 'ave a good day and enjoy the game.*'

'Well, if you're sure. Er . . . just one thing.'

'*Sure, mayte . . .*'

'Can I have a receipt? Just leave it blank, chief . . .'

I made the game with seconds to spare, by the way. Thanks for asking.

Next midweek it was Highbury. Now there's a place. The most wonderful stadium in Britain, a monument to football. As soon as you come up out of Arsenal tube station, a hundred yards from the main entrance, a special atmosphere fills your lungs – like walking past a posh restaurant.

Everything about the place reeks of history. Even the posters advertising the Next Home Fixture look like 1930s music-hall bills. The two stands along the sides of the pitch are original, in an art-deco style that says: *This Is An Established Club. This Club Has Heritage.* Everything's cream and red, with heavy steel gates and walls of pukka stone, not pre-stressed concrete.

But even the two stands behind the goals, the North Bank and the Clock End, have been built to fit in with their surroundings. Look at Ibrox. Magnificent as it is, had you never seen it pre-rebuild you could have no of inkling what it used to be like. But you can imagine Highbury *evolving* over generations.

The press box is opposite the tunnel side, to the left of the main TV camera viewpoint. It's far more cramped than most in the Premiership. Even the stairway up to it is like climbing into an attic. But the buzz you get in it is amazing.

With a full house of just under 40,000, Highbury is a true theatre. You feel close to the action, even though you're in the top half of a giant stand. At Spurs, in contrast, you're right down there with the players yet there's zip atmosphere.

The White Hart Lane press box is at dugout level, a couple of rows from the touchline, right next to the tunnel opposite the huge West Stand. You should get a fantastic feel of the game from there, but you don't. It always seems quiet, even when there are 30,000-plus in the ground. There's something ghostly about that whole stadium.

It's funny how two clubs with equally fanatical followings and grounds virtually the same size can spend similar amounts of money keeping their facilities up with the times yet end up with such different products. Highbury roars. White Hart Lane squeaks.

And Stamford Bridge *sucks.* Or at least it sucked then. Now it's getting near completion, a yuppie paradise called Chelsea Village, all hotels and restaurants and superstores. But my memory of it is as a never-ending building site – a collection of stands of all different shapes and sizes, where the diggers moved from corner to corner as they finished each job. Both ends were completed; fairly bog-standard '90s jobs, two-tiered and one-dimensional, half the seats filled with people who didn't want to sit and half with halfwits who never knew what it was like to stand. Opposite the tunnel they were halfway through the third stand, which was being built to replace an old shack of a seating area, like the Centenary Stand at Ibrox. The day I saw them play Newcastle, the bottom tier had just come into use, open to the public and the elements.

Which left the main stand, the biggest white elephant in British football. In 1974 it was space-age, three decks of far-out viewing for the showbiz types who *had* to be seen watching Chelsea every week. Dickie Attenborough, Raquel Welsh, pop stars, TV producers and MPs. The club put themselves millions of pounds in debt having it built and opened it just in time to get relegated and watch the celebs disappear like Charlie off a coffee table.

Now it hung round their necks like a ten-ton medallion on Tom Jones, sorer on the overdraft even than on the eye. From the front it still looks nice enough, or at least from a distance. But round the back you just *know* the architect took enough drugs to make King Kong giggle and eat endless Mars Bars. The service pipes run along the outside of the building. Pretty. There's also no visible entrance. Then you realise why. Go to either end and you find a tunnel running all the way along. You go in *there* to find the turnstiles and the pie stalls. The outside seems to serve no purpose; it's a bit like the cardboard town they build to fool the bad guys in *Blazing Saddles*. And all over the place, right round the concourse, were Portakabins and piles of sand and cones and yellow tape and all the other signs of a building site that never seems to go away.

All that and the press box is in the bottom tier, under the lip of the roof with pillars every six feet and a view like watching the game in Widescreen. Do you start to get an idea why I preferred to get the hell out of London on Saturdays?

Most weeks I'd plough through the early-morning shoppers to Euston or Paddington or St Pancras and head north to whatever game grabbed my attention most. How good a job is that, when the toughest decision you have to make is which sell-out games full of millionaire stars you want to be paid to watch?

Mind you, it wasn't all fun. *In Derby, I was thrown out of Argos for watching the telly.*

They were playing Man U and I arrived in town early. On the left, as the train pulled in, stood the Baseball Ground, with all its history and now with a giant petted lip at being abandoned. On the right, Pride Park, all new and shiny and chuffed with itself in the middle of a bulldozed engineering yard.

It was only ten past twelve, so I went into the town to look for somewhere to eat. Now, sometimes in a strange town, you turn a corner and there are more restaurants and pubs than you can shake a stick at. Not in Derby. You come out of the station, head along a landscaped walkway and into a '60s-style shopping centre that's had a roof added later on so a jungle of what once were sidestreets are now corridors. I could find no town square or High Street. So I wandered here and there and saw the usual Burger Bytes and Kwik Kafes and Ye Old Plastic Armes boozers and decided I rather have my wedding tackle used as target practice for William Tell than risk lunch there.

In the end I forgot about food and tried to find a bookie's. Could I? Would I be asking the question if I had? What kind of place *was* this? Winner of the 1997 Best Secret Amenities Award, presented by the Grand Masonic Order of Great Britain?

Eventually I was coming back through the shopping centre to end up where I started and head over to Pride Park early – because at least the press room would have a bar and by now I could have evaporated beer by looking at it – when I saw Argos. What's the time? Twenty-five past? *Footy Focus* time.

As it happens, I was thinking about buying a new Walkman, so I browsed through the display case of them next to the wall of tellies. Then I watched last Saturday's goals on *FF* and lip-read an interview with Harry Redknapp and caught a piece on the game I was going to see then heard dogs for miles around start howling because only *they* can hear Mark Lawrenson.

Then, from over my shoulder, I heard a woman's voice.

'*Excuse me.*'

Didn't think she meant me, so I went on watching.

'*Excuse me, sir – you at the TVs.*'

'Me?'

'*Yes, sir – I'm afraid you can't just stand there and watch telly.*'

Now, this girl was on the checkout. And if you've ever been in Argos you'll know there is always a queue a mile long at the checkout, so there were dozens of people all peeking out from behind the person in front, rubber-necking to see what was going on:

'What is it?'

'Ooh, I dunno.'

'She's told him off for watching the telly.'

'What's that?'

'I think he's trying to steal a telly.'

'What's she saying?'

'I think she said he's shown someone his belly.'

'Ooh, is that right?'

'What's right?'

'The man up there's a flasher.'

So I'm standing there, in front of twenty-four squeaking Mark Lawrensons, with Tracey on the checkout giving me dog's abuse and her mile-long queue ready to turn their slips for sprocket sets and indoor barbecues into flaming torches with which to run this pervert out of town.

'Why can't I watch the telly?'

'*Because you're not buying anything.*'

'What's that got to do with it? What if I'm *planning* to buy a telly?'

'*Are you planning to buy a telly?*'

'Well, no, but . . .'

'*You can't just stand there and watch it, then.*'

It was at this point that I remembered all my mother's teachings; when confronted by an uppity underling, always find the nearest high horse and get on it.

'Right!' I snorted. 'I've had enough of this *disgraceful* treatment! I demand to see the manager right now. Bring me the manager!'

So this woman in a feeshul Argos charcoal-grey suit came scuttling over and asked if we could sort this problem out quietly, because by now three-quarters of Derby and several thousand bussed in specially from nearby Nottingham were gawping.

'Quietly? I'll give you quietly – I've never been so insulted in all my etc etc. Who does that checkout girl [I point and the entire assembly turn to gawp at her] think she etc etc? I, madam, am a customer and do not expect to be treated like some kind of . . . of . . . of . . . *criminal.* Etc etc.'

The least I expected was a round of applause.

Charcoal-suit woman did a bit of umming and aaahing, tried to shush me, but by this time I was in overdrive: 'I mean, can't a person come into a shop and browse any more? Hmm? HMMMM? Can't a person look before he decides on whether or not to part with his money? Can't he?'

'*Well, to be fair, sir . . .*'

'To be fair? I'll to be fair you! [a saying lost on anyone outside Scotland] What's fair about that girl [I point dramatically again and the gawping thousands turn on her, then back to the mad bloke, like a tennis crowd] embarrassing me in front of a busy shop?'

'*Well, I'm sure she didn't mean to . . .*'

'I mean, are we under some obligation to buy in this store? Did I miss the sign on the door saying: "Looking at televisions on these premises will result in the full retail price being surgically removed from your wallet"? Did I? Hmmm?'

'*Of course not, sir. Was there something you wanted to buy? Because if there was I can organise it straight away. Perhaps a small discount as a token of our . . . em . . . regret at this incident.*'

'Actually, yes – there *were* a couple of things. A Walkman. Possibly two. A sprocket set, an indoor barbecue. And possibly even one of these fine TV sets. But I will tell you for nothing, madam, there is no way on earth I will be spending a single penny in this place after the way I have been treated by . . . by . . . HER!' Another point for luck. By now she had slid inside her overall like a tortoise. Game, set and match.

'*I'm sorry you feel like that, sir – I'm sure we can sort something . . .*'

But with that and a swish of my coat-tails I was off, pausing only to sniff: 'And I guarantee you I will never – *never* – return to Argos in Derby.'

And, dear reader, I never have.

Derby drew 2–2 with Man U that day after being 2–0 up before half-time. It was one of four times I saw United in the first couple of months of the season and they could have lost all four but instead lost none.

They were 1–0 down at home to West Ham, whose fans celebrated by slaughtering David Beckham. Mind you, they celebrated throw-ins by slaughtering Beckham, greeted news of every goal from every other game by slaughtering Beckham and prayed for their team to concede corners so Beckham had to trot over in front of them for an intimate chat about . . . well, I couldn't hear properly, but it was something to do with Posh Spice and Arsenal.

Away fans at Old Trafford are in a little section, about three thousand seats, curving round the corner flag to the right of the press box and at the opposite end from the Stretford and the tunnel. The West Ham lot were all trying to get down the front and hang over the edge, to get closer to Brylcreem Boy.

The stewards didn't seem too fussed; strange, as they control the home fans with an almost Nazi zeal. Even before you go into Old Trafford you're put on your best behaviour, like you're at your snooty auntie's. You're waiting for someone in a yellow jacket to lick his palm and slick your hair down. On the wall by every turnstile is a sign warning that standing is strictly prohibited and that failure to adhere to rules could result in the stadium's capacity being cut.

I have never heard this possibility being raised at any other ground. No standing or they'll shut the place down? You wondered how it could possibly be made to work, this sit-down-or-else policy. Football fans don't *decide* to stand up, our brains *tell* us to. Something exciting happens and we jump up. It's Pavlovian (*that's right – I also jump up when someone puts a dessert made of meringues and raspberries in front of me*). Yet at Old Trafford, the Theatre of Dreams, where the greatest players in Britain play the most exciting football imaginable, fans are expected to sit on their hands; in fact, as they languished a goal down to West Ham, I wondered when a steward would move in and huckle Fergie in case he got the capacity of the dugout cut with all his leaping and ranting.

Stewards walked up and down the aisles in synch every few minutes, their regimentation almost sinister. When the Red Army stood up to urge their sluggish heroes to greater efforts, the Yellow Army moved in. Quite how they decided which fans to pick on is anyone's guess – loud shirts? bad haircuts? – but they did, frogmarching this one and that one away to loud boos.

One section in particular, in the bottom tier of the stand behind the not-the-Stretford-End goals, turned the standing-up game into a protest. Little groups would stand up *en masse* at given times and make the security forces move in to shove them onto their backsides again.

Some of them must have missed Paul Kitson running clean through on Peter Schmeichel at the far end, bottling it and hitting the keeper's legs. It is at moments like this that you know Man U will not be beaten. You take your chances against them or die. United won 2–1 and the Hammers fans slaughtered Beckham.

Just after the winning goal, a whole swathe of the rebel stand stood up and chanted for all they were worth. Stewards moved in to sit them down. But now punters behind the protestors were standing up as well, because they couldn't see; and people at either side of the incident were standing up to get a better view of what was going on.

Happened every home game, apparently. The fans stand up to prove they can, the stewards move in and most fans eventually sit down again but for one or two who are ritually howked out and shown the door. It is a farce. Britain's biggest, richest, most successful club ploughing so much time and energy into stopping fans enjoying their day out.

Round about then they were talking about making certain sections of the ground Singing Areas because, they say, so many customers are complaining that their afternoons are marred by the chanting of a minority. Why do they come to football, these balloons? Did they think it would be like a couple of hours in the library, or a poetry reading or a golf tournament? What right do they have to *ssshhhuush* others who have paid the same money as they have, just because those others actually get involved in the drama unfolding in front of them? No wonder Man U get a bad name for having kiddy-on fans.

Not so Newcastle. There, punters know how to enjoy themselves – even when there's sod all to enjoy. The Toon Army – and I swear this is true – would genuinely rather see their team lose a thriller 4–3 than win a stinker 1–0.

They played Blackburn late that September and I took the train up. Aha – now there's something I nearly forgot. On the way from Euston to Manchester for the West Ham game, I noticed a little balding bloke sitting uncomfortably on a sports bag in the corridor. You know when you recognise someone but can't remember how? It was one of those. Did he work for a paper? Was he an ex-player? No one else seemed to be bothering with him, so he couldn't be famous. So I went back to my *Guardian* – they were sold out of the *Sport* – and I was looking at the team news for my game. Under 'ref' it said: David Ellery (Harrow). *Gotcha.*

Poor guy couldn't get a seat, so there he was, *en route* to handle a vital Premiership game in front of 55,000 punters, to make decisions changing the fortunes of players worth tens of millions – and he was forced to hunker up on his bag in a train corridor. The indignity of it all.

It wouldn't have been fair to share this discovery with any of my fellow passengers, especially the many scores of West Ham followers. But somehow it slipped out – don't ask me how – and spread like chickenpox in a kindergarten. By the time we got to Manchester, I'm surprised the wee fella hadn't decided to red card every Hammers player before kick-off. Stick? David Beckham could have sat next to him and got a break.

Mind you, that little cameo showed an important difference between football fans in Scotland and in *Laaaahnndahn*. Our fans are witty. Here we had three hundred West Ham punters with their country's most famous ref sitting on an Umbro bag in a train corridor, totally at their mercy – and the wittiest line they could come up with was: '*Oi, slap 'ead – wanna seat?*'

It was funny the first time. If you'd been locked up in a Bangkok prison cell for fourteen years and this was the first joke you'd heard since being released that morning.

But by the time the thirty-third crewcut, bull-necked throwback had returned from the bar and cracked it – to the half-drunk roars of his halfwit mates – it had somehow lost its Milliganesque comic genius.

All the same, you could see Ellery seething with hate at (a) not getting a seat, (b) getting clocked and (c) being condemned to nearly three hours of neanderthal humour. So that was a result.

And one more difference between our game and theirs. Many of our refs are petty-minded little schoolteachers. But *their* top man is a petty-minded little *public* schoolteacher. You see? A gulf in class we simply cannot bridge.

Anyway, Newcastle. On the way up I phoned my big brother, Ian, who's lived in the Toon since the early '70s when he came out of the army. He's been a club singer for donkeys years, though he's now also driving a taxi. He was waiting for me at Central Station, dumped the cab – well, parked it in the middle of a busy street with the hazards on, as they do – and we went for a beer.

In a boozer at the back of the Eldon Square shopping centre, they were showing the 5–0 game against Man U from the previous season. It was almost a year ago to the weekend, a year in which Kevin Keegan had been replaced along with half the team and the devil-may-care attitude that won the hearts of a nation.

God knows how often they'd all watched the video. The day it came out you'd have thought they were queuing for Cup-final tickets. Yet here they were, watching it with rapt attention as if it were being played out live. No one stood with their back to the telly and only turned round when their mate told them a goal was coming.

They were transfixed and utterly elated when each goal went in. It was 2–0 when we got there and we stayed for the final knockings. Then, stranger still, when the after-match interviews came on they called for hush.

Alan Shearer was talking.

They knew every word of what he'd said – and let's face it, it's not hard to memorise a Shearer interview as long as you know the phrases 'I don't care who scores as long as we win', 'it's not for me to say' and 'I'm only interested in Newcastle United' – yet they hung on every syllable like he was handing down the Ten Commandments.

'Well, to be honest, I don't care who scores as long as we win.'
'Aye – yee tell 'em, lad!'

'*England captaincy? It's not for me to say.*'

'That's reet, Alan – divvun take nee crap aff that Soothan shandy-drinkin' poof!'

'*Do I feel sorry for Man U? I'm only interested in Newcastle United.*'

'Gan on, man – stick it reet up 'em!'

We drained our beers, wandered up closer to the ground and went into the Strawberry. They were showing the 5–0 game against Man U.

Mad as they might be, there's something innocent about Newcastle fans. They don't ask for much – just a few beers, a good laugh and decent entertainment. Then they all go home and change into their best Away shirt and gan oot on the Toon fu the neet.

They don't have that 'who you lookin' at' mentality of punters in the south of England. But then again, they *are* just Scots with their brains battered in . . .

In Brighton, Scots get their brains battered in. And the Welsh, the French, gays, Jews, blacks, straights, gentiles, whites. They're a liberal crowd down there – they'll kick anyone to within an inch of their life.

On Saturday, 26 April 1997, I went there for the first – and hopefully the only – time. They were playing Doncaster in a bottom-of-Division-Three clash. It was the most important game in Brighton's history, until the week after anyway.

It was the final match before their Goldstone Ground – sold to a property developer by chairman Bill Archer without a clue where they would move to – was bulldozed. If they lost and second-bottom Hereford got a result at Orient, relegation to the Conference was almost certain.

The atmosphere was horrible. Three levels of horrible: the obvious fear of the drop, the feeling of nostalgia and injustice at losing their home, and an undercurrent of utter hatred towards Archer and people in general. Add to that the natural intimidatory talents of the local knuckle-scrapers and you've got a jolly spiffing day out by the seaside. Second only to Pearl Harbor.

Hey, and just as an added bonus, Chelsea were playing at nearby Portsmouth in the Cup next day, so plenty of them came down

early to pay their own disrespects. Guess it was the wrong day to be
. . . well, *anyone*, really, but especially Bill Archer. He was either
Benny from *Crossroads*-ly stupid, Bruce Willis-ly brave, Jock
Brown-ly arrogant or – more likely – a mixture of all three. Because
he turned up. At five to three he took his seat and it was all the
stewards could do to keep a little band of Suicide-Bomber Knuckle-
Scraping Special Forces from climbing up the enclosure beneath the
directors' box to chop him into bits.

There were 12,000 there, sad and bitter and angry and nostalgic
all at once, and the cocktail left an awful taste. They were photo-
graphing everything; the queues at the turnstiles, the turnstiles,
their mates. Then they turned the cameras round and took pictures
of themselves.

They videoed the cops who were videoing them. They had
pictures taken next to police horses in visors. Inside, a young bloke
in front of me in the stand placed his ticket on the seat with the
reverance of the Queen placing a wreath at the Cenotaph, pulled a
camera from inside his anorak and took a picture.

A lone bugler blew the Last Post and then we had two minutes'
silence, marred only by a plonker behind me going *sssshhhhhh* at no
one all the way through and drenching me with dribble.

Then the roar came up from their toes and the atmosphere
darkened like November in Helsinki and within twenty minutes
Brighton's captain Ian Baird – remember him at Hearts? – had
flattened his marker Darren Moore, who retaliated. Players and
subs and coaches and cops waded in and I feared the crowd would
come over the barricades.

But order was restored and Baird and Moore walked. Moore, a
huge black centre-half, was hit on the leg by a banana as he went.
Another flew by his head. Another followed, then another. A
second black player made to throw one back and he too was hit.

To hell with Brighton. Relegate them, close them down, torch
the place. I thought it, mind, I didn't say it.

All I can say is, thank God they won in the end that day. Or I
might not be writing this now (in which case many may say what a
shame they didn't lose).

Twenty-two minutes from time, a little winger called Stuart

Storer bobbled in the only goal; then news broke that Hereford were losing and from then on it was countdown to Armageddon.

As in, Armageddon outta here . . .

Long before the whistle, the cops formed a ring and pretended they were going to keep the fans off the pitch when the ref blew for time up. When he did, they were skittled. On they came in trickles, then a flood, then a tidal wave. From all four corners they came and tore up the muddy pitch with their bare hands, and when it was raped they set about pillaging the stadium. Back into the stands they climbed to liberate the seats they had paid for that day and warmed since childhood. It was touching. At first. Then mob rule took over and things verged towards the brown-pants side of terrifying. Seats were torn up, not for souvenirs but for frisbees. Time to retreat.

Down half a dozen steps to manager Steve Gritt's office, they were tearing Exit signs off the walls, trying to lift the pie-stall shutters, standing on each other's shoulders to rip out security cameras. So much for identifying the banana-throwers, then.

There must have been twenty of us in Gritt's executive cupboard. It was like one of those world-record students-in-a-phonebox stunts. Outside we heard them banging and stomping and hurling stuff. Something hit the door and we all ducked.

The players had grabbed their belongings and got the hell out of a dressing-room which fans were now stripping clean like lions on a zebra. Gritt laughed: 'They'll get everything but the sign on the door. I know that because I caught one of the apprentices unscrewing it earlier.'

We stopped laughing as someone – maybe more than one someone – banged on the door. Bang. Bang. BANG. Then they clicked there was a handle, found someone who walked upright and got him to work it. The door opened and a crewcut head popped round.

'*Awight?*'

'Yeah,' said Gritt.

And in squeezed this thing that would make knuckle-scrapers shiver, went over to the desk, snatched up the phone, pulled it from the wall and went out with it in his ham of a hand.

We stayed inside for another half hour, just to be sure. When it sounded like they had either gone or had fallen asleep after a hard hour's scavenging, I ventured up into the stand.

It looked like the morning after Ozzy Osbourne and the Khmer Rouge had gatecrashed a party round Keith Moon's place.

Cops had slowly, slowly, moved the last few hundred looters out of the frisbee-strewn strand, down onto what once was a pitch, behind where the goals used to be, over the wooden frame that used to hold advertising hoardings and onto the terracing whose crush barriers only remained because they were concreted down. Now they were moving them up, quietly and gently, to the exits at the top. After that they were another squad's problem.

I walked from the half-destroyed stadium, up a street of shabby terraced houses with election posters in the windows, past a corner shop cowering behind graffitied shutters and over a footbridge to the station. Never was I happier to be heading back to London.

And now, the football-fixture computer irony of the century. Brighton's final game, from which they needed a point to stay in the league, was at . . . Hereford.

I went and so, of course, did the knuckle-scrapers, on a three-train hike through the Midlands to the border with Wales. There were more police than sheep that day and everyone coming in from out of town was cattle.

Brighton went behind early on to a goal from Tony Agana (remember him from BBC2's fly-on-the-wall job about Sheffield United? He's the striker who played jazz sax in his spare time. Nice!) and it looked like their time was up. But then, halfway through the second half, Hereford's keeper hit a bad kickout, a shot came back in, he fumbled it and the rebound flew past him, right in front of a Brighton end which could not believe its luck.

The cops battled to keep Hereford fans from getting through cordons to battle the away lot at the end, but the away lot were too high to notice or care. They had stayed up and now there was no need to fight with anyone.

I just felt desperately sorry for Hereford, a lovely wee club who never hurt anyone – except Newcastle in the FA Cup all those years ago – but who were now out of the league, dumped by a club run by a charlatan and supported by a nasty, vicious, unfriendly bunch of thugs who never gave anyone any pleasure in their lives.

Funny how first impressions last.

Which is pretty much where I came in.

The impression London made on me from the off never really left and by October I was ready to head home. It was an unhappy time, but three great games made it at least some kind of happy ending.

At Highfield Road on a Wednesday night when breath came in clouds, Coventry beat a soulless Everton side 4–1 in the Coca-Cola Cup. But that wasn't the story.

At full-time, as his players slumped towards the tunnel, Everton boss Howard Kendall stormed onto the pitch, ordered them to about-turn and took them to the centre circle for a bollocking. They deserved one for their shambolic performance and Kendall never missed them, steam coming off his baldy head, finger wagging and purple cheeks puffing. Then he made a gesture which could only mean one thing, even from up in the stand: *Go lap the track, you shower of blarfs.*

Their faces said *whhhaaaa* – but off they went. Except centre-half Craig Short then stopped, shouted something, spun on his heel and headed for the tunnel. Kendall turned to see him heading his way and told him to get back out there. Short was having none of it and barged straight past.

Slaven Bilic, the big Croat defender, went after Short to put his arm round his shoulder and coax him back. Kendall looked round the team at more and more angry faces and seemed to give up. He walked away, exchanging angry words with Short, who then led the entire team off at his back.

Now that *was* the story. MUTINY!

Down in the press room, the Merseyside reporters were debating how to handle the situation. Local newspapers have to be a bit gentler with their clubs, because they have to deal with them every day. But I was for steaming in.

When Kendall eventually came in to speak, more than half an hour after the rammy, the local guys danced around what they really wanted to ask and stuck to the defeat itself, which by now didn't seem just as bad as what had followed it. Then I decided to brass-neck it.

'So, Howard, what exactly happened at the end? The players seemed to openly disobey your orders.'

'No, no – it was nothing like that. It was – well, some of them aren't used to doing a warm-down . . . and . . . well . . .'

'But Craig Short in particular refused to run round the track, had to be brought back by a team-mate, you had an argument with him and then he led the team off. Isn't that . . . well . . . a sort of *mutiny*?'

'No, not at all – we brought them off because we were worried for their safety with fans still around.'

'Riiiighhhhht . . . so what was the argument about?'

'Anything that was said was said in the dressing-room.'

There's an old Red Indian phrase that springs to mind at moments like these: My Arse.

So MUTINY! it was, all over the back page of the *Currant Bun* next morning – plus a superb picture of Kendall and Short pointing angry fingers at each other like loaded guns. That and Big Dunc walking away from a fight for the first time in his life. Get a copy – it'll be worth something in years to come.

Everton were playing Liverpool on the Saturday and anyone who doesn't know the game would have put them down as a banker to lose. But football being football, they went out and fought *for* each other this time and won, 2–0.

A couple of Saturdays later, the last before packing my bags for home, I went to see Leeds against Derby at Elland Road – and gathered final, conclusive proof that people who leave games early are deranged.

Derby went 2–0 up inside ten minutes thanks to two Dean Sturridge goals helped by two awful defensive pantomimes. When Davie Robertson pulled down Sturridge as he sprinted in on a hat-trick and Ali Asanovic made it three on half an hour, it should have been game over.

But the last time I'd seen Derby they'd chucked away those cast-iron three points against Man U and now they were in pre-Christmas sale mode again. Six minutes later, Rod Wallace got in the way of a shot and deflected it past Estonian keeper Mart Poom. Then the young Aussie winger, Harry Kewell, hit the crispest of knee-high volleys from the corner of the box to make it 3–2.

There was only one outcome from then on. It was just a matter of when the goals came. As it was, Derby held out until eighty minutes, when Christian Dailly stuck his hand up as a corner came in and Jimmy Hasselbaink scored from the spot.

That was when the fans started leaving. Hordes of them, streaming out to the carparks and the bus stops, as if they had *decided* the game was up. No more scoring, please, we need to get home for tea.

Hell mend them for missing the ball run loose deep into injury time and Lee Bowyer thrashing it through a ruck from twenty yards then running like a maniac to celebrate with those behind the goal who had bothered to stay.

I hope the rest got to their cars and switched on their radios and heard the score and banged their fat heads on the steering wheel until the airbag burst.

Derby's players couldn't believe it. They stood, hands on head, or hunkered down covering their faces. Three up inside thirty minutes away from home against the lowest-scoring team in the universe, and they had chucked it away.

I watched their faces, twisted in anguish, then scanned across to their stunned knot of fans, too traumatised to clap or to leave or even to sit down and mope.

How horrible it is to be a football fan who travels all that way and pays all that money and then sees their team collapse and their world with it. What a stinking game football can be sometimes.

I watched them finally drift away, watched the players peel themselves off the turf and trudge down the tunnel; all of them heading straight into a weekend from hell, when they'd want to speak to no one, see no one and do nothing but wallow in their own private anguish.

Served them right for what happened to me in Argos.

On the Monday, I came home with my worldly possessions packed up in an Avis van. Unloaded the lot at my sister Anne's place in Kilbirnie, arranged to stay Monday and Tuesday night then go back early on Wednesday because I had work to do at the *Currant*

Bun and a game on the Saturday. I'd stay with a mate down there and get a train back here from the game.

Tuesday night I took the van to the petrol station on the way to get fish suppers and, as I headed back, it started chugging like a chuggy thing. Thought little of it, had my fish supper, went to bed. Around four next morning I was away. For about twenty yards. Then the van chugged and chugged and chugged some more. It was like driving Skippy the Bush Kangaroo. Took me fifteen minutes to get to the end of the street, before it chugged its last and died. I called the AA and the bloke came out half an hour later. I explained what was what and he asked what I'd put in it last night. I said unleaded. He laughed. You know the punchline . . .

And so I walked back round to the house and got Anne out of her bed and the AA boy towed away a diesel Escort van full of unleaded to have its stomach pumped and to laugh with his mates about the pillock who poisoned it.

I lost my £250 deposit and three days' pay at Wapping, but it was God's way of telling me Rab C had been right. Get out of London before it turns terminal.

Now the only problem was Saturday and Sheffield Wednesday *v* Arsenal. I would have called off, but it was Atko's first game as boss at Hillsborough and not for the world was I missing a lecture in managerspeak.

Trains down weren't a problem. Trains back were. So Anne, kind sis that she is, got me insured for her trusty old G-reg Nissan Sunny, gently reminding me it was a diesel. Forty or fifty times.

I set off after brekky on Saturday, switched on the radio and found it wasn't working. Ditto the tape deck. It was a *looooong* drive. Five hours to the outskirts of Sheffield. Five hours of making up stupid songs and talking to myself. Parked on the edge of town and took a tram to the stadium. Realised once the game started that I hadn't eaten since before eight. Tried to get to the press room for a pie at half-time, but the punters were all coming the other way, heading for the bars. It was like swimming against a sucking human tide, so eventually I gave up and went with it – and was still queueing when the teams came back out, so I chucked it.

Near the end, the battery on my mobile packed up. Now I

wouldn't even catch Atko's act, because I needed to find a phone somewhere. Wednesday had won as well, making this one of Arsenal's last defeats on their way to the Double, so he'd have been in top tickets-and-tombolas form.

I found a phone booth just across from the stadium, but with a woman gabbing inside and four punters chittering outside. Don't houses in Sheffield have phones? The woman gabbed for five minutes that seemed like hours, the other four came and went quickly and then it was my turn. The box stank of pee (a cheeky wee 1997 Mad Dog 20-20, if I wasn't mistaken; it also smelled fresh. Had one of the five before me done it while they were talking?) and the copytaker took ages to key in my eight hundred words. Finally, it was over and I was on the tram back to the huge carpark, praying the Sunny would start.

Snow was falling now, through a fog. Suddenly I felt very weary, not just with today or the last week, but with six months of being away from home, from Kenny, from my mum and all the family and my pals. From my own house. From Scotland.

The drive home seemed to take forever. I went over the foggy hills to Manchester and hooked up with the M6. Thought about stopping for food so long that when I did, the service station Burger King was closed. Sod it, home was where the chicken supper was.

On and on the road went, on and on with me singing and talking to myself and wishing I was home with people I wanted to be with, people who weren't suspicious of me, people who wouldn't stab me with fish.

I almost drove myself mad on that last journey home, but then, near ten, I was coming down the hill into Kilbirnie and driving to Benny's chippie. Outside milled a gang of maybe thirty teenagers. They probably meant no harm, but I wasn't for risking it. London had me suspicious, too.

Went up the street and headed for the Chinese takeaway. Two blokes were having a square-go on the pavement outside. I drove on, round the roundabout at the end of the main street, first left and stopped outside the house.

I was tired, dispirited, fed up, hungry. I'd had enough. I trooped in, dumped my coat and took off my jumper and boots, then slumped in an armchair.

Sis came through with two big, fat square sausage sandwiches and a mug of tea made with proper Scottish water. We switched on the telly, just in time for *Sportscene*.

Home at last. It had almost been worth going away just for this moment.

I could feel that fracture healing already.

FIVE

ONCE IN A LIFETIME

You may find yourself,
Lying in a pile of sick.
And you may find yourself,
On a bus to entirely the wrong part of town.
And you may find yourself,
In a beautiful pad,
With a beautiful burd,
And you may say to yourself,
This is not my beautiful pad!
And you may say to yourself,
This is not my beautiful burd!
And you may ask yourself,
Well? How did I get here?
Answer: You have days like these. Once in a lifetime . . .

They've played for the Scottish Cup 114 times but only 113 captains have held it aloft.

In 1909, Old Firm fans rioted so badly after the second of two draws that the SFA wouldn't let either club have the trophy – so don't let anyone tell you fans were better behaved in the days when they wore suits and ties to the game. The only difference back then was they said 'Excuse me' before sticking a broken bottle in your neck then doffed their caps as you lay spurting blood.

So, 113 cup-winners it is. But wait – make that only twenty-three *different* winners. And wait again. Of those twenty-three, four – Vale of Leven, Renton, Third Lanark and St Bernard's – are no longer in the senior game, while Queen's Park, Dumbarton and Hibs have not won it since 1902.

Since 1903 there have been eighty-three completed finals and fifty-eight have been won by Celtic, Rangers or Aberdeen; leaving the other twenty-six to be shared among just thirteen clubs. Since 1962, when I was still sloshing around in my mother's stomach, only six clubs outside the big three – Dunfermline, Dundee United, St Mirren, Motherwell, Kilmarnock and Hearts – have won the cup. Only four others – Dundee, Hibs, Airdrie and Falkirk – have even made it to the final.

In other words, twenty-seven of our current senior clubs have not known in my lifetime what it's like to be there on the biggest day of the season; and of those only Morton, Clyde, Partick Thistle, Dumbarton, Hamilton, Raith Rovers, East Fife, Albion Rovers and Queen's Park have *ever* had the pleasure.

Which all means almost *half* of our clubs have *never* been to the Scottish Cup final. That's so sad it blows your mind.

Just think – if you follow St Johnstone, Clydebank, Ayr United, Berwick, Brechin, Alloa, Cowdenbeath, Stranraer, Arbroath, Stenhousemuir, Stirling Albion, Queen of the South, Livingston, Inverness Caley Thistle, Ross County, Forfar, East Stirling or Montrose, you've never known the feeling of waking on Scottish Cup final morning knowing it's *your* day. I fervently pray that each of those clubs gets there, even just the once.

For years, whenever the crack in our local in Falkirk got round to the cup, I'd stick on the old broken record about the day St Mirren won it in 1987; I never tire of talking about it – you might have noticed – and I'm happy to say the Bairns fans in the company never seemed to get tired hearing tales they already know by heart. Either that or they're just incredibly polite.

And each time the subject came up I'd tell them how much I hoped they got a day of their own to savour like I did, to give them an encyclopaedia of tales with which to bore the liver off St Johnstone or Ayr or Forfar fans in years to come.

In 1997, they got it. I was living in London then and came up for the weekend to go with them; but it was an odd feeling, like I was intruding. I always felt that way about the outsiders who swelled the Saints end in our year, and my mate Andy the Motherwell fan said exactly the same thing about their 1991 win which, like ours, was against Dundee United, who tend to be very obliging on these occasions.

*

I couldn't help but feel irritated when I looked round at all those strange faces, people I'd never seen at Fir Park or at away games. Loads of them were Rangers and Celtic fans or just punters who didn't usually go to see Motherwell.

It sounds stupid, but I kept thinking that they didn't deserve to be there, that it wasn't their day. Late that night, when we were settled in the boozer and the adrenaline had worn off and we were coming down off the high of winning, one of my mates went up and took the mike off the DJ and pointed out all the non-Motherwell fans. He was going: 'This isn't your night . . . or yours . . . or yours . . . you there, aye you, you've no right to be here . . .'

Yet it was probably that element of the support at Hampden who lifted the team to win the cup. We'd been 3–2 up with a minute to go when Darren Jackson chased onto a long punt from their keeper Alan Main, went in on Ally Maxwell – who had played on despite being badly injured – and scored. I felt like Mike Tyson had punched me in the guts.

All us genuine Motherwell fans, who'd been let down so often, were shattered. Stunned. We hardly made a sound. I knew for certain we had lost the cup. It had been within our grasp at last in our lifetime and we had blown it. No words could fully describe our feelings as we watched the players sit around getting rubs, listening to Tommy McLean trying to lift them.

Then the roar started.

It was so odd, because none of us was shouting. We were still too stunned to say anything. No, it was the hangers-on, the neutrals, the ones just there for a day out, who started the noise as the boys got back on their feet for extra time. The players looked up, guys who had been close to tears at losing that goal so late, and I swear in that moment their whole attitude to the game changed.

Then the rest of us shook ourselves and joined in the roar. Without the support of the people whom I didn't think belonged there, we might not have gone on and won it.

*

I know exactly what he meant. We had to go to extra time the year we won it and I know I was too nervous to cheer when the players ran towards us for kick-off. But the noise came from somewhere, because I'll never forget Campbell Money conducting it with a look of fiery determination all over his face.

Then I saw the other side of the coin the day I sat in the Govan Stand with about twenty Bairns-daft pals for *their* final with Killie and when they were 1–0 down and time was running out I was desperately trying to keep their spirits up with the mindless optimism which can only be mustered by someone who doesn't know what supporting *their* team is really like.

But I felt I had to do something to justify being there, to earn my keep almost. I didn't feel as if I belonged in that seat, that maybe some poor wee orphan in Falkirk had missed the biggest game of his life because of me, a neutral. Sure, I'd joined in everything and been made to feel more than a part of it. We'd got up at seven and gone down to Callander Park, a beautiful setting with a lake and mansion house and lush gardens which we attempted to carve to pieces with a pre-breakfast seven-a-side. It was jumpers for goalposts in the dew and the watery sunshine; guys putting their home-made top hats, all rosetted up, behind the wall at the back of the goals for safety. Laughter rang in the morning air and it was wonderful. I also scored with a magnificent back-heel, but that's by the by.

Then we ate breakfast for Scotland before going down to Brockville to wave the team bus off. I'll never forget the look of pride beaming from Alex Totten's face as he waved a fist of determination to the crowds.

From there we walked up through the town to High Station for the eleven o'clock to Queen Street and a few beers before the game. But I never felt as if it was right for me to say too much or nose to the front of the crowd as we headed for the stadium. I'd have hated it if they'd done that on our day.

It was afterwards, though, when they'd lost by a single scrappy goal and had one of their own wrongly disallowed that I really felt I had to distance myself. You can't tread on private grief and, not long after we got back to Falkirk, I sloped off and left them to it.

I wasn't among the 25,000 who lined the team bus's route to Callander Park or who crowded through the gates to see them stop the open-top team bus in front of the mansion house, but you could hear the cheers across town, even though there was no cup to be gazed upon. These were moments for diehards and diehards alone. People to whom it means more than just an excuse to bevvy in the street.

My mate Gordy, who worked at the *Sunday Mail* at the time, got to ride home with the team. He was utterly made up, just as I had been ten years before when I stood on the balcony of Paisley Town Hall with the team to cover the celebrations for the local paper.

You've no idea what it feels like to be a fan with privileges when your team gets to the Scottish Cup final, to have backstage access. You feel like their twelfth man, a part of it. I could have died happy on that balcony that night.

Andy the Motherwell fan and I sat down to talk about our finals for this chapter and the conversation burst here and there like a box of fireworks when someone drops a match in. He'd be halfway through telling me what they did that night when something he said would trigger a flashback to something that happened in the morning and before we knew it we'd been talking for two hours and realised you could write a book about days like these alone.

If you support one of the Old Firm or have followed Aberdeen through their glory years – or you're Bob Crampsey and happened to be around last century when Queen's Park won the thing ten times – you might read this and wonder where we dredged up all this emotion from. Maybe to you the Scottish Cup final is just another big game; maybe you're choked if you *don't* get there. But look again at the mere handful of unfancied clubs that have been there in my lifetime and try to realise how the effect it had will stay with them until the day they die. Or start wearing Littlewoods cardigans, whichever comes first.

IT IS BETTER TO TRAVEL HOPEFULLY THAN TO ARRIVE, ESPECIALLY IN A STRETCH LIMO

I love the cup. I love first-round games at tiny grounds on crisp Saturdays in December; I love it when wee teams turn over bigger teams, even when the bigger teams are still wee teams compared to *big* teams. I love the stories the cup throws up, tales of unknown nine-to-five guys who become famous for fifteen minutes by scoring a giant-killing winner.

I can't get enough of replays played on mudheaps under floodlights that actually seem to make the place darker; blood-and-thunder ties fought to the death at Boghead or Cliftonhill or on Highland grounds with snow piled high round the touchline. These games are what make football the greatest passion on earth.

In the second round in 1998 I volunteered to go down to Stranraer against Fraserburgh. It was Saturday, 3 January, a morning that dawned howling wet and windy. I had a hangover the size of a small village in Lincolnshire. Halfway down the A77, word came over the tranny that the game was off. I turned round and headed for home, deciding on the way to go to Stenny against Deveronvale. By lunchtime that was off as well. Briefly, I thought: sod it – I'd see us play Morton at Love Street in the league instead.

But at one o'clock *it* was called off because of the gales, which was God's way of telling me to get back on the trail of a cup game.

The ones left on were at Annan, Arbroath, Dingwall, Forfar, Inverness, Lossiemouth and Peterhead; only Arbroath and Forfar were accessible, so I headed for Gayfield. Got there at quarter past two – just as they were making the decision to postpone it because of winds which, even by that ground's standards (they get hurricanes there on summer days) were horrific. The ref bounced a ball on the halfway line and hoofed it towards the left-hand goal. It sailed over the bar, over the roof of the shed behind and landed two hundred yards up the street.

There was still time to get to Forfar, but the radio said it was almost certainly off. So I scooted to Dundee for the league game with Raith. It was dire. Right on half-time Raith scored with a free-kick from halfway which blew in about eleven different directions before swirling past Rab Douglas.

I left there and then and got to Forfar for the last half hour, although I'm ashamed to say that by then I was so cold and knackered I sat in the car and listened to the scores coming in.

So on the Monday I wrote about all this in *The Sun*. On Tuesday I saw Arbroath and Queen of the South draw 1–1 and on Wednesday I got a call from cup sponsors Tennent's. They said such endeavour should not go unrewarded and could they transport me to my next tie? Sure, I said, I'm having another crack at Stranraer and Fraserburgh on Saturday. And so it came to pass that photographer Colin Templeton, Tennent's PR bloke David Brown and I went to Stair Park in a white stretch limo.

It was magnificent: twenty-six feet of pure Texan tack, all crimson leather interior with telly, vid, hi-fi and an ice bucket built into the armrest. They gave us a Harrod's-sized food hamper and a crate of the sponsor's juice and we were sorted. With the tinted windows and the partition up between us and the driver, we hardly felt like we were moving. It is the only way to travel and certainly the only way to watch *Football Focus*; if clubs laid on stretch limos for punters every week every game would be a sell-out.

We swished into the carpark – I say *swished*; I mean *squeezed awkwardly then parked with our nose sticking halfway across the tarmac* – at half one, and were immediately surrounded by kids expecting to see Rod Stewart or Celine Dion or a gang of Colombian drug barons step out. They were highly disappointed.

'Jings,' said the grown-ups meanwhile, 'a hoose wi' wheels.'

Stranraer won 2–1 and afterwards, once we had chucked their entire team out of the back seat, we set about demolishing every scrap and drop of the food and drink; and as I write this I suddenly realise you'll be thinking words like *poser* and *prat*, but tough. If *you* ever go to the game in a free stretch limo full of free lager, *you* try keeping quiet about it.

That night they made the draw for the third round and Stranraer landed holders Killie at home. It is a vital night in the season, third-round-draw night, but too many fans believe the Scottish Cup only really starts when the big guns come in. They're missing out on so much excitement with that attitude, because the cup isn't just about getting to the final.

No one in the first two rounds – or in the Qualifying Cup that precedes them, for that matter – has any pretentions of going all the way. Boris Becker might have won Wimbledon as an unseeded qualifier, but as much as I would love that to happen in football, I firmly believe Jim Farry will appear on the stand-up comedy circuit first.

The equivalent of reaching the final for these teams is to land a top club in the third round and milk their few days in the spotlight for all it's worth; that and scrub their debts. Seeing them scrap it out to get there is as gripping as a semi-final for me.

It's only once you hit the fourth round, with sixteen teams left, that you start to wonder if one of their names is on the cup. Which is a silly phrase, really, as there are twenty-three different names on it already – including St Bernard's, surely the only team of dogs to have won a major national football competition.

But you look at the eight ties and you see two First Division teams playing each other or a Premier League outfit with what looks like an easy home draw, and you start to see little glimpses of what just might be.

Having said all that, I actually got my first inkling that St Mirren could go all the way in 1987 a minute before half-time in the third-round game with Inverness Caley at Love Street. It was 0–0 on an icy pitch when a winger called Wilson Robertson sprinted away from our back four and was right through on Campbell Money. If he'd scored then we'd probably have gone out. But he lost his footing and hit it wide, we scored three in the second half and as we'd never been a lucky cup team you just wondered . . .

Then we heard Rangers had lost at home to Hamilton and after that Celtic put Aberdeen out before losing to Hearts and some big obstacles were out of the way.

In the next round we went away to Morton and were 2–1 down but came back to win 3–2. The quarter-final was at Stark's Park and Paul Chalmers and Peter Godfrey eased us through.

Suddenly we were in the semis; us, Hearts and the two Dundee teams. We got Hearts.

Ian Ferguson put us ahead when he dragged Henry Smith out wide off his line, went round him and scored from an impossible angle. What a fantastic player he was at nineteen, all lung-bursting runs and cannonball drives and Flock of Seagulls hair.

Halfway through the second half, Gary Mackay scored through a ruck of legs and we wobbled for a while. But five minutes from the end, wee Frank McGarvey wriggled and twisted and popped every joint in his body to get away from his marker and slid in the winner and we were there.

We were in the final. My grandpa had seen us win it in 1926, my dad in 1959 and now it might be my turn. It was all I had ever wanted from supporting St Mirren.

Yet even as the players hugged on the Hampden pitch and the Hearts players sat and wondered when the hell they would ever get lucky, I still couldn't believe it. And on 16 May I still had to keep reminding myself it was really happening.

I was awake at six that morning, bolt upright, jerked out of sleep by some subconscious trigger that this was *the* day. If you've been there, you'll know the feeling. If not, I can only keep praying that one day you will.

You've been out the night before for a swift one to calm your nerves and ended up calm as a newt at one in the morning after wallowing in all the old telly highlights your mate has painstakingly collected on video. But still you're buzzing at 6 a.m.

And you think you're the only one, until you throw on some clothes and go for the papers and pass half the street already walking back with forest-loads of tabloids under their arms or people walking the dog or washing their cars or just strolling some too-slow fraction of time away until kick-off.

My year was 1987, Andy's and Motherwell's was 1991. But the day was the same. Just like it was for the Dunfermline fans in 1968, the Dundee United fans when they finally won it in 1994, Killie fans in 1997, Jambos in 1998. Days like ours don't happen very often, so you wring every last second out of them. You make twenty-four hours last a lifetime.

All morning I pottered and fidgeted and fretted until eventually I couldn't potter or fidget or fret any more. About ten I put my coat on and started walking the three miles into Paisley. It was a beautiful morning, in every way.

Yet I had to keep reminding myself what it was all about. It was as if my brain was trying to reject the concept of us being in the Scottish Cup final, that it was a dream I would wake up from any time. It was what I'd waited nearly twenty-five years for, yet now that it was four and a bit hours away I couldn't grasp the reality.

I'd been lucky, I'd been closer to it all than just about any other St Mirren fan. Working for the *Paisley Daily Express*, I'd had access to Love Steet any time I wanted – especially after regular sportswriter Stan Park went off sick and I was left to cover the football. I'd done the build-up to the 2–0 quarter-final win at Raith, then the weeks leading up to the 2–1 win over Hearts in the semi at Hampden – I'd talked them into doing an eight-page pullout for that one – and suddenly I was covering my team's preparations for their first cup final since I was still giving my mother cravings for coal.

I was there when they got fitted for their Hampden suits, when they recorded their cup final record – a dubious disco version of 'When The Saints Go Marching In' – and shared all the worries of the squad as they sweated over their places on the big day. This time, we did a twenty-four-page pullout and the rest of the normal paper was all Saints as well. It's an edition I treasure.

Then Stan got better, just in time for the final, and was given back the job of covering the game. I was gutted, Brian, well sick. They said I could do the after-match quotes and all the colour stuff; but it wasn't the same.

When I was walking into town, all suited and booted for work, I decided I couldn't watch it from the press box – not least because the height and slope of the place terrified me. I knew I had to go with the boys, on the bus, to the terraces. It was the best decision I ever made.

All the windows of the shops and houses on the way into town were black and white. Butchers had black-and-white sausages (an ideal ruse to get rid of that batch from 1965 they found at the back of a cupboard); clothes-shop dummies wore black and white tammies and scarves; everywhere were good-luck messages.

The pub was already heaving when I got there at half eleven. They had no seats on the bus, but I'd sit on someone's knee. Someone else had a spare ticket. Sorted. Then in came my mate Alex Moodie, a rabid Celtic fan, with the news that he'd just become dad to Lee. As if we needed an excuse to drink . . . But I'd made myself a promise that even if I hadn't been working I wouldn't have bevvied much, not before the game. I wanted to drink in every moment of the occasion.

Funny, but Andy remembered doing the same. He imposed a four-pint limit on himself. No hazy memories allowed. He and his busload left for Hampden before ten for a boozer they'd booked into near the ground. They were there for opening time, but no one wanted a session; they were all clock-watching, desperate to be at the game.

There was something about getting on the bus that changed the whole atmosphere of both our days. From being full of the joys, everyone went strangely quiet; it was like we were troops about to go over the top. We were lost in our own thoughts.

For me, getting to the final was the dividend for a quarter of a century's investment in my team; payback for all those days of losing at East Stirling and Alloa and Queen of the South doing us 5–0 at Love Street and Airdrie doing us 6–0 at Love Street and days when we had five hundred punters at games and most of them left long before the end because we were so bad.

Yes, we'd lost three semis in a row, in '82, '83 and '84 – first to a winner through Billy Thomson's legs in a replay, then to the goal that didn't cross the line in the last minute of extra time in the replay with Rangers, then to a bizarre deflection which looped in on the wind against Celtic. Each one piled hurt on hurt like some giant, sickening sandwich.

Yes, we'd been robbed in League Cup semis as well. Sure, we'd gone out of Europe to two goals in the last minute against the Swedes from Hammarby. But these were *good* times. For me, even being down to the last four of a cup or playing in Europe was huge success after all the other stuff we'd been through. It's what bugs me when I listen to fans at, say, Raith Rovers this last year or so. Okay, so things are going badly and they're suffering financially and struggling on the pitch. But this is just them coming back down from a higher high than they could ever have dreamed of; they've been far, far lower than they are now.

So for me, the bitterness I felt about losing big games wasn't wiped out by getting to a final. What that day did was fade the memory of those horrible, howling wet Saturdays coming back from defeats at the likes of Cowdenbeath and Hamilton.

It was the same for a lot of Andy's mates. On the bus to the pub that morning the boy next to him started trotting out their heaviest defeats, but Andy pulled him up short. That's not what it was about for him; for Andy it was about making up for being robbed of a place in the final before, when they were so close they could taste it. The boy argued back and babbled on about this defeat and that defeat, but Andy had stopped listening. He was staring out the window now, lost in his own bad memories – and suddenly he was back at Hampden on 31 March 1976, being conned out of a place in the final.

We were 2–0 up at half-time. Stuart McLaren and Willie Pettigrew scored. Pettigrew was taking the piss out of John Greig. We were cruising. And then they cheated us, them and referee J.R.P. Gordon. They got a penalty that wasn't even a foul and even if it had been a foul it was five yards outside the box. But Gordon gave it and Alex Miller scored. I think we all knew inside then that it was going to turn against us.

Derek Johnstone scored to make it 2–2, then in the very last minute we pumped the ball into the box and Willie went to pull the trigger, but Greig pulled him down. It was a stick-on penalty, but Gordon waved play on, Rangers went up the park and Johnstone scored again.

The next day there was a picture of the penalty-that-wasn't in the papers and it proved how badly we were robbed. Ian Archer in the *Glasgow Herald* called it 'the most criminal result ever'.

So getting there this time, fifteen years later, meant everything to me because of that night – I'd seen us lose other semi-finals, but none hurt like 1976 – and how badly it affected my view of football. Rangers got everything that night when it was Motherwell who deserved to go through. This was our day at last and no one could cheat us out of being there . . .

We got to Hampden at about quarter to two. Get there that early for any other game any other week of the season and you'll be a man alone, but that day it was the same as it had been at six in the morning; everyone else seemed to have the same idea as you except ten minutes earlier.

The Rangers End was two-thirds full when we got to the top of the steps, just as it would be when Andy and his mates arrived four years later. It was the first of so many moments that day when I wanted time to stop. Just to see all those faces I'd stood with and travelled with for years, all alight with anticipation, was magical. And there were so many others, people I knew but hadn't seen at a game for years, all with brand-new scarves and hats and badges. And I thought: Please, God, let it end here before we all have our dreams shattered.

The next time I felt like that was when the teams came out. At last, I'd seen it; St Mirren walking out of the Hampden tunnel for a Scottish Cup final. I felt so proud for the players, guys I'd come to know, whose excitement I'd shared for weeks. And I thought: Let it all stop *here* so they can take a happy ending into their old age.

My heart stopped every time Dundee United got over the half-way line that day. I've never known such fear at a football match and I guess the players felt the same because they never got started; it was an awful game. The morning sun had even run away and left us with rain that seeped through the clothes of those without a roof over them.

When I think back, I can't remember us doing *anything* worth while in normal time. All I can see in my mind's eye is United going forward and me willing them not to score, not to ruin it all for us. Then I think, though only for a fleeting second, how awful it must be for the United fans who had stood there with that horrible sinking feeling *five* times before they finally saw their team leap that final hurdle.

Beside me that day, Moodie – the ecstatic new dad and Celtic fan – kept touching me on the shoulder and telling me it'd be okay, that United didn't have the bottle for the big occasion. But I knew deep down he was wrong.

Still, ninety minutes came and went and we were still in it. Nothing in the least bit exciting or cup final-ish had happened, but we were in it.

Our day couldn't have been any more different from Andy's. By the end of ninety minutes, he and his mates had gone through every emotion you can imagine in what was surely the greatest Scottish Cup final of them all. Football's strange that way; you had two teams managed by the McLean brothers, two teams who normally cancelled each other out in sterile draws, turning on a show to match anything anyone anywhere on earth could have produced . . .

It was an amazing game right from the start. United hit the post, then had a goal disallowed – they always seemed to have a goal disallowed in finals. Then Jimmy Griffin slung one in and Iain Ferguson scored with a header. We went mental – but then Dave Bowman equalised and we were on a downer again.

The quality of the football was fantastic from both sides – all the goals were good ones. It was moving back and forwards so much that it was impossible to guess who'd win it for a while. But then we got at them.

Phil O'Donnell, who was magnificent all the way through, made it 2–1, then Ian Angus got a third and even when John O'Neil got one back we were pretty confident. With five minutes to go, we were knocking the ball around, playing out time. We thought the cup was ours.

We were all looking round at each other and not daring to say it was over, but the look on everyone's faces was so happy. The noise was swelling, ready for the final explosion. Then they scored. Did I say it was like a punch in the guts from Tyson? Wrong – it was a boot in the b**** from King Kong.

Ally Maxwell was holding his side after being thumped by big John Clark. We were sure he'd have to come off and Stevie

Kirk would have to go in goals. It turned out later he had damaged his spleen as well as his ribs, so he was incredibly brave to carry on. By the end of ninety minutes he looked like he wanted to throw up.

We had been so close, but now it was all going wrong. Yet those hangers-on I was talking about lifted the whole place and the team started extra time like a train. Stevie Kirk was on and causing mayhem in their box. We had two chances in the first few minutes – then he scored.

A corner came in, they claimed Alan Main had been fouled, but Kirky was there from about three yards to put it in. We had twenty-five minutes to hang on and they would be the longest of my life . . .

Back in 1987, we didn't start extra time any better than we had finished the ninety. United still terrified me every time they went forward. It was like in the war, when you knew there was a bullet somewhere with your name on it.

They fired it just into the second half. A ball came into our box away up at the Celtic End and, with that delay there is between sight and sound in huge grounds, we saw the ball go in the net then heard the roar.

Iain Ferguson – the one who went on to score for Motherwell – had scored against us, like he always seemed to. It was all over. I turned my back on their celebrations, wanted nothing else but to get away, to be somewhere else.

Then the silence from our fans broke. It was weird – a sort of muffled roar started away at the far end of the North Enclosure, level with the penalty box where the ball went in. They'd seen the linesman's flag go up.

And the noise spread along the huge open terrace like a Mexican Wave as more and more realised it wasn't a goal, they'd chalked it off. It had happened to United again. But sod them, it *hadn't* happened to us.

By the time realisation hit the Rangers End we almost took the roof off. From that moment on, I was convinced we couldn't lose, if only because United were probably convinced they couldn't win.

They must have wondered if they would ever get a break in a final – and God knows they deserved one. Just not against us, not that day.

As I write this chapter, I stop a lot and look up at the pictures on my dining-room wall. There's one of a blond boy shooting and a keeper diving in vain, another of the blond boy wheeling away with his arm aloft while the keeper sprawls and a defender throws his head back in anguish and a third of the blond boy blowing his cheeks out while his mates swamp him and a snapper captures the moment. Those are among the happiest moments of my life.

The move started quietly enough. Then Brian Hamilton, one of the two teenagers in our midfield along with Paul Lambert, had the ball and was hitting the most languid little pass over the top for our Ian Ferguson to run on to. The ball dropped over Fergie's shoulder and he hit it on the bounce. Billy Thomson leapt, the ball whistled past his hand and thumped high into those old, round-stanchioned goals right below us.

It was to be the last goal ever scored in those goals before they were replaced and there was never a sweeter one. My heart's racing just describing it. When it went in I let out one of those screams that come from your toes; the ones where you're trying to speak, to express your utter elation, but all that comes out is *yyyeeeeeeeehhhhhhhhhhghghghghghhh*.

Thirty thousand of us made that sound all at once, diehards and hangers-on, old and young. I hugged Moodie, new dad and Celtic fan, until he almost suffered the same injuries as Ally Maxwell and his eyes were popping like Marty Feldman. Then I went down on my hunkers and covered my face and stayed that way.

Andy told me he looked round with ten minutes to go and his mates had gone.

I went to say something to one of the boys and he wasn't there. It turned out a few of them had gone away up to the back of the terracing and sat on the steps, facing out the way. I stayed, but I could hardly watch – I was sure the game would swing away from us again. I couldn't even think about penalties.

Everyone was on edge. A few guys had even been criticising Davie Cooper, who'd done more than anyone to get us to the final, but who was having a stinker on the big day. Eventually wee Tam took him off and one guy shouted that it was quite right, Cooper was a nightmare. One of my mates grabbed him by the neck and yelled: 'THAT GUY WON US THIS CUP, RIGHT?'

Still, wee Tam must have thought we were there because he sent on Colin O'Neil for the last couple of minutes even though he was nowhere near fit. He shouldn't even have been on the bench, but it was his reward for everything he'd done to get us there – especially in the semi-final replay with Celtic. But he could hardly run and I just wondered if it would all rebound on us.

Then the ball fell to Maurice Malpas, eight yards out. It was a sitter, a cert to make it 4–4. He put it over the bar. Even then, Malpas got another chance – but Maxy somehow got to his shot and held it and this huge sigh of relief went round our support. It was the last action of the greatest cup final ever . . .

I thought Kenny Hope, on his last day as ref, would never blow for the end of one of the *worst* cup finals ever. Let's face it, that's what ours was if you were a neutral. For us, though, it was the 1970 World Cup final, 1967 at Wembley and every win we ever had over the Old Firm all rolled into one.

Or at least it would be if he'd blow the damn whistle.

All I saw in that last minute were the backs of people's knees as I crouched down, pals occasionally bending over to make sure I was still alive. Now I suppose I regret not having seen the last touch of the ball, the reaction of our players, 60,000 arms go up in triumph – but at the time I was petrified that if I stood up United would score for real and it would be all my fault.

I didn't even hear the whistle, just the *yyyehhhheeehhhhhh-ghghhhrhhghhhhh* and I sprang up and cracked my head on a barrier and couldn't have cared less. Everyone was hugging and leaping and crying and laughing and dancing and bouncing, and those who weren't in some bear-clinch were standing with their hands behind the heads, staring into space, dazed with the magnitude of it all.

It was all too beautiful.

This was the moment of a lifetime's supporting, the erasing of all the bad stuff, the summit of our football Everest. Top of the world, Ma, top of the world.

And suddenly I was numb, drained, washed out. I could have curled up and slept there and then on the rain-streaked terrace, if only I'd been sure all the streaks were actually rain.

Billy Abercromby went up and lifted the trophy and 30,000-odd of us let a lifetime of waiting rocket from our throats and into the damp air. Then each hero took a turn of showing off the prize and each time we *yyyyeeehhhh-eeehghghhhhhed* again and then they came down for a lap of honour as the Dundee United end stood empty but for crisp packets and broken dreams.

We stood there for a while after the last player had disappeared with fifty scarves and twelve hats on, just taking it in. No one wanted the day to end. Finally, I trudged up the steps, lost in a daze until a booming voice pulled me up sharp. It was Gordon Mathers, eldest son of my Uncle Sam, with whom I had travelled to games since I was in primary school; me, him, his brother Richard and our dads. We stood in the same spot on the North Bank at every home game, switched to the other end for the second half, met the same people on every away trip. We looked at each other, unable to speak and really having no need. Then we hugged till our eyes bulged. What more could words have said that the moment did not? It was what we'd wanted all those years of going to Alloa and East Stirling and Cowdenbeath to suffer the miserable and the mundane.

Since then, Gordon has been struck down by MS. He has lost it all. But when I think of him, I see the guy who hugged me that day, at the top of the Rangers End, until this time *my* ribs nearly popped. Football gave me that memory. Thank you, football.

Andy, meanwhile, got his mates back. They came hurtling back down the steps at the end, trying to find him, and they did all the dancing and singing bit just like we had. It was all really emotional; the build-up had all been like that.

*

First the town had been decimated by the closure of the Ravenscraig steelworks and wee Tam kept telling the players this was their chance to lift everyone out of the gloom. Then, right before the final, his father died. Both managers in the biggest game of the season had lost their dad. I don't know if that was the reason, but when I looked around the celebrations at the end he wasn't there. He never appeared when they were passing the cup round. And he never got his own chant from the crowd.

Some would say that showed he wasn't popular, but maybe it's to his credit that he left the players to enjoy their moment without him. They'd earned their moment. Davie Cooper, poor game or not, had been the man around whom everything had revolved. Tom Boyd and Phil O'Donnell grew into men that day. Wee Dougie Arnott had completed the set of Amateur Cup, Junior Cup and Scottish Cup winners' medals and that will probably never happen again. Kirky was getting a special reception for his goal and so was Maxy for playing through the pain. Colin O'Neil looked thrilled that Wee Tam had shown his soft side and played him. Then you thought about John Philliben, left out after playing every other game and you felt so sorry for him.

After it all, we got back on a bus that was pretty quiet considering what we'd just achieved. We were done in. The plan was to go back to Lanark, where we'd all started out, and go round a few pubs to take in all the celebrations. But on the way back we all decided we wanted to go to Fir Park because we'd heard the players would be there. The driver wasn't that chuffed, but it was our day and no one would have been rotten enough to stop us. When we started up Airbles Road, half a mile from the ground, we began to sing again. Everyone got a second wind. High up on the flats by the Civic Centre, they'd made a huge flag out of sheets and dyed it claret and amber. It stretched across about six windows. It was wonderful.

By the time we got to Fir Park the players had been and gone, but there was a turnstile open, so we went in; it would be great to be in there, just a busload of us, alone in our spiritual home.

There were about five thousand already in there . . . They were at their normal places on the terraces or sitting in the stand or wandering around the pitch. For me it meant even more to be there, because I had to work the following day and I'd miss the big homecoming parade. That still bugs me, because it didn't get much telly coverage. The local paper had a fantastic picture of the bus coming through a sea of people with Ravenscraig looming behind it, and it makes me sick when I think I wasn't part of it . . .

Paisley was heaving when we got back, about twenty minutes ahead of the players. It took me ages to get 400 yards from where we got dropped off to the Town Hall. Everyone wanted to hug you. And then I was inside, upstairs and on the balcony, watching the open-top coach come under the railway bridge and into Smithhills Street. And there was the cup, above Alex Smith's head, shining in the sun which had graciously come back out for our party.

It was hard to believe I was in there, waiting to greet it and them as they came through the door. And then, when they arrived, I couldn't speak. I was there to interview these guys but it took me half an hour to gather myself enough to ask a single question.

Downstairs in the Town Hall they were holding a real-ale festival, which the players dropped in to before heading off to their official dinner; next day they were going to Singapore for a four-team tournament which, by the way, they would also win.

I went back to Jack Daniels, a diehard Saints pub right across from my office, and it was chocca. The day before, I'd won two hundred pounds in a newspaper awards ceremony and I put it behind the bar and never saw change. But who cared? Half the pubs in the town had put the prices back to 1959, the last time we'd won the cup and even then guys spent fortunes. (There were also tales of pubs doing 4p a pint being empty, but with huge queues outside waiting for Happy Hour; these, however, are cheap jibes at the people of my town. As is the tale of a Saints fan throwing a coin at the ref and getting hit on the back of the head with it . . .)

Andy and his mates, by this time, were in the Crown in Lanark:

> We were standing at the bar when our old manager Jock Wallace, never really accepted by the fans, came in with his wife for a meal. He was wearing his Motherwell tie and was obviously looking for us to start up some crack with him. All that happened was that one guy told him he had no right to wear our colours, that he wasn't one of us. He slaughtered him.
>
> Big Jock looked really hurt. He just picked his drinks up and took them over to his wife. It was a bit harsh and probably ruined his night, but it was how some 'Well fans were feeling; that the celebration only belonged to those who'd paid their dues.
>
> We went to four or five other pubs before ending up at the Cora Linn, where we'd met that morning. We could have gone to Motherwell itself that night, but we wanted to be with our own mates in our own town and I'm glad we did.
>
> I finally got home at about two in the morning and put the video on. My wife Maureen had taped all the pre-match stuff – interviews with Willie Pettigrew, old games, all the build-up, that sort of thing – and I watched that, then the highlights from *Sportscene*. I was shattered by then, finished. But I saw it through to the end. You couldn't waste a second of a day like that. Not when you might never get another one like it . . .

I drank that night like I've rarely drunk before; but somehow I stayed sober. I drank Guinness and Drambuie and bottles of beer and as I went from pub to pub I slugged from bottles of champagne held out by pals and strangers alike. But my mind was so alive that the bevvy was a stimulant, not a sedative.

At midnight I went up to Dunn Square, with its statue of Queen Victoria wearing a Saints top-hat, and sat on the grass and talked the game round and round and round. Some of the boys were going on to the dancing, where the players would be before going straight on to the plane next morning.

Me? I checked out and started walking towards home, just like I'd walked into town fourteen hours before. There was something important I had to do. I hoped I'd get a taxi somewhere, but there was no chance. I got in some time in the early hours, having stood every twenty yards to hug someone new and slug more champagne.

I set the video on rewind then went to do my important thing. I told Kenny all about it. Five months old he was, snug and content, blissfully unaware of all the excitement as he rushed through the hours until morning. So I sat by his cot and told him the story of How We Won The Cup.

Then I got up and placed a kiss on his cheek and whispered that one day it would be his turn to be there when we did it.

The perfect end to the perfect day I hope you have once in your lifetime.

You will, of course, have to supply your own baby.

SIX

WHEN SATURDAY DOESN'T COME

For the purposes of this chapter, I have developed a new glossary of swearwords. This is partly to challenge the ridiculous nature of the curses we use so freely, to lay bare the myth that swearing is macho. I wish to expose the senselessness of the words we use to berate others or to describe situations when there are far more colourful and acceptable words within the grasp of the user. But mostly I've used different words because, as you know, my mammy's reading this and she'll slap me. Therefore, I give you:

DOOF: Commonest and most multi-functional of swearwords in daily use. Can be a straight expression of surprise/disgust/pain (Aw DOOF! or For DOOF'S sake!); an adjective (he's a DOOFIN' blarf) (BLARF: see below); a noun (What a DOOFER; or the more abusive still, MOTHERDOOFER).

LINESMAN: Someone whose parentage is up for question.

SPLANJE: One who is held in contempt or an act which may make you blind. Note also SPLANJER.

SPLODGE: Smelly stuff. Also one who is held in contempt.

BLARF: A much-despised person. Also often used as an exclamation at the beginning of a sentence (Ya BLARF! Did ye see that game last night?)

Now, let us begin . . .

*The greatest thing about being a footballer
is that you never have to grow up*
– Gerry Britton

So I'm watching training and suddenly there's a shout.

'Hey, you!'

'Who, me?'

'Yeah, you – got your boots? We're a man short for a vital seven-a-side session.'

As it turns out, I do have my boots. Can they give me some spare kit? Excellent.

Five minutes later I'm ready and we're off. I get an early touch. Easy pass. Move into space for the return. See a harder pass and go for it. Perfect. Hang back as our team pile forward. Then make the run.

Ball comes in from the right. Striker shapes to shoot, but defender gets a head-flick to leave him frozen in ballet. Ball loops up and drops at me. I don't panic, not me. My pulse *slows*. Blood *chills*.

Take it at knee-height, cutting under the ball with the bridge of my left, arm and thigh coming across my body in easy balance. Watch it arc left to right, see team-mates and opponents half-turn in slow motion like passers-by following Superman's whoosh.

Keeper leaps, back arched like a Fosbury Flopper, fingers stretching like a drowning man clawing for a rescuer's hand. Ball beats them by an inch. Hits the net just inside his left post, six feet up.

Unstoppable.

And at the side they're nodding at each other and going: 'Hey, he's not bad – from now on we'll take his opinions much more seriously.'

Then I turn up to cover their game on the Saturday and the manager comes bounding up to the press box at half two with a desperate look in his eyes. He grabs me and says: 'Look, I know this is unusual – but we've had a flu epidemic and you're our last hope.'

'But I'm not registered or anything . . .'

'That's okay, after your goal in training we took the liberty of getting you signed up as an amateur just in case we ever had an unlikely emergency like this or you ever needed a way into a chapter of a book.'

So I say yes and they hustle me downstairs to get changed and rubbed down and poured into one of those huge subby suits like a toddler's winter all-in-one. I fidget on the bench – they'd managed to patch up eleven to start – and watch them go three down with twenty minutes left when their midfield general faints from the effects of his virus.

They've already used the only other two fit subs so I get stripped and all around me I'd hear fans asking who the hell I was, like in the *Roy of the Rovers* bubbles when punters on opposite sides of a stadium packed with 50,000 would reply to each other's shouts.

'Who's the little podgster in the No.46 shirt?' asks a bloke in the South Stand.

'Why, I think it's the witty and strangely good-looking sportswriter Bill Hingmy,' replies a voice from the North Stand.

'Yes,' confirms an old guy with a muffler scarf and a pipe behind the goals, 'it is.'

And on I go and within two minutes I've repeated my training-ground volley goal. 3–1. Two minutes later I've played a one-two in the centre circle, nutmegged a lunging defender and dinked one into the path of our one fit striker. 3–2. They're rattled now, and our crowd are going tonto.

We win a free-kick on the D. Instinctively the lads know I'm the one to hit it. And I do, outside of the right like Cubillas beating Roughie in Cordoba, whistling past the right end of the wall, leaving the keeper with his weight on the wrong side. Hits the inside of the post. Single fit striker slides to push it in. 3–3. But he's collided with the post and is dragged off, howling.

They go for the jugular against nine flu-flattened wheezers and a podgy amateur. Corner against us, swings over our keeper and drops to an away foot. He's twatted it and they're shouting Goa— when I get my head on it and it rebounds into the mêlée. I sprint off the line, crunch the guy going for the scraps, see the ball spin free.

The boys around me are out on their feet, it's got to be me. So I'm up and chasing and nicking it round a sliding tackle. Halfway inside my own half. One mate makes it out in support. I shape to find him, make the next defender shift his weight left and go outside. Over halfway now.

My one mate comes looking, so I find him. Keep going. They've been left short at the back. My one mate knocks it through. Last man slips. I'm in. Keeper stays big. I could try and go round him, but I'm shattered. Could try and slot it, but the park's too heavy. So I put left foot behind right, jab with the toes and the ball curls up and away past his startled left shoulder. There's not even time to kick off again.

Back in the dressing-room I sit for a long time, taking it in. Knackered.

Eventually I peel off my muddy kit and hit the showers. I'm still letting it lobster me when the manager comes in and says the press want me. I say let them wait.

Twenty minutes later, I'm humbly telling them it was a wonderful experience, but a one-off. I have a real job and my work here is done . . .

That's the daydream.

I'm lost in it every time I watch a team train. Always the same, to the tiniest detail. Then reality bites. A stray ball bobbles at me and even though I can keepy-up no bother – honest – I'm so self-conscious I can't even flick it off the deck and end up giving it a half-hearted sidefoot back towards them and walk about for the rest of the day with mud on my shoe, a Mitre-print on my trousers and shoulders heavy with regret at not having their confidence, their ability. Their *freedom.*

There's something very intimidating about being around the objects of your dreams, like the gallus teenager who fancies the sultry divorcee next door then runs a mile the day she comes on to him. In his dreams he'd got all the lines spot-on, acted smooth, walked cool, pressed all the right buttons. Now all he could stutter was *ffflennen.*

You never mess it up in your dreams. Reality is scary when it leaves you out of your depth. Which is why I was standing in the foyer at East End Park at 9.40 on Monday, 26 October 1998, trying to look invisible. This was the dream made real. And I was terrified.

A few weeks earlier I'd asked Dunfermline's assistant manager Dick Campbell if I could come in and watch them prepare for a game. Research for a book. Sure, he says, put it in writing.

A week or so later the phone rings. It's John McVeigh, their first-team coach. McVeigh is the football maniac's football maniac. The obsessive's obsessive. The psycho's psycho. Dunfermline had just got him back into football, four months after he was sacked by Partick Thistle at the end of a trying season. Yes, he says, Bert and Dick are happy enough for you to come for training. Next week okay?

'Excellent. Cheers mate.'

'Only one condition,' he says.

'Uh-huuuu . . .?'

'You get stripped and train *with* us.'

Thus I spent a restless Sunday night, running the old daydream over and over – except this time I couldn't pass water. If I'd had six shots at John Lennon etc. They ran me ragged for hours, after which I crawled behind the goals and, like a dyslexic alcoholic, vimtoed my load.

The players laughed at me. Laughed me off the pitch. Not just ordinary laughter, either, but the kind in Swinging '60s movies when it echoed and swirled and the faces went all fish-eyed around you.

Some time in the night, sleep wrestled my mind away from the torment, he wrote cheesily . . .

Monday morning I agonised over everything. What to eat, what to wear, whether I had everything packed. Went through that bag again and again. Screw-ins, check, mouldies, check, trainies, check. Shinpads, towel, woolly hat (players always look cool in woolly hats at training, always leaning back with their hands on their thighs and laughing at some killer in-joke), trunks. Toilet bag, check.

Ate toast, drank tea. Got changed. Looked in the mirror and got changed again. Went through bag again. Brushed boots again. Watched the clock move far too slowly until, at last, it was time to go.

Slung the bag on the back seat, climbed in, clunk-clicked, revved up. Handbrake off. Handbrake on. Got out, pulled bag from back seat, checked through it one last time. Check.

Got stuck behind an Eddie bloody Stobart lorry on the Kin-cardine Bridge and cursed it rotten. It's always an Eddie bloody Stobart lorry, isn't it? With its green and yellow and red and black that they turned into Carlisle's away strip and their girl's name on the radiator. Every Eddie bloody Stobart lorry wears a girl's name. Eddie bloody Stobart also has a fan club. Did you know that? Can you *believe* that? There's something like 20,000 members, half anoraks and half bored housewives, who have to wave every time they see one of the fleet and who get a flash of the lights in return.

Or they run down their little driveways, wiping rubber gloves on pinnies, to say hello and hope against hope it's the one with their name on it. And every time there's always someone stuck behind it, cursing like an aircraft hangarful of drunken Scots Guards.

Three miles and what felt like an hour later I got past. Now I could relax. Saw cars going the other way and wanted to yell out that I – *me, yes, ME* – was on my way to be a professional footballer for the week. With a Premier League club.

Now I'm excited, gagging to get started, to be part of it. To *share* their freedom. Then I'm standing in the foyer waiting for McVeigh to come and get me and I'm wishing I could climb inside my Nike bag and hide. Do the players know I'm coming in? What if they don't and I walk in and someone says what the rest are thinking?

What the doof's HE doing here?

I'm dreading anyone coming out of the white-painted door opposite me with the sign reading HOME DRESSING-ROOM in black. Where's McVeigh when you need him?

Then he's there, pumping my hand and taking me along the corridor, through the connecting doors and into Bert's office.

I'm expecting the rules to be laid down early. No going in there, no asking this guy questions, no interviews without permission. But it doesn't happen. There's no grilling, no suspicion about why I'm *really* here. I tell them I'm not here to dig any dirt, but they're not bothered. Bert just shrugs and says: 'We've nothing to hide.'

There's a knock at the door and Joe Nelson, kitman for nearly thirty years, pops his head round. He needs a car to take striker George Shaw to hospital. He was helped off ten minutes into Saturday's 2–2 home draw with Celtic after keeper Jonathan Gould landed on him and gave Dunfermline a penalty. George has come in complaining of terrible pains in his side and lack of breath. Bert reckons it's a rib. They all agree that's one of the worst injuries to get, because the docs can't do anything for it. All they can do is let him rest, although they know he won't be able to get comfortable.

Bert's looking at a list of eight injured players. Irony is, only Shaw and defender Jamie Squires – who's had six stitches in a gashed shin – got injured against Celtic. The rest?

'Ya blarf!' says Dick. 'We had two weeks off because of the Scotland games and when we came back half a doofin' dozen were doofed. Scott Thomson's fallen downstairs in his house and broken a bone in his doofin' hand.

'We pride ourselves on meticulous preparation, but we've never been worse prepared than we were for the Celtic game. Couldn't name a doofin' team till Saturday morning when we usually do it on Thursday doofin' lunchtime.'

'Aye,' says Bert, 'and losing Geordie and Jamie early on just summed up the doofin' week.'

The injuries mean training today will be light, just a loosen-up, get the lactic acid out of their muscles. Seeing who's been on the steamed puddin', they call it.

Then Dick checks his watch, claps his hands at me and barks: 'Right, go get your overalls on – it's time for work.'

The coaches change in the ref's room down a corridor between the home and away dressing-rooms. It has three chairs, a row of pegs on the wall by the door, two wall-mounted hairdryers and a phone on a table beneath a frosted window which opens onto the enclosure beneath the main stand.

(*Most teams come out of tunnels beneath where the fans sit. At East End Park they come out of the dressing-rooms, along a small balcony and DOWN a flight of stairs to the pitch.*)

They've laid out royal-blue polo shirt, sweatshirt, shorts and socks for me. John sends a YTS boy to get me tracky bottoms. I pull on my boots and look at myself in the full-length mirror which stands beside a side door leading to a series of shower stalls and a loo.

Now I'm *really* nervous.

McVeigh and I go in Dick's car to the training ground at council-run Pitreavie Sports Ground. It's a sprawling expanse of football and rugby pitches with a small athletics stadium and a gravel carpark. A band of high trees away at the bottom of its expanse separates it from a busy road.

Dunfermline have no training facilities of their own and are allowed to use Pitreavie free of charge. But this means there are limitations to where they can work. Jimmy the groundsman, a burly wee bloke in a Pars woolly hat, scopes their every move.

But Dunfermline are not poor boys. They're not even in a minority; for all the money sloshing around in transfers and wages, hardly any top clubs have their own training ground. Rangers had one years ago, right opposite Ibrox. They bulldozed it to give their new breed of affluent fans somewhere to park. Dunfermline used to have training facilities of their own too, but when the club ran up massive debts in the 1980s it was sold and is now a junior club's home. And so they do the work painstakingly designed to let them challenge the élite on a council site where they get a row for churning up divots.

'Sometimes I pray for £100,000 to buy a new player,' Bert sighs as the players arrive in a white minibus that has seen better days, 'but then I think it might be better if they spent money like that on the biggest empty shed they could find and made us an indoor gym.

'How can you get ready for a doofin' Premier League game against Celtic when the wind's howling and the rain's pouring and the doofin' parkie comes and moves you off the pitch because there's a schoolboy game on it on the Saturday? Believe me, he's doofin' well done *that* before!'

The players stretch and chat and yawn and then split into pairs for a passing and moving exercise to warm up their muscles. There seems little pattern and they don't move out of second gear. I stand at the side, juggling a spare ball and waiting for the shout to join in.

Dick whistles for them to stop and split into two teams. He hands one lot red bibs. They play a game of three-touch, then two-touch and then all-in. Dick and John agree the game slows up when there's no limit on the number of touches they can have.

Bert and Dick have been in charge here for six and a half years. They took over when the club was £3.8 million in debt and a couple of stumbles from the knacker's yard. Neither had a contract then and they still don't. Bert says he's happy to work on trust, but he's also not the type to knock on the chairman's door begging security.

He was a classy inside-forward in his playing days, leaving school in Fife to sign for Leeds then coming home to Dunfermline under Jock Stein. He missed the 3–2 Scottish Cup final defeat by Celtic in 1965 through injury, but was in the team that won 3–1 against Hearts at Hampden three years later.

Four years on, after two broken legs, he left and signed for Berwick Rangers. 'The manager there was Harry Melrose, who had been here,' he said, 'and I decided to give it a try. They were an okay team, but there was one boy – a right-back – who was terrible. We all knew it.

'Anyway, I'm playing this day and it's not going right and then I hear this voice slaughtering me – and it's the right-back. It was like hearing a voice from above telling me: "If he's slaughtering you, it's time to chuck it." So I told Harry I wouldn't be back and that was that.'

Bert and Dick go back a long way. They played together and ran Rosyth Juniors, renting the gravel carpark at Pitreavie for training, before coming here. Bert became No.2 to Alex Totten at St John-stone before coming home and hooking up with his pal again.

'It upset me when I came back here and saw how low the club had sunk financially,' he admitted. 'When I played here we faced the like of Valencia, Borussia Dortmund and Bordeaux on big European nights and they were still up there with the best while we were in the dumps. It wasn't right.

'So we accept not having contracts or much money to spend because we know the place has to be straightened out. The board have had to make tough decisions and sometimes that affects my plans. But in my time here I've never been to a board meeting. They let me concentrate on the football.'

On the pitch, they're practising shooting. Keeper Lee Butler, a big, grinning Yorkshireman signed from Wigan in the summer, hurls himself at drives with Monica Seles grunts and wrists like cricket bats.

'These are the best days of their lives,' Bert says, 'but some of them don't realise it until they're working in a pub or driving a van. Then there are players who look fantastic in training but can't do it on a Saturday. We had a lad called David Bingham here. He went to Livingston during the summer. In training he was brilliant, but some Saturdays he'd let himself down. So we'd leave him out – and then we'd see him in training and wonder if we'd regret it.

'Some of them are like that. You see them, all wanting the ball, all confident in their own ability. If they all wanted it the same on a Saturday, football would be a different game altogether. But the tricks stop with so many when it's for real. Out here it's only their pals who see if they go wrong. On a Saturday there's the big crowd and the media and the pressure of big bonuses hanging over them.'

Now the players have split into pairs, opposite each other. McVeigh faces them on the edge of the box. One plays a pass to the other, who puts a pass in to McVeigh. Then the pair cross and shout which one wants a pass back for a shot at Butler.

Greg Shields, the ginger-haired right-back signed from Rangers the previous season, has hurt his foot and hobbles out before the routine starts. Which make *this* the moment.

'Right, Leckie,' shouts Dick, 'you're in.' Something inside me falls over.

Andy Smith, club captain, star striker and £400,000-rated Scotland B international, had been partnering Shields. I played him a ball. He mishit it at McVeigh, who yelled 'Stop!' and made the pair of us lap the pitch.

Midfielder Marc Millar, squatting at the post with striker Gerry Britton shouted: 'Go on, Sinbad.' It took a second to realise he meant me.

Back at the line, we swapped over. Andy played me in, I found John, but forgot to cross over. Third time we got it right. John played off to Andy, Butler saved his shot. Next time he laid off to me, perfect for my right foot but I only stand on that one, so I took it on the outside of the left and Butler could have thrown his cap on it. Next time, same ball, same option, same bobbling outcome.

But I was in there. I was kicking a ball and no one had laughed me off the park yet.

We went to a two-touch game. The first surprise was that the other players were willing to pass to me, not to freeze me out because I'd been foisted on them by the gaffers. The second surprise was that my first couple of passes went where they were meant to. Couple of nice easy ones to start with, like in the dream. Then one with the outside of the left, aimed between two bibbed opponents for English midfielder Richard Huxford. Right on his instep. *Piece of cheese, this.*

Then I made a run, never got the ball, turned back and realised I had no gas to keep up. I had used my one gear. So I stuck to getting and giving, being a wall for the real players; until the last couple of minutes, that is, when I got second wind and brass neck.

Played one off to Huxy. Shouted for the return and never got it. Shieldsy did. I ran on, made an angle, showed. Good on him, he played me in. I've got my back to goal, only reserve keeper Davie Hay to beat. Turned like a juggernaut in a phone box and couldn't lift it past him.

All over.

On the side, Dick and Bert are laughing about me screaming for a return ball from Huxford. It dawns on me that I haven't heard anyone else *demand* the ball all morning. I thought everyone shouted and bawled in football, especially up here at the sharp end. But I watch them troop back to the bus and suddenly realise how quiet Dunfermline's players are.

Back in Bert's office, word comes that George Shaw does have a cracked rib. There's no point in him even trying to come in this week.

'Tell him to go to Majorca,' Bert tells physio Pip Yeates, 'but not to send us the doofin' bill.'

Talk turns to tomorrow night's Under-21 League game with Hearts. The Under-21 League has replaced the old reserves now that we have the new EssPeeEll with hot and cold running groovy ideas. Clubs can play three over-aged players and Bert's giving a trial to Chris Jackson, the former Hibs midfielder who's had a few games with Stirling Albion after coming back from a spell in Iceland. Centre-half Andy Tod needs the game as well after his stint on Saturday. The third? 'Big Andy Smith will want to play,' says Dick. 'That's a doofin' stick-on after he was suspended for Saturday. It means he won't train tomorrow morning, just come in for the game. They'd all rather play than train.'

'Aye, but there's a risk,' says Bert. 'What if he gets injured? And what if some young doofin' ref sees a big-name player and wants to make a name for himself? It's a helluva risk.'

I go for a shower as Dick talks to Norrie Gray, a reporter with the *Courier* newspaper. Outside, McVeigh is giving Smith and Scott McCulloch – Bob to his mates – some extra sprint work; ten yards to a line in the blaes, back to the start, up to a mark twenty yards away, back to ten and so on.

Bob's coming up a foot short of the line each time to get the jump on Andy. Maybe he thinks McVeigh and Dick don't clock it. McVeigh claps his hands and sends them in.

Dick tells me out of nowhere that Bob has no spleen. Lost it in a car crash. The boy himself is amazingly so-what about something so major. He said: 'It happened when I was eighteen and playing with Rangers. I suppose I'm lucky to be walking, never mind playing.

'I was heading back home to Cumnock from training, going through Newton Mearns, when I lost it on a bad bend. I was in hospital for two weeks, had my spleen out and lost a year from the game. But I know it could have been worse. Anyway, the docs said I didn't need my spleen to carry on playing and there'd be no long-term effects. I take penicillin every day, but that's about the size of it.

'Rangers were great. They gave me a new contract while I was recovering and looked after me superbly. But by the time I came back there was no way into things – so when Iain Munro came in to take me to Hamilton, I jumped at the chance.

'Iain was a big help and so was Sandy Clark when he took over. Last season we were flying until about October – we were top of the First Division and looking good – but they had no money and that meant players had to go. Hearts came in for Jose Quitongo and Dunfermline wanted me.

'My last game was at home to Dundee. We lost 4–0 and I scored *two* own-goals. What a way to go out – maybe Bert should think twice about selling me if that's what happens!'

He laughs, but the pressure's growing on Dunfermline to do just that. Dundee United want him and, within a week, Aberdeen would make a player-plus-cash offer worth £500,000.

Meanwhile, sure enough, Andy *has* come and asked to play tomorrow night. Dick listens and tells him to go and talk to Bert. He winks at me as the tall striker walks away. He and Bert have already planned for this and made their decision. Like Toshack and Keegan or Morecambe and Wise, they play situations as a pair.

Then, again, we're in Bert's office. Pot of tea, pile of toasted cheese and non-stop football crack. They're on former players. Who was the best drinker, got the most women, made the biggest arse of himself. Round comes the name Paul Kinnaird; a legend, one of the funniest, mental-est, drive-you-off-your-nut-est guys in the game.

McVeigh says: 'He was away with the Ayr United boys after they won the Second Division the season before last and he kept calling one of the other lads Butter Bean. It was Butter Bean this and Butter Bean that. So the boy's taking it, but after a while it riles him.

'Eventually, PK calls him Butter Bean once too often and the boy turns on him. "Why d'you keep calling me Butter Bean?" he says.

'And PK says: "Have you ever met anyone who liked Butter Beans?"'

Dick stands up: 'Ever seen PK's Savoy Shuffle? [The Savoy, or Sav, is a Glasgow nightclub where men are men and women are even more like men.] Doofin' superb. When he signed here, start of the season we won the First Division three years ago, someone told me to ask him about it. So at training I pull him aside and tell him I want the Savoy Shuffle as our warm-up.

'Fair play to him, out he comes and asks for two volunteers. No one comes forward, so he grabs big Norrie [McCathie, legendary club skipper who died of gas poisoning that season] and Tattie Cooper [Neale, now Ross County manager]. Tells them to copy what he does.

'So he's like this [puts hands on hips] then like this [left shoulder down] then this [switches to right shoulder down] and he's got the two of them giving it all this [puts the three moves together with exaggerated tosses of the head; Dick looks more than a bit like Freddie Mercury without the tash, but give him a feather boa now and he'd be a spitter for him]. Next thing the whole doofin' team's doing it. Thank doof there were no doofin' photographers there.'

'What about the boy at ******?' says McVeigh. He tells us the club, but let's protect the innocent. Okay, it was Hearts. 'They had a thief in the dressing-room, right? So they put in a security camera with a bloke watching the pictures. So they get a shout to go to the security office to check out a tape.

'The video runs and this YTS kid comes in the empty dressing-room with a broom. Has a look about, checks no one's there – then grabs the broom like a mike and starts singing away! He's giving it laldy! Then he stops, has another look round, sits down, pulls out a *Daily Star*, whips the trackies down and has a splanje!

'They haul him in front of the manager and show him the tape. He's mortified. At the end they ask him if he's got anything to say – and he says: "Aye – thank doof ah wisnae the thief as well!"'

And on that note . . .

The three of them are taking the young players out for a session at Pitreavie after lunch. I'm going home. My muscles have asked for the afternoon off.

TUESDAY

It's freezing, but I'm sweating.

Steam is coming off me in the bitter morning chill like a Grand National winner. My back aches. *Everything* aches. But I have to go on, have to will myself to get the job done. Can't let it beat me. Can't admit defeat.

Not long to go now. Just a few more big efforts. Keep pushing it, forcing it. Ignore the muscles screaming for mercy. Tell the wimps: No pain, no gain.

Not long now. Not long now. Keep chanting it inside, like a mantra. Mibbes you'll convince yourself, this thing that you are, grunting like a mum-to-be in the final stages of giving birth to an XXL bowling ball.

And . . . then . . . it's . . . it's . . . iiiiiiiiiit's . . . *done.*

I exhale for what feels like three hours, until my lungs have turned inside out and my chest has caved out behind my spinal column. Every tendon, every vein, every *hair* is on fire.

But the feeling of pride, of achievement, dulls the agony.

I've done it. I've scraped all the frost off the windscreen.

Now I have to go to training.

Fitness? It's a stupid word. It's like saying restaurants serve food. Yes, they *do* serve food – but does that mean there's no difference eating at a burger joint or the Café de Paris? (Not that I've ever eaten at the Café de Paris, but I assume they don't do Dead Dog Burgers'n'Non-Potato Floppy Fried Sticks On The Side with Thick'n'Glowin' Nuclear Sludge Shakes and Apple Pie heated to 400 degrees Celsius by a flamethrower.)

The term *food* just means anything eaten for nourishment or gratification. It covers a huge range, from Pot Noodles to . . . well . . . *food.*

And so it is with fitness.

You need fitness to get out of bed in the morning. To stand up. To brush your teeth, to wash your hair, to get dressed, to . . . okay, you get the point. Millions get puffed walking upstairs, hundreds of thousands start peching when they run for a bus, many thousands jog round the block then cave in, thousands manage a game of tennis.

And then there are the top few per cent who are *fit* fit. Athlete fit. Fit like the boys at Dunfermline are and like I am not. If I played ninety minutes with my mates, I could last the pace. Pick my runs, take a breather when I needed it, wait for the second wind and go again.

But that's among people whose fitness isn't too far above or below my own level. Here, training with a Premier League football team, I am a Pot Noodle and they are *filet d'agneau en croute avec jus de frambois.* When they run, they are good on the eye. When I run, I am like a poke in the eye.

Reading this, you might *think* you are fit. You may well actually *be* fit. But all but a few would realise, once you have worked with professional athletes, to what *degree* you are fit.

Which is not to say that just because these guys are properly, gen-up, kosher fit that they always *look* as if they are. Take Gerry Britton.

Gerry Britton is six foot, skinny, with black hair that flops over his ears and eyes. He has a sort of hollow face with a permanently sad look about it, a cross between Johnny Depp and *The Scream*. And he always, *always* looks knackered.

This morning, he and nine others from the first-team squad are sprint training on the gravel track round the East End Park pitch. Dick and McVeigh have put little markers, like Chinese coolie hats, at twenty-yard intervals down both sides. The players pair up and dot themselves by the markers.

The rest of the squad are either injured or are part of the Under-21 League game tonight. Dick says there's not much point me getting changed for all the time they'll be out, and I'm disappointed.

I feel a bit of a fraud, walking across the pitch in civvies while the rest stretch and jog themselves ready for work. One or two ask me why I'm not stripped and I shrug. They tell me to ask away. Then Dick shouts for them to get into pairs for sprints.

Each man has a different stride. Greg Shields moves like a Rolls-Royce. Scott McCulloch and striker Scott Thomson run within themselves ('soft fitness', the coaches call it). Some are explosive, others lumbering. Even if you'd never seen him play, you'd tell from the off Lee Butler was the keeper. They always look different, heavier, their strength in different places from the rest. Hamish French, oldest of the squad at going-on-thirty-five, isn't the quickest but is definitely working the hardest.

Then there's Gerry. The first thing you notice is his head, lolling from side to side like his neck's broken. He seems to have no bones. Take the languid, puffed-out gait of Chris Waddle and throw in a bit of Frank McGarvey's wibbly-wobbly touch-me-and-I'll-fall-over style and you have Gerry. Yet he's no slouch and, if anything, his awkward look is one of his main weapons on the pitch, that and his deliberate finishing style of *passing* the ball into the net. On

Saturday, he took the penalty after George Shaw was crocked and it was his first goal of the season.

You might not think it to look at his hunched running style, but a huge weight lifted from his shoulders when he beat Jonathan Gould from twelve yards. He had missed most of last season with a knee problem and a striker who is not scoring feels as useless as that little light in your fridge when the door is shut.

Now he was buzzing, putting a shift in, clouds of breath and peals of laughter hanging in the cold air of an empty football stadium.

Dick and McVeigh follow the pairs round as they get into the rhythm of their complex little exercise. Bert stands in the centre circle, keeping an eye on them. He's telling me about the next raft of plans for the ground; astroturf pitches in the far left-hand corner opposite the main stand, a hotel off the main street, new dressing-rooms and a new tunnel in the stand behind the home goal.

He's assuring me – or maybe himself – that the outlay won't bite into his already-meagre transfer budget when there's a yelp from behind us. Andy Smith's leaning on the perimeter wall at the away end stand, taking the weight off his left side. He's done his ankle in during the sprints.

'The pair behind were coming through us,' he's explaining, 'and I moved aside, stood on the wee step up from the track and it just twisted.'

None of the coaches needs reminded of the irony that he was only training this morning because they knocked back his plea to play in tonight's reserve game.

I expected them to make a fuss of an injury to their skipper and one of their top earners. But after finding out what was wrong they as good as ignored him. He limped away gingerly on his own, shaking his head, to see Pip in the treatment room.

'If you make a fuss you can make the injury worse,' says Bert. 'You can make it a bigger thing in their minds and then you've got a real doofin' problem. Best to let him go and get it looked at and then we'll see what's what.'

The rest have been stretching, keeping warm in the early chill, while Andy's little drama has played itself out. Dick and McVeigh set them going again. Bert watches and I watch the look on his face, an expression that never seems to change. It's like someone just took him by surprise with a camera.

'I like players who've known a job outside football,' he says, motioning at winger Stewart Petrie. 'He used to work in a warehouse, so he knows all about getting up at six in the morning in winter and grafting all day before training at night. Some have never known anything apart from a couple of hours' work a day.'

Then he says something that surprises me. 'But we still worry that we work them too hard.'

I give him a look that is a question mark above my head.

'The game is harder and faster now and there isn't much time between matches to train. You can't hammer them on the track when you're playing maybe twice a week, because they need to have plenty in their legs when they play again.

'The real hard work is done pre-season. That's when they build their fitness. After that it's just a case of ticking over and working on their touch, on set-pieces and finishing.

'Some days we just take them to a café for a bacon roll or send them in for a rubdown from wee Joe Nelson. Just get them loose and relaxed. Other times we'll run them pretty hard, but not that often.'

Andy comes back after twenty minutes, walking more easily. His ankle's not as bad as he thought. He walks and jogs, but Bert tells him not to push it, to go and get changed.

The rest finish off with shorter sprint drills, then pick up the marker cones and wander back in to thaw out. Some head straight for the showers or the bath. Gerry, Derek Ferguson and Craig Ireland go to pump weights in the gym.

Andy Smith and Andy Tod join Dick and McVeigh in the warm room that doubles as kitchen and laundry. An urn bubbles, a giant teapot stews, the toaster blasts non-stop. Dick slams in hunks of plain bread and steaks of cheese for roasting. Steaming mugs of tea flow. Bliss.

Then we wander along to Bert's office, but McVeigh diverts to the small games hall that adjoins the gym to watch a game of heady-tennis. It's Scott Thomson and Scott McCulloch *v* Gavin Johnson and Hamish French. McVeigh shouts abuse at every shot.

Gavin and Hamish win and head for the door after handshakes. McVeigh blocks their path. Dick's appeared at his back. Gavin and Hamish swap withering looks; there's no escape from this challenge.

Coaches cannot get enough of heady-tennis against their players. It's their chance to put one over on them. I've seen games go on for hours until the coaches win. I once made a snide comment to Alex Miller about it when he was manager of St Mirren, and next thing he had me and my colleague Stan Park down for a ritual humiliation from him and his No.2, Drew Jarvie.

Now it was Gavin and Hamish's turn. Or so the coaches thought. The players beat them. No, they *whupped* them. McVeigh cheated like a sprinter on extra steroids who's nailed his opponents' shoes to the blocks. It ended up 21–11, but Gavin and Hamish scored about 34 points. At one stage they were getting two taken *off* every time they scored a winner.

Eventually the coaches only gave up because we were going out for lunch. Bert, Dick, McVeigh, me and club secretary Paul di Mello. Baked potatoes, fish, all that healthy stuff at a little bistro up the road.

Afterwards, Bert went home to walk his dogs and Dick went to give a talk to a local school. McVeigh and I went back to East End Park and saw the games hall empty. I knew what was coming next.

'Fancy a game of heady-tennis?'

Those are the words he said, but he said them like: 'Fancy an hour or so of me taking out my frustration on you at losing to the players?'

But I'm in there like a shot, because this is what being at a football club is all about. Research for a book my erchie – I'm living out the daydream.

The hall is narrower at the far end because of an alcove at the near. A door on the right, halfway along, opens into the gym. On either side of the high volleyball-style net, beams come down four feet and all the way across. These features are all weapons for the regular, but nightmares for the rookie.

In heady-tennis you serve to the court diagonally opposite. The ball has to bounce once before being returned and after that if it bounces twice it's dead. You get two touches. If it hits the wall before bouncing, it's out.

On an even court I'd have done better, honest. But McVeigh, playing at the wider end, took about three points to suss I was all left foot and played everything into my right corner.

Still, I'm doing okay. Hanging in, though a chainsaw would have been handy to hack those beams off. And to cut a hole in the wall to my right. McVeigh's done this a hundred times and knows how to play his serves right into the very pipes running round the skirting.

The first set ends 21–11. We swap sides. Now there's a bigger surface to cover. But he still puts nearly everything into the right-hand corner and kills me. When I do get in shape to return, I'm hitting those damn beams nine times out of ten.

And I'm feeling it; this is what I mean when I talk about degrees of fitness. The really fit would breeze a few sets of this stuff. The semi-fit could play through to their second wind. But I'm suffering in the legs and in the head.

I know the shots I want to play, but tiredness is stopping me, and as I get more tired, the brain slows and I'm not sharp enough to think out the shots I would be able to play if I wasn't so unfit.

The second set ends 21–1, we swap again and I'm happy to be back at the narrow end. But he knows I'm knackered and he's playing on it. He's a pro, no room for sentiment. He wins the third 21–0 and is as happy as if he'd won the Scottish Cup.

'Well, you've found out a lot about us so far,' he says, pumping my hand, face right in mine, 'but I've found out something about you as well – you're doofin' splodge at heady-tennis.'

He's already shouted to a YTS boy to fill the two baths that sit side by side in a shower room which also houses two toilet cubicles. We soak for ages. I feel brilliant, happy. *Free*. It's just after three now, four and a half hours to the reserve game. The rain has started. We go back to Bert's office and sit talking to Paul di Mello.

Paul's a chartered accountant from Kenya, a small, slender bloke with sticky-out ears and a cheery smile. He always looks chuffed to bits to be around a football club. He's called club secretary, but does the job to which other clubs give the grander title of general manager or chief executive.

Bert goes to him with the names of players he wants and it's up to Paul to try to get them. To work out the finances, make the approaches, sit down with players and agents, thrash out deals. He writes up all the contracts from club captain to YTS kids.

The contracts come into three categories: a top bracket of stars on more money than the rest; then the rank-and-file of the first-team squad; then the youngsters. He's working right now on a rewording of the deals given to some of the better youngsters because of the Premier League rule that two under-21s must be on the bench in first-team games.

Paul's concerned that some might get first-team bonuses because the club are forced to put them in the sixteen, not because they've earned the right to be there. He and McVeigh agree the player market has changed out of all recognition because of the Bosman Ruling that makes everyone over twenty-four available without a fee after they're out of contract.

'It's like a Kay's Catalogue of players now,' says McVeigh, 'there's hundreds of them out there, all fighting for a job.'

Paul nods: 'I think it's ridiculous that come 1 January players who will be out of contract in June are free to talk to anyone they like. What if they get a move set up and decide not to try any more? We can't do anything to stop that.'

'It's getting to the stage when players will be asking for a notice period,' says McVeigh. 'They'll come in one morning and tell you they're leaving and there'll be doof all we can do but watch them work their tickets.'

Paul goes home for something to eat but is coming back for the game – if it's on. The rain's been falling steadily for over an hour and a sky the colour of the *Ark Royal* says there won't be a let-up.

'Snooker?' says McVeigh.

When you come out of Bert's office and turn left, there's a door that leads to the main corridor. Through it on your left is the Away dressing-room, opposite the boot room. Next there's the side corridor down to the ref's room and a double swing door to the pitch. Back on the main corridor, there's the Home dressing-room, then a stairway to the executive lounges, then the treatment room and finally the players' lounge.

Before we go in, imagine what it would be like. Cosy, lively, warm; a place where the team can get away from the gaffers, where opponents can come in and share a beer after they've kicked each other up and down for ninety minutes.

Now put all those thoughts out of your head.

The players' lounge is a dingy, white-emulsioned chipboard room that's long since exhausted itself crying out for a fresh coat. There's a scratched bar with no beer, a remote control with no telly and a pile of broken cues for a ripped snooker table with only six reds.

When you cue over the right centre pocket, you're blocked by a beam sticking out from the wall. So, over the years, they've battered a hole in it at shoulder height.

Word is that when the new dressing-rooms in the West Stand are ready they'll come with an all-singing, all-dancing playroom for the stars. But right now their only private meeting place is a miserable sight, like the social club in a derelict factory.

We set up the six reds and break off with tipless cues. The white rolls drunkenly off-line, giving me an excuse for being duff. My only unerring talent is in going in-off. McVeigh beats me 3–0.

'So now we know *two* things about you,' he grins, 'you're splodge at heady-tennis *and* snooker!'

It's now gone half five and the Under-21 players are arriving. Still the rain batters down. We go along to see Bert, refreshed by a wet afternoon's dog-walking, and Dick, back from school.

'What were you doing?' asks Bert.

Dick loosens his tie: 'It was a project on strategy and teamwork.'

'I hope you learned something . . .'

There's a knock at the door. It's Chris Jackson, the trialist. He's a delicate-looking boy, with curly red hair cropped short and a business-like grey suit. Shirt, tie and shoes are immaculate. He looks like Something In The City. Bert asks him if he'd prefer to play right midfield or centre. He says centre.

'Just you go out and enjoy yourself,' says Dick, 'and don't worry. If you're useless we'll just take you off, okay?'

Dick grins. Jackson looks round the faces, unsure. Then he grins too and gets up to go and meet his latest bunch of new team-mates, another special offer in Kay's Catalogue, easy payment available.

They're worried the game's not going to start. It's heaving down as we go out the ref's exit to the park. They're afraid the lines will be washed away. The ref and linesmen arrive just after six, all looking young enough to play in an Under-21 League game. They dump their bags and venture out into a downpour made even more dramatic by the floodlights.

Hearts have arrived, led by ginger-haired coach Peter Houston. They hold off getting changed while the cherub-faced officials do their stuff, wandering the sodden pitch, hands jammed in anorak pockets. The rest watch and wait.

Eventually the thumbs-up comes and players disappear back into the dressing-rooms. Dick gives them a few minutes to start getting changed before doing his stuff.

Joe Nelson is scurrying around getting this player underpants, that one longer socks. No club could survive without a Joe Nelson, the wee bloke who knows where everything is and everything goes, who can produce a tie-up or a stud key like a rabbit from a hat. He's – what? – early sixties? A bustling little bundle of perpetual motion with endless patience and understanding. His enthusiasm is as striking as his full head of nearly-black hair swept back like DeNiro in *Goodfellas*. Dick, balding long since, asks him where the justice is.

The players go out for a kickabout in the downpour. One of the three over-age players for Hearts is one-time Scotland right-back Dave McPherson. He's played in the World Cup and doesn't look ultra-thrilled to be playing in a game like this on a night like this.

After McVeigh shouts them in, Joe throws them towels and they pummel hair and legs dry, take off training tops and slip into match shirts. Then Dick claps his hands for attention. 'Right,' he barks, 'tonight will tell me more about your attitude than your ability. How much you fancy it on a doofin' horrible night. Are you up for it?'

He doen't wait for an answer. He machine-guns them with his eyes and his words, telling them they *will* be up for it, they *will* be first to the ball.

Then he starts on Edinburgh.

'Edinburgh?' he yells, 'Doofin' Edinburgh? I doofin' *hate* doofin' Edinburgh, the buncha blarfs. Soft linesmen, that's what they are. They've come across here, thinkin' they're doofin' smart, thinkin' we're country boys – well, it's our doofin' job to doofin' show them, isn't it? *Isn't it?*

'Doof me, they played our youth team the other week and gave us a doofin' doin'. Beat us to every ball! Them! Edinburgh splanjers! Any of you play in that game? You? And you? Did you enjoy it? Naw, did ye doof! So don't let it doofin' happen again . . . *right?!?*'

All through this I've been watching Edinburgh boy Chris Jackson sitting, head bowed, right below the coach's pointing finger. After he's finished he has a quiet word with the boy. Nothing personal.

And then they're on their feet, clapping and stamping and giving each other slaps of encouragement. They snake behind skipper Andy Tod, who gets a final fist-up cajoling from Dick and Bert.

Joe reaches into one of his Aladdin's Cave cupboards and throws me out a black-and-gold padded substitutes' jacket, and damn warm and cosy it is, too. Who would want to get stripped to play on a night like this when you could be snuggled up in one of these? *Er, me.*

McVeigh stands in the dugout with Joe and the cosy subs. Dick is banned from the touchline, so he and I stay on the little balcony outside the dressing-room. Injured first-team keeper Ian Westwater arrives beside us to watch. Bert is up in the stand with Hearts manager Jim Jefferies.

There are a few dozen fans in the stand, plus a handful of scouts and managers. You can hear every shout from the players, every thwack of boot on ball.

Sweeties are passed round our balcony, caramels and chocolate eclairs. Football people seem to love sticky sweets. Dick grips a Silk Cut between his teeth as he thrusts freezing hands in pockets.

Then, not a lot happens. Followed by not very much, then squiddly poo and a fair bit of the square root of sod all. It's awful stuff, admittedly not helped by the weather, but one of those games you just can't see coming to life.

Hearts are playing Juanjo, the pencil-slim winger signed on a free from Barcelona a few weeks before. Bobby Robson, the former Barca boss now at PSV Eindhoven, says he can't believe they let the boy go. Watching him, even in these conditions, you can see glimpses of his talent.

The only real incident of the first half comes when Jackson and the Hearts No.6 thunder into a tackle and only Jackson gets up. You could hear the contact and the yelp. Pip Yeats grabs a foldaway stretcher and races round to help treat the injured player, who's being dragged to the track like a dead weight. They lift him gently onto the stretcher. *One, two, three – hup*. Pip and two Hearts subs carry him round the track, into the Dunfermline dressing-room and through to the treatment area.

'Can someone find the boy's dad?' Pip's saying. 'He's up in the stand. The boy's done his knee but it looks worse than it is. Jackson's boot has cut the kneecap like a Stanley knife.'

Pip is still at work dressing the wound when half-time comes. He pops his head round to warn Dick not to mention what happened in his team talk, as the boy can hear everything.

Dick claps for silence. He scans the team, some drying soaked hair or changing shirts, some slumped on the bench drinking juice or water.

'So what's the first doofin' thing you notice about the boy Juanjo?' he says.

Silence.

'Come on? What is it? What do you notice?'

I know the answer, me sir, please sir; but I'm saying nothing. I just hope no one says the wrong thing if they break the silence.

'Okay, I'll tell you,' he says eventually, lowering his voice. Then the volume booms back up as he rasps: 'He's doofin' *quick*. He's got doofin' pace to burn. So what do we not let him do? Run doofin' in *behind* us!'

He picks out the defenders, tells them to get it organised. He goes to a tactics board with magnetic draughts-pieces on it to show them how he wants it balanced. Then he's looking around: 'Where's doofin' Davie Hay?' The keeper mumbles that he's behind him. 'Well, listen – *if you stay on your line one more time I'm doofin' taking you off. Understand? Doof me, get out there, make it doofin' yours*.'

The keeper nods his apologies, head bowed.

Then they're all stamping and clapping and let's-get-into-them-ing again and they're back into the rain. Dick gets the reserve keeper stripped – just to ram his point home, just to show Davie he's not kidding.

The second half is no better than the first. Pip finishes work on the Hearts boy and puts him on crutches. He asks if he's missed any action. Dick just scowls.

Marc Millar, the third over-ager, is also booked for a clumsy tackle and the danger now is that he could be sent off. With the first-team squad already thinner than a hermit's address book, they can do without that. He's taken off and complains of a calf strain.

It all peters out to the 0–0 it had looked from the first few minutes and they trudge off with heads bowed. In the dressing-room, they sit like schoolboys outside the headmaster's office, waiting for six of the belt. But it doesn't come.

Dick plays it all softly-softly, calling it a poor game, a bad night. Rotten conditions. Says they'd done well at the back against a strong team. And all the time he was scanning, scanning for signs of who was hurting. Or who was thinking: Hey, we're off the hook; the gaffer's not worrying, so why should I?

'Overall, you did okay,' he finishes, but then grins: 'And you're all in tomorrow.'

Then he goes and crouches by Faulconbridge and Nish to talk about their performance together up front. He speaks quietly and calmly and says if they want to give him an argument he's listening. Faulconbridge starts to speak back on some point or other only for Dick to promise him what they call in Fife 'a rap aff the puss'. The boy might be English, but the message is universal.

As they peel off sodden kit, McVeigh calls one or two over to the magnetic board, running them through wrong moves they had made or right ones they might have but didn't.

Only Jackson goes out for a warm-down and halfway through his lap the floodlights go out. By the time he jogs round to the dressing-room, someone's shut the double doors to keep the heat in and he has to knock hard to get back in.

Along in Bert's office, the result doesn't seem to matter much. They're talking more about performances. 'We've got a saying,' says the manager. 'Players put themselves in the team and players put themselves out the team.'

Tonight the feeling is that Faulconbridge, after all his good work against Celtic, has put himself back out for Saturday's game at Dundee.

They would start looking at a team for real tomorrow. Once they saw who was fit to train, knew who was up for it.

I left East End Park at 9.52 p.m., having clocked in at 9.08 a.m. John McVeigh had been there the whole day too.

I tell him he won't granny me at heady-tennis tomorrow.

WEDNESDAY

Rain's still hammering. Dick's been down to Pitreavie at eight to find a piece of grass dry enough to do some decent work on. Andy Smith is jogging round the East End Park track. He's told Dick and McVeigh he's fine to train, but they watch and disagree.

The worry when a first-team player has an injury is whether he's really over it or whether he just wants the money. Win bonuses can double or even treble the wage packet, so the difference between being out there and not is huge. They agree Andy's convincing himself he's ready. He'll never train.

The six-foot-odd Aberdonian, blond hair and ears like the Scottish Cup, comes in and insists the ankle's fine; the only trouble's a twinge in his back from when he hurt himself. But he's okay, honest.

The gaffers were right, Andy didn't train. Just jogged round the outside of the soggy patch of pitch, feeling his back now and again and shaking his head.

After today's session, Bert will call them into the boardroom to dissect the Celtic game; a slaughtering followed by a gentle pep talk to get them going again.

They work under a sky which can't decide whether to wear blue or black and on a surface turning rapidly from green to brown.

High-tempo ball exercises take them up through the gears towards Saturday and Dens Park. They start with the usual two-touch, rain driving across them, before Dick shouts a halt.

He gets goals put back-to-back and splits the squad into reds and blacks. The red keeper, Davie Hay, bowls the ball to start a move that's meant to end up with a goal in the net at the other side. If the ball goes out of play, Lee Butler plays out and the blacks try to get round and score past Hay. They scuffle about for a few minutes before Dick, all urgency, yells stop again. 'That's doofin' lazy,' he shouts above the howling wind. 'Lazy! Ya blarf, there's some of you not moving, just hanging about the goals. So now we go man-to-man. Let's see you get someone and go with him. No stopping.'

They're off again, shadowing each other, but it's still sluggish. Another stop, players hands on hips in the biting wet and cold. 'Okay,' says Dick, 'now I want two from each team standing twenty yards out on their attacking side. You can't shoot until you play them in and get a return ball. Okay? Let's go again . . .'

And *now* they move. Now it zips. Ball out, quick passes, runs away from markers. Get round the other side and play your outside man in. Move for the return or make a decoy for someone else to take a pass. I chase round, fielding balls that are flying a hundred yards high and wide in the gale. Bang them back to Hay's goal when the play's on the other side.

Then they do a shooting exercise, using both goals at right angles to each other and players hitting shots at the first keeper then spinning to fire at the second. It's punishing for the man in the middle. Butler flings himself to parry with those huge wrists and smacks them on the turf when he's beaten. Hay watches more shots curl over in the wind than hit the net.

Then it's a game and I'm in. Same story as before; couple of good early passes then I'm blowing out of my backside. It's two-touch at first. I take one from a Derek Ferguson pass, use the second to find Hamish and overlap as he flicks round his marker. I see Scott Thomson far post and in my mind the cross is already on his forehead.

But I don't get through the ball, hit the first defender and there's a sharp pain across the bridge of my left foot. Then Gerry's first touch lets him down and I nip in, chipping it over his outstretched leg in a neat little arc to McVeigh.

We go behind. Near the end, Ireland hits a crossfield ball for Bob which I've read early. I'm out, taking a touch on my right instep and watching it bounce up nicely. But I'm too knackered to shoot and tall, dark Davie Hay watches it roll towards him. He picks it up in one hand, grinning.

Losers get to carry the goals back to the pavilion.

Back at the ranch, the debate over Saturday's team gets up steam. Dick has picked a line-up in 4-4-2, with Andy on the bench, but Bert wants three or even four up front.

'Nah,' says McVeigh, 'don't tinker with the system that did well against Celtic.'

There's a knock at the door and Shieldsy's head pops round. 'Er, can I have a word?'

'Sure, what is it?'

'Em . . . I crashed the minibus.'

We're waiting to hear some horror story about six first-team regulars in hospital, big-money men out for the season.

'What d'you mean you crashed the minibus?' asks Bert.

'Well, I've never driven it before and . . . well, I was coming out of Pitreavie and caught the slab that juts out the top of the pillars at the gate and it's scratched right along the side.'

'Was it the old minibus or the new one?' asks Bert.

'The old one.'

'Thank doof for that . . .'

They send him on his way and laugh. They're not sure whether they'd have owned up if they'd done it or if they'd have kept schtum and hoped no one noticed.

Bert's jotting a team on a pad in front of him. I'm waiting for him to pronounce, but instead he stands up and says it's time for the team meeting.

In the corner of the boardroom, with its display cases full of trophies and medals and trinkets and its walls covered in the pennants of old European rivals, they've set up the tactics board with its little magnetic men, blue for Dunfermline and yellow for the opposition. The players file in and sit in an arc of chairs round the top end of the darkwood conference table.

They look uneasy. They know the gaffers are raging at the goals lost against Celtic. Huxy's in for it; he was meant to pick up Henrik Larsson on free-kicks, but lost his bearings and let the Swede in to nick an equaliser straight after Gerry's penalty. He had been told and told before the game. It had been written on the dressing-room wall. But he lost his man and a goal and now he's for it. I can't look at him.

Again, though, the kicking doesn't come. Furious as Bert is when he thinks about the incident, he says that those responsible *know* who they are, *know* what went wrong and what they were meant to do.

The words hang in the air over Huxy's head like a swarm of bees making an arrow in a Tom and Jerry cartoon. The gaffers keep telling me what a deep lad he is, this dark-haired Englishman signed on a free from Burnley. He likes all his food steamed, will only eat it at nanosecond-specific times. He's quiet, painfully so, an introvert. He's the only one I have never yet heard speak. And he's off the hook, except maybe in his own churning mind.

Bert takes centre stage for the first time this week. He goes through the second goal with little figures on a magnetic board; he says it was a mess. Just after Hamish had put Dunfermline back in the lead, a long Tosh McKinlay ball let Brattbaak in behind Toddy. Butler pushed the striker wide, but Brattbaak twisted and turned as the keeper scrambled before placing a shot past three men on the line.

'We need to be tighter than that,' Bert's saying, showing the path of the ball and the gap between the centre-backs on the board. 'We talk about the strengths of players and McKinlay's delivery is an obvious one. Yet we leave a hole for him to hit and let Brattbaak run in to.'

The three of them drum home how Craig Ireland and Bob were too far to the left. Bob mumbles that they were watching Larsson and Donnelly on Celtic's right. McVeigh says those two were no danger out there, then Bert looks at Shieldsy and says he should have gone to Brattbaak instead of the line. 'You made a good run back,' he tells him, 'but we've already got two on the line. Why do we need three? Why? Especially when Buts is on his arse trying to grab the ball off the striker. Someone should have gone out there and closed him down.'

He looks round, leaving a pause like half-time. It's his way of bridging between the down stuff and the encouragement. Then he talks them up, tells them how big Saturday at Dundee is, how they have to fancy themselves after playing so well against Celtic. How it's all about learning, about listening, about looking at what's gone wrong and putting it right.

Afterwards, I sit with Gerry Britton in the perspex home dugout. I've been told he was studying to be a lawyer. 'Naah,' he says. 'I *was*. But it was too much, it would have been six years and that was too much of a commitment. I'm doing a degree in Social Science with the Open University and that's hard enough. I study about twenty hours a week – that's longer than we train! It's all economics and politics, useless except I get the degree, and that helps if I want to move into business later on. I want to stay in football, though. Probably, anyway. I've started my coaching badges and I can see myself on that side.

'The money as a player at a club like this isn't great. Maybe £500 a week, though the bonuses are excellent – when you get them. If you don't, your basic's your lot.

'People think we all get thousands. But it's not like that for most players, even full-timers in the Premier League. They think we come in and just fanny about for a while then sod off again. I don't think they really have the right impression of our lives.'

Then I ask him what I've wanted to ask all of them all week. '*Is this really the best job in the world?*'

I've wanted to ask, but then I've also been scared in case they sneer and say no way, forget it – it's *a* job, nothing more. That they all just do what I always dreamed of doing because they do it, because it came along.

'I mean, I always wanted to be a player, but I was never good enough, so to do this is like . . . like, a *dream* for me,' I'm gabbling. 'But I'm not sure if that's how you all feel or if . . .'

'Don't worry,' he smiles, 'it *is* the best job in the world. No danger. I get to come in at ten in the morning, have a laugh with my mates, go out in the fresh air to keep fit. I could be away home at twelve if I wanted. I get to play football in front of thousands every week. And I get paid for it. Of *course* it's the best job in the world.

'Sure, you sometimes get pissed off, days when you can't be arsed. But that happens to everyone, in every job, doesn't it? The training facilities are crap. It's ridiculous that we should be begging for a corner of a public park when we're trying to match Celtic and Rangers.'

I tell him as gently as I can, not looking at him as I say it, that he doesn't look much like a footballer.

He gives a little shrug and admits: 'You're right – I've always been told that. At Celtic, when I was a kid, they thought there was something wrong with me when I ran, and tried to change how I moved, but it's just the way I am. Derek Ferguson was in the stand on Saturday and it's the first time he's actually sat and watched me play. He said I looked knackered after five minutes. Then he said I got a burst of energy, then looked knackered again. But I was fine all the time, really. I've had that in the past with managers wanting to take me off because I've looked done in and I've had to convince them I was fine. Chris Waddle's the same – he always looks like he's going to drop. Until he gets on the ball, that is – and then he flies.'

I ask him what the bestest thing of all is about this best job in the world of his.

He thinks for a second, then says: 'The best thing about being a footballer is that you never really have to grow up. I get to run about in shorts carrying on like mad, having a laugh and a joke like most people never have at their work. Yet it's funny how we're treated; sometimes like men, but other times like wee boys, when they're having a go about stuff. I've been in dressing-rooms where players have been close to coming to blows or even actually scrapping. It's not that way here now, though last season we had a big centre-half called Dave Barnett who came up from Birmingham and who was always wanting a fight. Unfortunately, quite a few took him up on it.

'Now? We have a laugh, but on the pitch we're quite a quiet lot. The gaffer's right about us not doing on a Saturday what we do in training. But it's pressure, it's not wanting to be seen making mistakes. In training it's just the boys and they laugh at you whatever you do.'

Everyone's packing up early today. Time to think, to put the final touches on the team. Before it's definite, they need to sort out a few things. Huxy's to see a specialist at half nine tomorrow morning about a pelvic problem. And they say Andy and Jamie Squires *must* train to have a chance of playing.

That night, watching Arsenal *v* Dinamo Kiev in the Champions' League, I find myself watching for things the coaches have been shouting about all week. I'm shaking my head when defenders don't block the runs of forwards or strikers don't work in pairs. *I need a right good slap.*

THURSDAY

The morning is wilder than a dingo who's come home to find his house ransacked.

Tea warms us as we sit in Bert's office and dissect the Arsenal game. I say the tackle Tony Adams made on Shevchenko – sliding in on the edge of the box at full pelt, taking the ball and getting up to pass it clear – was one of the best I've ever seen.

'Ya blarf!' says Dick. 'What about it? Did you see it, Bert?'

'Aye.'

'What a tackle.' Dick's out of his seat to re-enact it. 'The boy's clean in and Adams is behind him like this [he makes the shape of being on the striker's shoulder] and slides in like this . . . you want to have seen it, Bert!'

'I *did.*'

McVeigh watched Man U beat Brondby 6–2 on cable. He's waxing about Solskjaer's goal, with his first touch after coming on as a sub. Then they get down to the real business: Saturday's team.

Bert still fancies four up. Dick would go with three. McVeigh still says stick with 4-4-2. Dick's twin brother Ian, a former striker with the club who's known as Pink, comes in on his way to work. He's around on matchdays, helping with the warm-up. He wants to throw in his tuppence-worth about Saturday, but every time he puts forward a player's case, Dick or Bert tell him the boy's injured or out of form. They argue against his every formation, winding him up. By the time he leaves he's suggested about 17 players in 4-3-3, 5-3-2, 2-3-5 and 6-3-3 Squadron. And the only solid decision is that he's buying lunch.

Down at Pitreavie, the ground they've been allocated is sodden. The huge puddles are an obvious injury risk if they do high-tempo work. Dick and McVeigh walk up to the next seven-a-side-sized area to check it out. I go the other way to see if there's a drier patch – but everywhere seems to be under water. If directors or fans could see it they'd maybe cut the team some slack if they lost come Saturday. This is no way for a Premier League club to prepare, no way for pros to reach their peak.

Dick and McVeigh decide the next pitch is slightly less of a bog, so the players lug the goals – they're using full-sized ones for the first time this week – fifty yards further up. Then they're off and playing two-touch, but yet again Dick reckons they're slack, so he changes it to one-touch and the pace lifts. You wonder why they have to be put under pressure before they step it up.

Bert watches Andy and insists he's 100 per cent fit, but I'm not sure if he's trying to convince himself. He's swearing like a lorryload of navvies about the conditions – and no wonder. Mud is clogging, water lying, wind whipping in our faces and carrying stray balls for miles. They had wanted to work on set-pieces, attacking and defending, but all they can do in this weather is keep the boys moving and get their sharpness up. 'You can't even call them in and have a doofin' chat about things,' Bert says. 'They get cold and stiff. So we just move them, keep the ball moving, get some shots on target and get the passing going.'

Gerry looks good, so too Craig Faulconbridge. He was in the plans after Saturday and out again after the reserve game – but now he's flying. Jamie Squires is training forlornly with Pip. Five days after getting those six stitches on his shin, he still doesn't look comfortable. He's not kicking a ball yet.

Half an hour later and the pitch is like the Somme. They're slithering, struggling to turn. Balls are bobbling and sticking and doing any kind of quality work is almost impossible. The rain's driving harder than ever and the wind's like fifty lashes.

Then the morning *really* turns bad.

Over the horizon and down the hill marches the groundsman, all wellies and woolly hat and indignation. He's heading for Bert, comes right up in his face. 'We're gonnae fa' oot, Bert,' he's saying. 'An' ah dinnae want that. Ye know the bits ye're meant to play on and the ones ye're no'. Ah need ye aff.'

Bert takes an executive decision. He blames Dick. 'Ah know, ah know,' he shrugs at the parkie, 'ah told him. But you know Dick. He doesn't listen. Me? I'm only just here. I didn't know he was going to use this bit. He just never listens – go and tell him.'

So the wee man splooshes his wellies round the pitch to where Dick and McVeigh are comparing notes and leaves Bert with his shoulders shaking: 'Now you'll see something – Dick'll tell him to go take a doof to himself. He'll probably belt his puss.'

Dick knows two words of diplomacy and one of them is 'off'.

We watch him and the groundsman square up. McVeigh's laughing. Dick's listening and nodding as a finger wags in his face, like a player who's trying to show a lecturing ref he's really, *really* sorry for a foul but who's actually thinking: 'What a splanjer.'

Then the groundsman's marching back round to Bert, leaving Dick and McVeigh laughing and the boys still splashing and slithering for all they're worth.

'It's up to youse,' the groundsman's saying. 'You can either move or I phone my boss and I don't want to do that because ye might end up with no pitch to train on at all.'

I motion to the Pars badge on his hat and ask if it bothers him that the players he supports could be injured sliding in puddles on the pitch he *wants* them to work out on.

'Maybe,' he says, 'but there are kids playing on *this* park on Saturday and I'm thinking about *them*.'

And there you have it, sports fans. Dunfermline's professional, Premier League team are thrown off the only available training facilities in their town because they don't pay to be there and schoolkids do. *Crazy*.

Dick carries on while the groundsman watches and seethes.

They're split into three teams of five, rotating in what's now an all-in game. I watch Derek Ferguson, the former Rangers midfielder, come off with his five and immediately get a spare ball and jog round the pitch with it. He's the only one who keeps moving while he's out of action. Ferguson has carried the reputation of a troublemaker for a decade like a bad smell. As a kid at Ibrox he was labelled a bevvier and never really lost the tag after a £750,000 transfer to Hearts and a couple of indistinguished further moves. Persistent injury hasn't helped him fulfil his potential. Now he's better known as the big brother of Barry Ferguson, the twenty-year-old wonderboy of Dick Advocaat's new-look Rangers. But he's still a hell of a player and a hell of a trainer. There's something about him that's more professional than some of the others; the way he stretches, the effort he puts in, the precise way he makes his passes. You watch him and wish so many years hadn't been wasted, be it through his own fault or fate.

He's just played another sliderule ball when Dick calls time. He's made his point and now it's time to cut his losses. They go behind the goals to the original pitch they'd been given and split into threes to hit long passes in the constant squall.

Ten minutes later and enough is enough. Dick shouts them in. Gavin Johnson chips a ball towards Lee Butler, who dives headlong into the biggest puddle on the entire complex. He is utterly soaked and grins from ear to ear as his mates cheer.

I watch Fergie boot a ball fifty feet into the air, drop to the press-up position and catch it on the back of his neck. That's talent.

I walk back with Shieldsy and ask him what it's like waiting for the team to be named. He's say it's nerve-racking. 'You hate this time, even when you're playing well,' he says. 'You don't know what's going through the gaffer's mind, whether he's going to change everything from the last game. I'm fairly confident about my place just now, or as confident as you can be in football. I reckon I could have a couple of stinkers and still get the shout, but you can never be sure. I hope I'm in. You don't know the team, do you?'

I shake my head.

He shrugs. 'There was a spell last season, not long after I'd come here, when I was a bit –'

I never got to hear what he was a bit of, because up ahead they had revved the minibus and a gaggle of grinning faces were disappearing as the sliding door was pulled shut without him.

He looked at me apologetically and sprinted off. He banged on the door as they went to pull away and they let him on.

Bert, Dick and McVeigh are going for lunch on Pink and want to know if I'm coming. I say no. I'm not sure why. Maybe I just don't want to leave this place. The nearer it gets to matchday, the more I want to be part of it.

The players have showered and changed and are heading off, but I'm still hanging about in my sodden training kit. A couple of press boys are around the foyer, looking to speak to Gerry about him facing his old team on Saturday, but I feel different from them today. I'm not a sportswriter, I'm part of a football team.

The gaffers have *made* me part of it, excluded me from nothing. The players greet me in the morning the way they do each other. I know secrets, I know the routine, I'm in on the debate over who's playing and who's not. I've even found myself throwing in opinions and not being told to doofin' shut it.

And it's struck me that pretty soon I'll have to stop pretending and go back to real life. *Sigh.* I peel off my kit in the ref's room and stand, eyes closed, under the scalding shower for a long time. Then I'm dressed and leaving reluctantly, out to the car and away, as happy and as unhappy as I have ever felt in my working life.

The most horrible feeling in the world must be that when a footballer is told he is not good enough, no longer wanted. To leave a club, to leave the game, for the last time when you thought – *knew* – you could make it does not bear thinking about.

Maybe it's better that I'm only playing at it.

FRIDAY

The day of relief for eleven, of resignation for some and of huffs for others.

By nine-thirty, the team has been decided at last. After all the ifs and buts, the to-ing and fro-ing, the agonising over formations and personnel, they have done what you always had a sneaky feeling they would. *They've stuck by their guns.*

Bert has a 4-4-2 side written on a sheet in front of him:

Lee Butler

Greg Shields   Andy Tod   Craig Ireland   Scott McCulloch

Hamish French   Richard Huxford   Gavin Johnson   Stewart Petrie

Gerry Britton   Craig Faulconbridge

It is the eleven who played the bulk of the Celtic game. Fergie, Marc Millar and Andy are all on the bench. Jamie Squires is not in the sixteen.

'Andy needs a wee jolt,' says Bert. 'He's only got three goals compared to twenty-six last season and he needs a break. Anyway, he missed last week after getting sent off and that's not our fault.'

'Players put themselves in and players put themselves out,' says Dick, again.

I wander out to the gym. Gerry and Fergie are working the weights. Although I now know the team, I ask them what they think it might be. Fergie says he thinks it will be the same as last week, in fact he reckons the boys would be unhappy if it wasn't; there's no reason to change it.

Meanwhile, Dick is telling Jamie Squires he's not needed for Saturday. He takes it badly. When Dick then names the team in the dressing-room, Squires makes to walk out. He says he's not part of it, so doesn't need to stay. Dick, using all his diplomacy, says otherwise and Squires sits back down.

There's no chance of the first eleven training anywhere decent on grass this morning. Pitreavie's a quagmire and they can't risk it with the groundsman again. Bert's fixed up the use of half an astroturf pitch at nearby Dalgety Bay, in the shadow of the Forth Bridge. Only the first eleven will go, the rest staying for running at East End Park. On Fridays they keep the subs and those left out altogether away from those who are playing. The first eleven and the Huffy Squad.

'We don't want anyone with a grievance nipping away at the rest,' says Dick. 'We don't need anyone upsetting anyone else, rocking the boat. By Saturday most guys who aren't playing are right up for it, they motivate the rest no bother. But Fridays are difficult – they're down and some let it show.'

At Dalgety Bay the sun is shining, but it's freezing. Half the pitch, outside a sports centre, is being used by an assortment of podgy guys like me in a variety of replica strips, playing six-a-side. I feel so chuffed to be with who I'm with.

McVeigh's firing shots in at Lee while the rest pass and move and stretch. Then Dick calls me over. He wants to try me out. The outfield boys go in a circle with him and the deal is that someone chucks me a ball and I have to first-time it round them clockwise without it touching the deck.

The first couple of goes are sketchy, but then I get into a rhythm. Johnson to me, header to Ireland, side volley to me, side volley to Shieldsy, back to me, on to Bob, to me, to Hamish, wide of me, so (check this) a little heel-flick at knee-height straight back to him. Nine times I kept the ball up.

I had got through the week without them laughing me off the pitch once. Yet.

Then it was match-situation time. They play Six-by-Four – the back four defending against the six outfield men, getting as close as they can to real situations. A ball gets played wide to Petrie, who's clearly offside – but no one appeals. Dick stops them and roars the place down. 'Never doofin' mind if it's only training,' he yells. 'You *all* get your hands up, every one of you. Shout for everything. Did you see Arsenal on Wednesday night? They got away with a perfectly good goal for Kiev by all appealing together. Get shouting, for doof's sake.'

Then they're working on corners, from either side, attacking and defending. Gerry and Craig are coming short and going to the back post, leaving holes for others, for Toddy and Ireland running for the header and Hamish and Stewart to nick chances.

Dick calls a halt, then spreads them out to use the whole pitch and finish the session with Shadow Play. Lee stands alone in the far goal, the rest work as a team with no opposition.

They play it out from Toddy and Craig to midfield, back to the full-backs, in to the strikers, back to midfield and on to men running in on goal. It's crisp, precision stuff. The front boys are moving smoothly, the men running on timing it perfectly. If they can do this tomorrow . . .

The rest of the day is theirs after this, time to look after themselves and keep their legs fresh for the game. The week's work, faltering and stuttering as it has been, is over. Now only the real job remains.

It's been a long week for Pip Yeates, cherub-faced physio here for seventeen years and for Scotland since 1994. He's kept a non-stop watch on an army of walking wounded and hasn't seen many come through ready to play. Of his casualties only Andy and Fergie are even on the bench.

Scott Thomson's arm will need another week, Squires is down in the dumps over his damn shin stitches, young midfielder John Fraser isn't kicking a ball yet. Chris Templeman, the seventeen-year-old midfielder they rate so highly, isn't quite there for tomorrow. George Shaw hasn't been around the place all week. Keeper Ian Westwater, the Grant Mitchell lookalike who did in his knee at Parkhead on the opening day of the season, is back in the gym.

Andy Smith's one of Pip's quickest healers. That same day away to Celtic, he went off with an ankle injury that needed crutches. He wasn't on them for long; Celtic only had one set and they had to go to Westy when *he* came off.

'Andy could hardly walk,' says Pip, 'but the following week he was fit to start in the League Cup at Livingston. Some players are like that, with others you can't tell. Some tell the gaffer to ask me if they're fit. That's a cop-out. Others desperately want to play when they clearly can't.

'If I ever wrote a book, it'd be called *Gie's a Minute* after an injury our old winger Kenny Ward got. He took a real thump on the ankle and I knew it was bad but he wanted up. He was shouting: "Gie's a minute, I'll be fine." I had to hold him down – and thank goodness, because he had a double break *and* dislocation.

'Physios can't afford to panic. You can't let the importance of the game or the desperation of the player rush you into letting them up early. That can make it far, far worse for the player and the team.

'But it's hard – there are injuries on a football pitch that a full casualty staff might take two hours to look at and diagnose, yet a physio has maybe twenty or thirty seconds to assess the damage and make a decision.'

Local boy Pip was twenty-one and shuttling between clinics in Edinburgh and London after graduating when the call came to help out at Dunfermline. At first he only went to training nights and played rugby on a Saturday, but eventually gave in to pressure to go full-time. The club allow him to run a private clinic from his treatment room at East End Park – otherwise there's no way they could afford a man so in demand. As his reputation grew, he was called in by Craig Brown to help the Scotland medical team for the Euro 96 qualifier in Greece in 1994 and has been the main spongeman since the finals.

'The big-name players made it easy for me from the start with Scotland,' he says. 'On my first night in Athens, Andy Goram came up in the hotel corridor and introduced himself. Of course, I knew fine who he was, but it was just a nice thing for him to do and I always remembered the gesture.

'The big difference with Scotland is the equipment at your disposal. Here it's very limited because there's no way the club could afford the gear I'd like. But Scotland have all the latest advances, a full high-tech kit. And it was decided a while ago that a Scotland player is a Scotland player – so every team at every level, even the women's team, have the same medical equipment.'

Pip has also worked on movie sets and on the strains of big-screen stars. A former partner did work for film companies and when he called off from one assignment, Pip stepped in. 'A few years back I got seven days' notice to do three months' work on *Gorillas in the Mist* with Sigourney Weaver and Bryan Brown, the guy off the Citroen ads. We were in Rwanda a lot of the time and it chills me when I read of all the trouble that has happened there since. Even in our time there, one of the locals working for us was taken away by the police for several days before being released. I think they were upset about him ordering other locals from different tribes around. I still dread to think what might have happened to him after we left.

'Oh, and I also worked on the *Muppet Shop of Horrors* and *Who Framed Roger Rabbit?*'

Er . . . but wasn't one a puppet movie and the other a cartoon?

'Yeah, but they still had their physio needs. Roger was a bugger to catch, but massaging Jessica made up for it. Another time I got called to the Caledonian Hotel in Edinburgh on the morning of a game at Brechin – Rudolf Nureyev was staying there and he felt stiff after a performance the night before.

'The guy was about fifty and in fantastic shape, but the flexibility had gone. I spent about ninety minutes getting him sorted – and by the end of it I was knackered. I drove up to Brechin, but when I went to give the boys rubdowns, my arms and wrists were done in. They weren't having it that I had tired myself out massaging a ballet dancer!

'Jimmy Nail also got me across to Edinburgh to sort out a muscle problem. He was a great guy, not a big-time Charlie at all. Most stars I've met have been like that, actually. I've been lucky.'

Pip only has one hard-and-fast rule about treatment. He will *not* give players injections. For years, players have had cortisone pumped into their bones and muscles to kill pain and let them play through knocks. But the effects of long-term use are there for all to see, particularly in the stars of the 1960s when the pace of the game quickened and the pressure grew and talent was no use to anyone in the stand. There is a frightening number of players from that era who find it hard to walk because cortisone has disguised the damage eating away at their joints. Allan McGraw, the former Morton manager and their top scorer in the '60s, walks with the aid of two sticks and suffers constant agony. Knees, ankles, hips and backs have been wrecked in the name of grinding out another win here, another point there. Play through it, son, and we'll look after you. Like hell. Football has used players up and worn them out for too long.

Now, thankfully, managers and medical men are being educated. Pip Yeates and many like him will not have players injected. It is far harder these days for a manager to force a half-fit player out onto the pitch these days. And a good thing too. A short-term huff from the gaffer is better than a long-term inability to run in the park with your grandkids.

SATURDAY

Bert wished he could have taped his voice as an answering-machine message.

'East End Park?' he chirped for the dozenth time in five minutes. 'Aye, the game's still on. Dundee've told us there's no inspection planned. Bye.'

Click. Pause. Ring.

'East End Park . . .'

It was just him and Bob Drummond, his spy on opposition sides, alone in the rain-lashed stadium at noon. Or so they thought. Suddenly Bert heard banging and was out of his chair like a shot, leaving the phone ringing off the wall with fans desperate to leave for Dens.

Five minutes later he came back. It hadn't been a burglar. 'Can you believe it?' he's saying. 'Ya blarf! Huxford's in there training. I didn't have a clue he was coming in early. He never said a doofin' word.'

The players aren't due in until 12.45, but Huxy's doing some extra stretching. His place was safe as soon as his pelvic problem got the all-clear from the specialist on Thursday, but he's obviously worried.

'A deep boy, very deep,' says Bert and he's about to tell me why when the phone rings. Again: 'East End Park? Aye, the game's still on . . .'

Then he goes out of the room and when he comes back the phone's still ringing. Only this time it's to tell him that ref Martin Clark's on his way to Dens for a 1 p.m. inspection after all.

He hangs up and shakes his head: 'Would you believe *that*? Dundee said ten minutes ago it was raining, but that the park was okay. Now we're up in the air.'

Dick Campbell and Pink arrive, soaking. They agree it's a great day to be a forward. The phone rings again and Bert rolls his eyes and says doof. He motions pleadingly for Dick to get it.

'East End Park? Aye, it's on,' he looks at Bert, who mouths 'inspection' and holds up one finger, 'but there's an inspection. Phone Dens after 1 p.m.'

The team are leaving at one o'clock. It's only a fifty-minute drive, so there's no pre-match meal. Bert and Dick are debating how long they can hang around when Dens manager Jocky Scott calls. Dick listens and puts the phone down with a shake of his head: 'The pitch is playable, but they're worried about water lying around the turnstiles and the terraces. They're worried about the safety of the fans.'

Bert leans back in his chair and sighs: 'It would be a nightmare if it's off now. It's the worst thing in the world. You've worked all week for nothing. Sometimes we'll have them do a bit of training when a game's off – but in this weather . . . ah, doof it.'

A fan on a mobile phone calls from a supporters' bus. They wanted to leave at half twelve, but once Dick tells them the news they decide to hang on. 'They should call games off early and be done with it,' he says. 'That'd be fairer on the punters. They want to get up and get parked and have few pints and some lunch. It's their doofin' day out.'

Behind the team coach, a bus filled up with punters whose bubble of enthusiasm got a slow puncture as they heard the latest. In their heart of hearts they *knew* it'd be off, though no one would say so. Because, in football, fatalists or even realists are not welcome.

Across the country, thousands like them idled on buses whose drivers drummed fingers impatiently on steering wheels, waiting to find out if they had a hire or not. And dozens of supporters' club treasurers fretted over their chances of a refund . . .

Bert's disappeared outside. He comes back smiling. 'The rain's eased right off,' he says, 'so if it's the same up there we could be okay. We want this played today, not midweek.'

McVeigh, Andy, Gerry, Fergie and one or two others are already heading towards Dundee by car. We'd pick them up on the outskirts. Those who live locally are in the dressing-room or hanging about the foyer. Directors and their wives wait in their Sunday best. Bert stands up, grabs his coat and says: 'Let's go.'

As the engine rumbles into life, he tells me how in the 1960s Jock Stein once chucked the Dunfermline team off the bus at the first roundabout outside Dundee and made them walk a mile up the road before picking them up again. 'I can't see me asking this lot to do the same today . . .'

We pull away and immediately there's a new tension. This is what the week has been all about. This is why I came here. Now that I'm here, I want to win as much as anyone. It's a huge game. Dundee are the only team Dunfermline have beaten all season, though they've only lost twice so far. All seven other games have been draws, but as the week has gone on the feeling has grown more and more positive and now Bert's praying the skies on Tayside are as clear as here.

We're not even two hundred yards up the road when a mobile rings. It's Jocky Scott again. Dick Campbell listens. Everyone else falls quiet, knowing the worst.

'Okay, driver, turn back . . .'

The pitch is playable, but the stadium is unsafe for fans. The directors sigh. Their investment has not only made East End Park's pitch perfect – there's a drainage expert on the board – but their new all-seated stadium is too, even on the wildest day.

It takes us longer to go right into a side-street, turn at the end, come back and go left again in busy lunchtime traffic than we had actually spent travelling with hope of the game being played. The players who got off the bus looked a different lot from the bouncy, confident athletes who'd swaggered on ten minutes earlier. Now they looked dispirited, crestfallen. Cheated.

'It's a nightmare when this happens,' says captain-for-the-day Hamish. 'You're right up for the game and then you're knocked down.'

'All you want to do on Saturdays is play football,' says Shieldsy.

Now they're hanging around, expecting more bad news. Like being told they're in for training next day – or, worse, there and then. They fall silent as Dick appears. 'Monday, 10 a.m., then. We were going to have you in tomorrow, but forget it.'

Now the hunt starts for games to watch. Westie and David Hay want to go to Tynecastle. Paul di Mello goes to fax for comps. I make a call to find out what's left on out of the rubble of a fixture card. Dick and Bob would go to see Stirling v Alloa and Bert and Pink to St Mirren v Hamilton.

Bert rings Jocky back and they agree to play on Wednesday night at 7.45, but for a team trudging back through the puddles to their cars, it might as well be next year.

I drive Shieldsy and Bob home to the brand-new, 2.4-kids estate on the outskirts of town where they live round the corner from each other. They're fed up. At first Bob was talking about going to see his old Hamilton mates, but now neither can get themselves up to go anywhere. Dundee at Dens was the only game that mattered.

They and the rest went home to pull off club ties and dump blazers and watch telly or spend a rare Saturday with the kids or fill the void with beer and snooker. But no one really wanted to do any of it. Their week's work had been for nothing. All the slog in the wind and rain and mud, the worry over their places, the graft to perfect set-pieces, the will to get that elusive win.

All that adrenalin, down the drain with the rivers of rain.

POSTSCRIPT

Six days into 1999, Bert Paton resigned and Dick was handed the reins with McVeigh as his No.2. Late that night I called Bert's house and Dick answered. He sounded in shock.

I spoke to Bert for a while and he told me he had quit for one reason. He had fallen out of love with football and he always vowed that when that happened it was time to go.

I asked him what it was that had done it. He said there were too many things wrong with football to start explaining. It was a sad night for him, for Dick, for Dunfermline and for the game.

Were you to draw up an identikit of the kind of person this book is about, it would look pretty much like Bert; a football-daft punter from a working-class background who loathes posers and whingers and bigots and time-wasters. A bloke who'd watch any game, any time, anywhere because a game's a game.

And Bert Paton will still go to games every night that he can, still check out the talent and shake his head at those who don't use theirs.

A good man is like a bad curry. You can't keep either of them down. And to prove it, Bert returned in the spring as chief scout. But he couldn't bring a change of luck with him. By May they had won only four games, and too many draws, too many might-have-beens, saw them relegated. Bob McCulloch went to Dundee United, Gerry was freed along with Marc Millar and others. And McVeigh left to manage neighbours Raith Rovers. Tin hats were immediately ordered for the first derby.

SEVEN

CHIMPIONIS

Getting the 1 a.m. train home from Bordeaux seemed like a good idea at the time. Couple of beers after the game, bit of a knees-up, wander to the station round midnight, drift into dream-filled kip as we rattle hypnotically through the night.

A superb idea; thought of only by me and the entire Scottish and Norwegian nations.

Thus there I am, just about first on and ready to wrestle myself into position zed, when every door flies open and peace is shattered.

Suddenly every carriage is a trifle of kilts and rucksacks and Viking helmets and bevvy and sleep-mutilating noise. In minutes the place is reeking of kebabs and earlier-on's kebabs, beer cans are shhhttshing open, fourteen different singsongs are fighting for space in the fuggy air, conversations are being shouted above conversations. It's like Karachi at rush-hour.

Then, above all the din, comes a series of piercing shrieks. It sounds frighteningly like someone is kicking a monkey; not that I had ever heard someone kicking a monkey, but if I had I'm sure this is how it would sound.

The place falls silent as we fix on the noise and, sure enough, someone *was* kicking a monkey.

In the mêlée, we haven't noticed this Arab bloke and his missus sprawled across two double seats with a chimp on a chain. Well, you wouldn't, would you? The wee thing's obviously been asleep, but when mayhem strikes he wakes and is now scared silly. He's shrieking like a hundred-strong hen party watching Dion Dublin get his kit off, rattling his chains like a ghost on *Scooby Doo* and squirting bodily fluids all over the shop.

But Johnny A-rab is having none of it, so in a bid to silence his imprisoned primate he pushes it down below the seat and batters seven colours out of it.

Now, football fans may not be the most sensitive on earth – especially after about a zillion consecutive nights on the sauce – but they're outraged at this breach of ape rights; one wee woman with huge Olive-from-*On-The-Buses* specs in particular. 'Rat's terribul, so it is,' she's yelling, 'you lee that wee monkey alane, ya blarf – ur ah'll kick *your* heed in and see how *you* like it.' Her man grimaces across the aisle at me as if to vouch from bitter experience that she means it.

Another woman joins in the hectoring, then a couple of blokes and soon the whole carriage is yelling at Johnny A to not only lee the monkey alane, but to get aff the train and stay aff.

Johnny, meanwhile, is still smacking Charlie the Chimp round its ribs, while Mrs Johnny screams in French: 'It's our monkey! We will kick it if we like!'

Think again, hen. Next thing she, her man and the punchdrunk monkey are being shown *le* door by the combined moral presence of the Tartan Army and Noggin the Nog's Animal Liberation Front.

Four Norges in pointy hats watch them go, then slip into the vacated seats, plonking feet and bottoms straight into the EC Monkey-poo Mountain. It's going to be a long, long six hours home.

I had come onto an empty train imagining myself as this mysterious loner, lounging in the dark with an air of mystique. I arrived in Montpellier at ten to six, bolt upright in the fallout of sweaty socks and stale beer.

The Vikings were shouting. They always do. Vikings are incapable of speaking at everyone else's normal decibel level. It's a disturbing sound, for conversational Norwegian sounds like two or more people having a vomiting contest.

'Bloooch greeech kooog boooorgle?'

'Haaarckh yoo blooooof whaaaaaarghhh!'

'Ghhhhhllllaaaaaaaaaarrrrrrrrrrrrrffffffff!!!'

I often think about that monkey, about what happened after he and Johnny A-rab and Mrs Johnny got howfed off the train. Did Johnny give him a withering look and sigh: 'Well, minkey – that's anither train we've been chicked off of. How many times, huh? Why do you always have to embarrass me? Sometimes I wish you and I had never gone into partnership to show Marie-Claire here off at the circus . . .'

Or maybe the monkey waited till Johnny's back was turned, pulled out a person wrench, whapped him on the back of the napper and eloped to Acapulco with Marie-Claire and the profits from the circus act.

Who knows? But my mother always wanted me to be a minister and one of the great talents of the minister is to take two totally unrelated subjects and somehow weld them together using only the phrase *'you know* . . .'

So. *You know,* when I think of that little incident it tells me a lot about being a Scotland fan. England fans would have joined in kicking the monkey, having stabbed Johnny for being an A-rab and called his missus a *slllaaaaaag.* German fans wouldn't have sat in the same carriage as an A-rab in the first place. French fans would have sautéed the monkey and opened a cheeky Côtes du Rhône with which to wash it down.

But Scotland fans demanded nothing more than justice for the frightened animal. Champions of the undermonkey, they couldn't stand to see a defenceless creature suffer – not after all those years of watching our goalkeepers.

Seeing dozens of your countrypeople, most of them strangers but for the common bond of football, rise up in indignation against the torture of a chained-up beastie which was being cynically exploited by a ruthless master did wonders for the soul.

Because, *you know,* that monkey could have been ourselves. *Hmmmm?*

For were not we Scots for hundreds of years the trussed-up Charlie Chimps of the football world? A nation bonded and smacked into submission by an overbearing, unfeeling master? Told when to dance and booted when we got uppity?

It is surely true – except that when the World Cup comes around our chains are broken. Before devolution, it was Scotland's only chance to come into its own, freed from the tyranny of our London ringmasters. And out we'd march into the big wide world, self-sufficient and strong, independent and proud in equally fierce measure. Bold, determined, patriotic, revivers of a glorious heritage.

Ready and willing to make an arse of ourselves on OUR terms.

Yes, sports fans, going to the World Cup with Scotland is the greatest lesson of all in how football fans suffer for their love.

Plenty write us off before a ball is kicked, sneer that we'll never make it through the first stage, that we'll be home before the postcards. They understand nothing of what the World Cup is all about for this country.

It's not about winning the damn thing, because once we did we'd be judged in every game we ever played on being the greatest team on earth and as soon as we lost we'd come tumbling off our pedestal and within a year we'd most probably be forced to disband the SFA, shut down Hampden and start doing something new and stupid like orienteering or underwater badminton or elephant-strangling in rum.

No, what the Sammy Sneers don't understand is that going to the World Cup with Scotland is simply an extension of the crap so many of us go through every week of our football lives.

Most of those who knock the ritual of spending your savings on what you know will be a losing cause are the kind of Old Firm fans who don't get what following Scotland is about any more than they understand what following Raith Rovers is all about. The basic difference between them and the rest of us is that they go to football every week expecting to win. We go hoping to win. Thus when we *do* win, it is a wonderful experience; whereas winning for your Old Firm punter is a *ho-hum, so-what* experience. But when your Old Firm fan loses . . . Oh My God, the world is ending. They look around, wide-eyed, for someone to blame. A religiously bigoted referee, a one-eyed linesman, an opposing team who dare get their tactics right instead of lying down meekly. Whereas when the rest of us lose, we're over it by the first sip of our second pint. That's the best way to approach life when you support most Scottish club sides and the *only* way to be when you follow Scotland.

It is about hoping against hope, dreaming the impossible dream, refusing to admit defeat even when the game's long over and we've lost 3–0. It's about everything I've tried to write about in this book; the investment of eighty-nine minutes and fifty-nine seconds in gloom in return for – maybe, just maybe – one moment of golden sunshine.

That night on the train home from Bordeaux, we were still basking in one of those moments. Just when the Norway game looked beyond us, just when we looked like we were going home, big Davie Weir lobbed elegantly down the inside-right channel and – at the far end from where we stood on our seats – Craig Burley's toe lifted the bouncing ball over the head of Frode Grodas.

A realist would have come out of the Stade Lescure shrugging *so what?* and telling you drily we'd scrambled a draw against an average side, that we only had one point from two games, the odds were against us qualifying and even if we somehow did we wouldn't be nearly good enough to go any further.

And he would have been a very lonely man in a heap.

The rest marched off into the early-evening sun gabbling excitedly of a great little team who'd been unlucky to lose to the World Champions, who'd played off the park a team unbeaten in two years and should have got more than a draw, who would now frighten Morocco to death, go through and take on either Italy or Chile, neither of whom were too scary.

Call 99 per cent of Scotland fans fantasists if you like. But if we weren't we wouldn't bother our backsides going all that way and spending all that money in the first place and if we didn't go we'd miss out on the party of parties. Which, after all, is the reason for being there in the first place. Take away the knees-up and all you've got is thousands of bizarrely dressed lunatics watching their team lose.

Most Scotland fans you meet seem to follow Thistle or Falkirk or Hearts or the Highland clubs. They know pain. Going to the World Cup just lets them endure it in better weather.

There are Rangers and Celtic fans as well, but certainly not the ones who turn up at five to three and are away again with quarter of an hour to go. Not the ones who start the party songs; most of *them* would rather support England or Ireland. The kind of Rangers fan who goes with Scotland is one of the handful left at Ibrox when they're into injury time. Everywhere I go I meet a squad from Aberfoyle and most of them are Rangers fans and I've never once heard them argue over whether Morocco is a Proddy or a Tim country, which is nice.

There are loads from up north, from Aberdeen upwards. The ones you just *know* believe their bit of the country is the *real* Scotland. The ones who have family-sized bags of chips on each shoulder about West Coast clubs, the West Coast media, West Coast accents, West Coast food, houses, women, dogs, cats, shoes, bananas, drinking chocolate, sticky-back plastic, pubs, music, hedgehogs, telly, teabags, amphibious landing craft, beaches, peaches, carpets, mice and men.

In the company of big, hairy sixty-two-pints-for-breakfast, fingers-like-a-normal-bloke's-leg growlers from Inverness or Peterhead, you know how Londoners must feel when we start on them for being Soft Southern Shandy-Drinking Poofters.

But when we all come together, from the north and the east, the west and the south, the cities and the isles and all points abroad, there is no tribalism. Not for us the English clique system of a St George's Flag with Bradford City or Chelsea or Forest painted on it; our lot's St Andrew's crosses may bear the names of towns, but few Scotland fans take their team affinities with them. (Partick Thistle fans are among the few exceptions. I usually give them the benefit of the doubt by thinking maybe they wear the Jags kit as a service, to try and prove there's always someone worse off than yourself.)

Go abroad with Scotland and you're a Scotland fan, not a Bluenose or a Buddie or a Jambo or a Bairn. Admission to the gang is by production of national strip, some tartan and an acceptance that *Que Sera Sera.*

That's Spanish for What's Fur Ye'll No' Go By Ye . . .

It must seem bizarre to an outsider that thousands of ordinary working men and women would scrape up a minimum of a grand a head and use the bulk of their annual holidays to follow a football team whose chances of glory are about as slim as the Venus di Milo's of winning the Embassy World Darts Championship.

Every four years the same writers – mostly women, but mingled with a few men writing like women – dig out the same old pieces from the archives, dust them off and change the place names; the ritual pre-World Cup assault on our brave boys at the front:

'*Why oh why oh why oh why must we celebrate the stupidity of these thousands of halfwits in their kilts and their football tops, beer-bellied and red-faced, giving foreigners the impression that all Scots live on a shortbread tin. They spend all that money and booze themselves silly for three weeks, leaving their wives and kids behind to fend for themselves. And for what? To watch some wee men in shorts chase a bag of wind about a bit of grass . . .*'

Then these same writers batter out their next article on how women should get over their shoddy treatment at the hands of men by getting a new hairdo, buying a new dress for a girlie night-out and screaming their lungs out when they get there. If only they had the wit to realise the two processes are the same.

Scotland fans go abroad, dressed stupid and acting stupider, for the same reason women go to the Chippendales. One lot go crazy to relieve the tedium of being stuck in the office or the kitchen or having kids running them ragged or husbands mucking them about. The others go to the World Cup as an antidote to four years of suffering at Firhill or Central Park or Tynecastle or Love Street.

The World Cup is total escapism, a fantasy world of dressing up in a way you never would dare to at home, a world where there are no rules, where deadlines and clocking in and out don't exist. Watches don't work at the World Cup, which is just as well as most punters fall over and smash theirs on the first night.

Best of all, because you go knowing in your heart that Scotland will fall at the first hurdle yet again, there is no letdown at the end of it. There will be disappointment, sure, but it is fleeting. A few beers dull the pain and by halfway through the next day you've packed your misery away with your kilt and started thinking about the next time. Believing with all your heart that it *will* be our year.

It is a fantastic feeling to be in among innocence like this, especially in people who for the rest of their lives are as cynical and suspicious and anxious as the rest of the world. Everyone should be a Scotland fan at the World Cup once in their lives. It is an unforgettable experience.

Especially when someone else pays for it.

I'm walking down Sauchiehall Street with Melanie, then my girlfriend and now by some lapse in her sanity my wife, one day in

February when my mobile rings. It's Steve Wolstencroft, Geordie *extraordinaire* and sports editor of the Scottish *Sun*. He is also a newspaperman beyond measure and to prove it he asks me: 'How d'you fancy going to the World Cup?'

Of course, I hedged my bets; asked what the arrangements were, discussed terms and checked my diary to see if I had a window for the whole of June.

Like chocolate I did.

If I could have climbed down the phone and shaken his hand I would have. Other people you might have kissed, but you've not met Wolsty . . .

The World Cup. The greatest show on earth. Watching Scotland – and, he says, anyone else I fancy – staying in nice hotels, seeing France. All of it not only free, but with dosh on the hip too. Throw in *The Great Escape* and a fat guy and you've got Christmas.

They booked me on the team plane, nineteen nights in the pleasant Mercure Palais des Papes hotel in Avignon, an hour from Marseille in the warm south of the country, gave me a three-week rail pass, a cash advance and expenses. All I had to do was wander around watching football and write down what I saw. And they paid me *for the things I wrote*, on top of all the rest.

Gor bless ya, Mr Wolsty – yer a real toff, so yer is.

The original deal was that I'd write three columns a week on whatever I fancied, plus pieces after each Scotland game. But I ended up writing every day, because anyone who doesn't have ideas oozing from every orifice during a World Cup has blancmange for brains.

So I'd get up and wander down through medieval Avignon for breakfast and the papers, decide where to go that day and hit the tracks. Pick a game, any game, haggle for a ticket and charge it to the company.

If I'm labouring the point of what a wonderful job this is, my apologies. But I still have trouble taking it in myself sometimes . . .

My tickets for Scotland's game weren't even for the press box, because they wanted me to get the atmosphere as well as the action. Against Norway and Morocco I was in amongst the punters, which was a total blast. But for the Brazil game . . . oh yes, there is a God.

My mate Gordy, who worked for the *Sunday Mail*, had got his hands on a ticket at the last minute through his office. He appeared at my hotel in Paris the night before and we went out for a few with big Eck McLeish and Alex Smith before leaving them and heading to the Champs-Elysées.

It was a magnificent place to be, a bubble'n'squeak of nationalities and songs and dances. We walked the length of the famous avenue, then back up and started all over again. We were drunk with the atmosphere. Mind you, the Stella Artois helped.

Back at the hotel, we lay awake gabbling like kids on Christmas Eve before finally nodding off with the telly still on. We woke early, eyes wide with excitement, desperate to be at the game *now*. That morning went *soooooooooooooooooooooooooo* slowly.

For some reason I got it into my head that I wanted a pair of sports socks and dragged Gordy up to the Champs to find some. Maybe I shouted this need in my sleep and some French sports sock collector passing our room overheard and went round all the shops bribing them to say they didn't sell that kind of thing; or maybe we just looked in the wrong place. But there was not a normal, single white ankle sock – never mind a pair – to be had. But the wild footwear chase used up an hour and a bit and maybe in the end that's why I had such a stupendously pointless idea in the first place.

Back at the hotel, the press guys were milling around in the lobby. Because I didn't have to sit in the media seats I was in civvies; well, Tartan Army civvies. Grey baggy combat shorts with loads of pockets for stuff, Scotland shirt, white sports socks (Gordy had a spare pair all along; the fact that he didn't tell me after breakfast suggests he too wanted to waste as much time as possible) and trainers.

Some of my colleagues said they envied me, but I know fine well many more looked down their noses and thought it was a disgrace for one of their party to dress that way. If I'd been in a lime-green polo shirt, red-and-sky-blue checked trousers and yellow-and-brown diamond Pringle V-neck they'd have approved, but to look like a . . . a . . . *fan*, that wasn't on. Gordy knew they were giving him the bad eye as well, in his kilt and his retro Scotland shirt and his Timberlands, but we both bit our tongues.

The press bus was late. A couple of times a coach would pull into the other side of the carpark and some of them would grab their holdalls and bustle across only to be told it was actually there to pick up a party of Japanese architects on a tour of Parisian bordellos and so they'd bustle back across and chuck their holdalls down again and *harumph* a lot.

(Two hours after the game, when the rain was tipping down, they would finish filing their copy – I'd done mine in a downpour right outside the stadium ten minutes after the final whistle – and find out the bus was still half a mile away in the media carpark where they'd been told to meet it and some would refuse to walk that far. Gerry McNee, in fact, would refuse to even walk a few yards in the rain when the driver finally got the message to go round to the stadium. The Voice of a Football then stomped back to the hotel, booked a room and wrote about it in his *News of the World* column on the Sunday.)

Anyway, the bus to take us to the game finally turned up and crawled through the mental traffic to drop us in that carpark, right across from the Nike Village where the Brazilian fans had set up camp; it had hot-and-cold-running samba music and a non-stop barbecue and women with pneumatic busts squidged into T-shirts that looked like knotted hankies.

We listened to the beat of the drums for a while; then, along with squad PR man Stuart Thomson, wandered across the road to a little asphalt playground where a forty-a-side game between fat Scottish people and Brazilians who looked like Rivelino's superfit cousin was in full swing. Then we stumbled on the one tiny bar open in the whole area and helped drink it dry, which wasn't hard as they had about nine bottles of tepid beer in their bubbling, buzzing old fridge.

After that we had a Big Mac at a table with two Cameroonians and a Korean and wandered round the outside of the Stade de France until an hour and a bit before kick-off. What a time that was, what a riot of colour and noise and laughter and food smells; all the tartans on the map mixing with the sunflower yellow and clear-sea blue, all the flags waving and the touts loitering and the TV cameramen darting in and out of the crowds.

We were on our second lap when I experienced a moment which will never, ever leave me. In front of us, the crowds parted and we realised we were walking in the middle of the road and then, looming before us, was a bus. Our bus. The team bus. Scotland were going to run us over. And I think that right then I'd have let them.

For there, by the driver, was Craig Brown and his face was beaming like a wee boy who'd just opened his Christmas present and found Sharron Davies in a clingfilm bikini.

We leapt towards the kerb as the bus swept past and there, spread across the entire back window, was Colin Hendry; arms spread and fists clenched, the veins on his neck thicker than some people's thighs, his face contorted in a expression which would have had the Brazil squad's washer-woman on overtime had *they* been there to see it.

We stood stock still, our hearts pounding, as the bus disappeared round the bend and into the ring-of-steel inner sanctum of the Stade de France. Suddenly both of us were eight feet tall and, while that isn't too much of an improvement for Gordy, it would certainly make me Most Stretched Boy in the class of '98.

And then we realised we were the only members of the Scottish media party to see it and as Gordy wasn't even really with the party that only left me and our hearts sank a little.

At the end of our first lap of the stadium we'd met Kenny MacDonald from the *News of the World* and David Hardie of the Edinburgh *Evening News* as they surveyed the scene. But every other person who'd been on that bus with us had gone through the first security check, across the concourse, through the second security check and headed straight into the Media Centre, never to reappear. There they stayed to scoff free food and free drink and to watch TV pictures which were being beamed live from about a hundred yards away. The miracle of technology, eh?

Neither of us could believe that attitude. To be here, now, two hours before the opening game of the World Cup; and not just *any* opening game of the World Cup, but one with Scotland in it – and not just Scotland but Brazil as well. Probably the greatest football occasion our country will ever know and the people paid to report back on it to the nation spend the build-up sitting looking at each other in an air-conditioned room.

Sadly, though, that is the way of it with some of our media people. Some – and they know who they are – would rather douse themselves with petrol and have a conversation with a fire-eater than mix with the punters. It's as if those who pay to watch football, the people it exists for, are not part of their world. They forget these are the people who keep us all in a job by buying newspapers and watching TV and listening to the radio, and that we are the link between them and the stars. Instead, some have this image of the media being about themselves and the stars and no one else.

This I could understand, but still not accept, if they shared some phenomenally close relationship with the Scotland squad and with the Old Firm and the like and felt they couldn't jeopardise it all by being too close to the ordinary folk and maybe – just maybe – criticising The System sometimes.

But it's not that way. What actually happened in France was that every day they would all troop up to the Scotland training camp and a couple of players would be wheeled out and they'd get enough out of them to fill the required space and that would be that.

During the season, Rangers and Celtic each have a Friday press conference at which their management grudgingly part with as little information as they can get away with and at which a player might – if the clubs feel like it – be made available to answer questions. And after games at Ibrox and Parkhead the managers come in and grunt some more and then players might – just might – come up and talk for a bit, until the PR people hustle them away for fear that they might be forced to answer the occasional difficult question.

I don't think this is the way the media should be covering football. It should not be a lobby system like in Parliament, where you're fed a party line and that's your lot, and where everyone gets everything there is to get and if that means you get nothing then that's politics, Brian. We've got to get back to writing about *football*, about the whole game, from our hearts and not from some photocopied, officially approved press release.

And here is a warning. If thirteen journalists from thirteen papers continually go to press conferences and all come back with

223

the same story, then some day the media barons will get together and ask why the hell they need thirteen journalists to ask one question and they might just decide to chip in and send one guy instead.

It's time for individuality in the media, for papers with different agendas, for TV and radio stations who don't just shuttle their equipment back and forth between Ibrox and Parkhead, and for those with the privilege of access not just to act like a pack, accepting whatever handouts are chucked our way like stale bread to the ducks.

In Scotland we have a Football Writers' Association and I'm not sure of all the work it does because I've never been a member, but I do know that the last time they had a heated vote about any issue, it wasn't the availability of players or the off-hand treatment of the press by top clubs or the lack of decent facilities for us at many grounds. No, the last row they had was over whether or not to admit women members. There was much harumphing when the men-only brigade lost; but honour was restored when an amendment was passed saying that any woman who *did* join would not be allowed to bring *other* women to the annual Player of the Year dinner. I know, I was speechless too.

Anyway, back at the game . . .

Gordy and I held off the moment of finally going into the stadium itself like we were keeping our favourite sweetie in the box for last. We wanted to time it just right, to enjoy every last moment we could outside before taking our seats. Eventually, we agreed the time was nigh. The team was in, so now we should go too. We showed our tickets, then queued for bottles of water and shook hands (don't ask me why) before going up a small flight of stairs which opened into the huge bowl that was the theatre of our dreams.

I was a stride ahead, so I saw it first. A sight to take you from eight foot tall to making you duck your head for fear of bumping the floodlights.

The players had emerged in full Highland dress to test the pitch. It was a magnificent, awe-inspiring sight. They looked so cool, in their kilts and Bonnie Prince Charlie jackets and big socks and brogues and, yes, even in their shades. Reservoir Jocks, ready to go to work.

We just stood there at the top of the steps, transfixed by our boys as the French and the Brazilians stood to cheer them. Then we checked rows against tickets and found our seats, a few yards in front of the press area that stretched most of the way along one side of the arena. Right above the centre circle. And smack bang in the middle of Superstar Central.

We weren't meant to be sitting together; Gordy had got his ticket from somewhere-but-don't-ask-too-many-questions and was a row or so away from me, but we jiggered-and-pokered with other punters and ended up next to each other. You couldn't come that far and then be split up.

Right behind us, directly below the press box, were rows of executive boxes. And out of them as time passed and the opening ceremony began came more and more famous people to ease their Yves St Laurent-ed backsides into reserved seats. Wenger, Papin, Cruyff, Basile Boli, Luis Fernandez, Neeskens, Tigana and more; football heroes, then actors, then pop stars. To the left, about twenty yards along, was the VIP area with FIFA top brass and politicans and royalty. We were close enough to Jim Farry to tell you he didn't join in the Mexican Wave. If he'd known what was going to happen to him a few months later he might well have got blitzed and joined in with the rest.

And then there it was, the World Cup itself.

A few months earlier I had held it in trembling hands at Hampden during a day when I followed it all over Glasgow on a sponsored tour of schools and sports centres and supermarkets. But this, somehow, was different.

Somehow it was even more special to be looking at it, sitting up on its little plinth, half an hour before Scotland played Brazil in the opening game of the tournament.

Suddenly I got something in my eye.

The opening ceremony was bizarre, because it was organised by the French. It was all giant dancing flowers and abseiling insects and dogs and cats on concealed trampolines; this was what the second day of Woodstock must have felt like.

Then, when the teams could be seen at the mouth of the tunnel and there were ten minutes to kick-off, I phoned Kenny and he told me he was sitting in front of the telly wearing his kilt, and that was me gone. My eyes are too near my bladder at the best of times, but this was something else. Gordy, meanwhile, was on the mobile to his dad and he was off as well.

When they played 'Flower of Scotland' we put our arms round each other, and if they'd told us the day was over then and to please disperse we would have gone home happy men. It is a moment I will never, ever forget.

The privilege of being there was enormous, especially as so many others suffered the terrible frustration of being there in Paris, on the concourse of the stadium even, but not *there*. It was awe-inspiring to be part of thousands upon thousands of Scots and Brazilians partying together in the hours before kick-off – but depressing to know that only one in three would be inside to see it in the flesh.

They danced in a McDonald's forecourt, played five-a-sides on the pavement, gave it pelters to the samba band practising behind locked gates at the Brazilian Village. And then they watched the lucky ones go off for the greatest experience many will ever know in football.

Other hadn't even gone as far as the Stade. They cut their losses and hung around the bars of central Paris, unable to put themselves through the torture of being within touching distance of *the* game. Many had come without tickets and were content to watch on TV, but the ones you really felt sorry for were those let down by the rats who set up fly-by-night agencies which fleeced millions from the trusting. We met two of the unlucky ones in a pub by the Arc de Triomphe on Tuesday night. They had paid £810 each to be at the three group games, but the tickets never appeared and their hard-earned dosh may never be seen again either. They were hanging around in the hope of picking up a pair for the next day, but the prices being asked for the few available were scary. I was offered £850 for mine by the concierge at our hotel. Multiply the frustration of those two pals by twenty or thirty thousand and you start to see what a disgrace the allocation of places for this festival of the so-called People's Game was.

Then there were the tales of heroism; like the legend of the two lads standing outside the Stade de France an hour before kick-off. Ticketless, soaked, bladdered. They've seen *The Great Escape*. Steve McQueen on the motorbike with only a fence between him and freedom. They have no motorbikes, but are laden down with the super-strength bravado issued only to the very, very drunk.

So they go over the top.

Except the first boy is halfway up the perimeter fence, kilt somewhere round his ears, when the security guards spot him. In a second he's on the deck, a baton tattooed on his ribs. His mate has two options. Stay and back him up at the risk of a tousing – or nip in the gate while the guards backs are turned. No contest.

So the first boy gets up, alone, and woozily focuses on a Cockney standing over him asking if he's looking for a ticket. He says yes, unless he's got an ambulance in his pocket. The spiv has a furtive look round and hisses that five hundred sovs and it's his. The boy pays up and staggers in, soaked through, skint and clutching his battered guts. Can't believe his luck.

Meanwhile, his pal realises that although he's inside the main gate, there's another ticket check to get through. He thinks on unsteady feet. Suddenly, he spies a row of wheelchair fans waiting to be shown in, goes up behind the nearest one and says: 'If anybody asks, I'm wi' you . . .'

Some boys in the boozer afterwards swore it had happened, that the boy with the broken rib was sitting along from them. I hope it was true. You have to admire anyone who got round the ticketing scandal that blighted a wonderful opening to the World Cup.

Sports paper *L'Equipe* waxed: 'To the rhythm of the samba from the Copacabana and the songs of the Highlands, the Stade de France lost its virginity and found a lover.' It reported warmly of Scots openly wearing the shirts of their rivals, of posing for pictures as they recreated Marilyn Monroe's famous skirt-up pose above air vents.

'Thank God,' writer Bernard Lions gushed, 'football is beautiful.'

'If every game has spectators like these,' said TV station France 3, 'then this will be the happiest World Cup of all time.'

Memories of the game that day, historic though it was, don't make me shiver the same way memories of the *occasion* do. Yes, when John Collins tucked that penalty away we were in heaven and when Tom Boyd ran smack-bang into the ball as it flew off Jim Leighton's hands for their winner we were in hell; but that happens every week in football. You're up, then you're down.

These things don't rouse me the way remembering Broon's beaming face at the front of the bus does or Hendry's fired-up salute at the back window does. Not the way that first sight of the boys walking around the pitch in their kilts does.

It was the occasion that mattered that day, not the game, not the defeat. Isn't that what being Scottish is all about?

Which leads us nicely to. . .

WHAT BEING ENGLISH IS APPARENTLY ALL ABOUT

Two days later, on the Friday, I jumped on a train for the forty-five-minute journey to Marseille.

That night, France would open their World Cup campaign against South Africa in the Velodrome. It seemed the whole country wanted to be there, but I would try to buy a ticket anyway. It was a game not to miss.

France had gone bonkers for the World Cup and so far all I had seen was happiness and helpfulness and togetherness. People could not do enough for you, could not wait to talk to you about football, about your country. It was heaven.

However.

The next game in the Velodrome would be on Monday; England *v* Tunisia. By tonight, English fans would be arriving in town. And then we would see how far the spirit of goodwill to all *hommes* lasted. It didn't take long to find out . . .

The bar L'Arc de Ciel is a shady place in a shady city. A giant message painted on the wall reads: F*** Off PSG. They don't like the prosperous north of France down in Marseille – they don't much care for anyone but themselves, in fact, and even then they give themselves a good kicking now and again just to show who's boss.

It's like Newcastle with smellier tabs.

There's a volatile mix on the streets; French, African, Spanish, Arabic, living together in uneasy truce. Even on that Friday, party night as the World Cup campaign began, you got the feeling it wouldn't take much to set it all off.

Enter the English.

With immaculate timing, I arrived at Saint-Charles railway station early in the afternoon as the first of them hit town. They wondered why the signs were all in foreign. Soon the trickle would become a stream, then a flood and finally – by the morning of the match – a tidal wave. Judging by the first few scraping their knuckles into the bar at Saint-Charles, you feared for Marseille at their hands. However, after being in L'Arc de Ciel later, you feared almost as much for them at the hands of the Marseille people.

It took about a day before it All Went Off and every TV channel was showing pictures of neanderthals in 1966 replica shirts or topless like tattooed walruses, hurling bottles and making come-ahead signs to riot cops who'd been gasping for a fight for days.

It isn't easy to pick a venue where the English hard core – plus the beered-up sheep who follow their lead – will not cause trouble. Were you hunting the perfect place *for* trouble, however, Marseille during France '98 would have won hands down. The wide boulevards, the bars full of people more wary of outsiders than even the English are themselves, the searing heat – and, of course, the security hordes. It was Fisticuffs R Us.

The pecking order of those security people went like this. First, red-blousoned and rosy-cheeked volunteers who checked tickets and gave directions. Then came the local police, whose job was basically to direct the traffic and tell you the time. The real stuff was left to national police riot squads, the ones whose eyes you can't see for reflective visors, backed up by – most worryingly when the English were around – a massive private army of bull-necked bouncers. They could have been straight off the terraces themselves; skinheads with a wage, a logoed bomber jacket and a muzzled Alsatian. Far from stopping trouble, they looked like they'd welcome a scrap; them *and* Sabre.

On Friday night they stayed in the background, watching

through narrowed eyes as nation mixed with nation in per-fect har-mo-nee. The muzzles stayed on, and on the dogs too. Twenty-four hours later, though, both were let off the leash. A minor incident between an England fan and a motorist sparked off running battles which looked worse than they were – but which were enough. The war had begun and whether it remained a war of nerves or became a bloody one, the sad fact was that the wonderful party that was France '98 had been gatecrashed.

And then, to increase the chaos, loitered the touts. They were everywhere on that Friday, flogging tickets by the handful – and this before France's opening game, which you'd have thought would have been a certain sellout.

You thought then, if they have so many for *this* match, how easy will it be for one the locals don't care for? Like one with England in it.

I was offered my first in the underground. Eighty quid. I said no. Outside the Velodrome, a huge black bloke munching a sandwich offered another for sixty. I said no again and watched Denmark *v* Saudi in L'Arc de Ciel. (The name, by the way, means Rainbow, possibly because the scar on the face of the Thing serving the drinks made it look like Zippy. It carried eight beers at once and sloshed them on the bar, then nodded towards me, flicking Gauloise ash at the bloke in front. Still, I'm sure she's good to the kids.)

Outside again, another tout says fifty pounds for a good seat. I say no. He says, okay, forty, last price. I ask to see the wares first. He gets his mate, who produces a wad that could have choked a donkey, all with watermarks and holograms. They bear the legend: FA of Liechtenstein. How can I refuse?

I pay the 400ff, only for yet another shady little *homme* to offer me a seat for 300. Pah. It's like taxis; once you get one, you see millions. Suddenly I noticed touts on skateboards, touts on bikes, touts lounging shadily under trees. They were playing fair. Forty quid is face value. But when the English moved in? The answer comes on the Saturday – boys from Bolton were on telly boasting about picking up tickets for £150. Some ended up paying even more, only to find they've been palmed off with a seat in the back row of last week's Sasha Distel gig in Strasbourg. Trouble is, too many English fans cannot – will not? – break down language barriers and thus are taken for a ride. And by the time they realise it, they are usually so drunk they'll take it out on anyone within punching distance.

Which brings me back to the bar at Saint-Charles, where the barman had just slapped my change down like it was a glove and this was a duel. You can't take things like this personally. It's the way they are in France. But you wondered what the reaction would be the first time he tried it with an English fan – and there wasn't long to wait till we found out.

Banging through the swing doors came four of them, all Three Lions hats and Factor Blow-torch. Boys fresh from the sophistication of the Landahn suburbs.

John the First (they were all called John) asked a well-dressed guy leaning on a high table what game was on the telly. The guy didn't understand. John the First gave him a look, peered at the screen and, even though it said 'Bulgaria' and 'Paraguay' in the box up in the corner, he seemed none the wiser.

John II and John III were arguing over whose shout it was. John IV cut in and motioned the barman: 'Oi, four beers.'

The barman shrugs that French shrug at John IV, who does what the English do in these situations. He gets louder: 'Four beers, chief. FOUR. F-O-U-R! Heineken!'

He holds up four fingers. The barman counts them slowly. Then he pours four Amstels and says: '*Cinquante-deux francs, m'sieur.*'

John IV says: 'Wot?'

The barman repeats, *cinquante-deux francs.* The Johns look at each other and scratch beneath their hats. Wassee onabaht? Whoi cannee speak English?

Eventually, John IV half-pulls a 100ff note from his wallet. The barman taps it, as if to say: 'Yes, that's the one.'

John III lunges forwards: 'Did you see that? That thieving blarf nearly had John IV's doofin' wallet, John I. Wanna do the splanje, John II?'

'Nah,' says John II, 'doofin' forget 'im.'

'Ee's forgotten,' says John IV, 'anyway, no use getting nicked now. We'll miss the game. Do it on the way back, when it don't matter.'

The English had arrived. Without the language, without manners, without a clue. Wherever they lay their beany hats, that's their home, and the locals were warned not to forget it.

Scientists later claimed England replica shirts were too thin to save the wearer from the effects of sunstroke. Sadly, from what I saw that day, you couldn't protect some of them with a wet suit and a diver's helmet.

Since everything that Went Off in Marseille and the skirmishes that followed in Toulouse and Lens and St Etienne, endless English fans have come out with their side of the story; tales of indiscriminate attacks on innocent revellers by riot cops, of how knife-wielding locals and blood-thirsty Tunisians were allowed to lay into them while security forces cocked a deafy. Of lying awake in their hotels rooms, fearing the door would be kicked in at any time and they would be beaten, robbed or worse.

I am sure many of these accounts are true. But the fact is, no other nation's fans were picked on by French police or by local residents. And that is because no other nation's fans, barring the indescribable animals masquerading as German supporters who crippled a policeman in Lens, had an element who went with the intention of intimidating their hosts. Not even those fans of countries whose hatred for each other makes us and the English look like passionate lovers.

Long before going to France, a few of us decided we *had* to go to the USA *v* Iran match. It was in Lyon, less than an hour away from St Etienne where we were due to play Morocco two nights later. But even if it had been in Uzbekhistan and we were playing in Florida, we'd have made it.

We had the scene all worked out in our heads . . .

Across a balcony at the Stade Gerland stretches a huge banner reading: Death To The Great Satan.

Along a bit, another flag unfurls. It says: Death To The Great Santa. The Dyslexic Iranian Supporters Club have arrived.

At the other end, American supporters spot some Iranian women among the crowd and yell for them to get their faces out for the lads.

The Iranians, quite rightly, are not having this slur on their ladies. They strike aggressive poses and shout for the Yanks to Khomeni Have a Go if they think they're hard enough.

The Yanks are unimpressed and taunt the Iranians with chants of: 'You're Shi'ite And You Know You Are!'

How we laughed. And how we'd have gone mental had we walked into a boozer in Teheran and heard them giggling about mean Scots in kilts doing the Highland Fling.

It would hardly be a footballing classic. Eleven college boys still trying to remember not to pick up the ball against eleven moustaches. Arguably the two poorest sides in the tournament.

But there was so much more to it than kicking a ball. It was about twenty years of Cold War thawing for ninety minutes – and the risk of 200 years' more tension if it all went pear-shaped.

Washington had done its bit to cool the jets that week, extending the hand of friendship, calling this accident of the draw a perfect window of opportunity for them to talk truce. Their players then came out and gave it the full Bob Dylan Megamix in the build-up: Why can't we all just live in peace, man? Why can't we just love each other?

The Iranians joined in, saying this would be a happy occasion. A chance to heal old wounds and forge new friendships.

Then the French went and chucked in a wee hand-grenade to spoil the fun. One of their TV channels showed a movie called *Not Without My Daughter*, a weepy about a Yank lady married to an Iranian bloke who gets stuck over there after the Islamic revolution and how she plans to get away, but not without the aforementioned sprogette. To the TV people it was just an innocent space-filler between live games. To the Iranians, though, it was like having their moustaches pulled out hair by hair with blunt pliers. The doors of their training camp – never exactly Russ Abbott's Madhouse at the best of times – were slammed shut on the world. Coach Jalal Talebi and his moustache called the film an insult and an outrage.

Barry Norman said it wasn't *that* bad, though the acting was a tad wooden.

Talebi and his moustache claimed the screening had been a political act designed to upset their preparations for such a big game. With every sentence, each bristle pointed further towards the ground.

And for twenty-four tension-filled hours, rumours abounded that Iran and their moustaches would pull out.

Then, out of the blue, Talebi and his moustache held another press conference. This time he and it laughed and joked, saying they loved America, that they used to live on the West Coast – and even ran a supermarket in California, with his missus and *her* moustache. Wonder if he took out a bank loan to buy it? Debt to the Great Satan!

So, calm returned. The match would go ahead. The Iranian players and their moustaches were even allowed out for a day's shopping.

(*'Hey Ali – what's French for: Which way to the nasal-hair-trimmer shop?'*)

Then they and their moustaches posed for pictures with the townsfolk of picturesque Yssingeaux where they were based and signed endless autographs for children who then asked their parents why those funny men had eaten paintbrushes.

ARE YOU TALKING TO ME OR CLEARING YOUR THROAT?

Two amazing things happened to me that night. First, an Iranian bloke and his moustache came up trying to flog tickets to me and my mates Craig and Clarky. He spoke like he was constantly clearing his throat.

'Chwere chyou cam fchrom?' he asked.

It took a second for us to catch what he'd said. Then we clicked and told him: 'Scotland.'

He shook his head and his moustache took the skin off a passing woman's back. 'No, no – *chwhere* in Scotland?'

So we said Falkirk, thinking he'd never have heard of it. Hah.

'Chwere abouts in Falkirk?'

We were looking round for the hidden cameras now. This is Jeremy Al-Beadali, right, and we're on *Chyou've Been Fchramed.*

Then he held out his hand and announced: 'You are my fchriends – I chome fchrom Broxburn.' By this time our bottom lips are on our shoes. He can tell we're shocked, so he says: 'Well, not *fchrom* Broxburn, obviously.'

Well, obviously. That's more of an *East* Lothian accent, eh?

'No, I'm acchtually from Bargeddie.'

Now the street sweepers were scraping us off the pavement. The boy wondered what the joke was. He asks us if we wanted the tickets or not, but we couldn't answer.

So he wandered off, waving his hand in the air and muttering something that sounds like *Ach-ach-ach-achachh*. Or maybe his moustache was actually Bagpuss and it was trying to get rid of a furball.

So we were just about getting ourselves back together when Amazing Thing No.2 happened. This couple stroll up, spot Craig is wearing the kilt and strike up some chat with him and Clarky while I'm looking for tickets. The couple are Irish.

You know that moment when you think you know someone but you can't for the life of you remember how or who or where? I got one right then. I looked at the bloke. He looked at me. His missus looked at me.

Then, as they say in Teheran, it chhits me like a chammer. He's called Bernie, he runs a chippie in Dublin and we met at Italia '90. Me, Big Geordie and Ush stayed on to have our livers ruined by him and his seven pals after Scotland went out.

A week or two after the tournament, I went to Ireland to stay with them, met his wife Carol, got on like the proverbial h-on-f. Screwed up what was left of my liver and threw it away with the empties. But after that we lost touch and I hadn't seen them since.

God knows what the odds were of meeting them eight years later outside the USA *v* Iran game in Lyon. But it restored my faith in the Lottery, men on Mars and even Scotland winning the World Cup one day.

Bernie and Carol had won tickets in a competition. Only in Ireland, eh – an all-expenses-paid trip to the first night of World War III. What did they chuck in as a bonus? A personalised Scud missile through their hotel window?

They'd arrived in town that afternoon and, like all good Dubs, had been drinking just to be sociable ever since. Another hour or so and they'd be sociabled out of their boxes.

'Jeyzuz,' says Bernie, 'what a stert we hed t'noit. Forst ber we go intu, there's not a woman in soight. Takes us about foive seconds t'click that it's a gay joint.'

'Sure it was a noitmare,' Carol chips in. 'Oi've never seen a gayer place in me loife. Even the barman's dog wouldn't look at me!'

So then we were all full of hugs and handshakes and all that stuff before they were off to their seats and we to keep hunting tickets. I arranged to meet them the following lunchtime for a swift gargle. Just when that new liver was taking, as well. (When I got there, they already had two drinks on the bar for me. You can guess the rest – I'm still trying to.)

So there you are. Inside five minutes you meet an Iranian from Bargeddie and pals you haven't seen for eight years. And you remember what a wonderful, wonderful place the World Cup is to be.

By then I'd been in France eighteen days and they'd flown by. I'd seen games in Paris, Marseille, Bordeaux, Montpellier and Toulouse, and now I was in Lyon with St Etienne to come and who knows where after that, and I'd marvelled at every occasion.

On the eve of the tournament I wrote that the French were anxious about the amount of punters from different nations criss-crossing the country between venues and with days to spare between games. As it turns out, it was one of the elements which made the event so special. I'd been on trains with Norwegians and Danes and South Africans, the Dutch, Italians, Cameroonians. They were all great crack – even the Yanks were entertaining, as long as you just listened to them and bit your lip.

I sat across from two New York college-boy types coming back from Italy v Cameroon in Montpellier. They'd been supporting the Italians. 'Hey, Perruzzi did well as goaltender, huh?' said one.

Perruzzi was injured and at home. His mate seemed to know this. 'Nah, Perruzzi didn't play. He got sent off in USA '94, so he's barred.'

I closed my eyes and hoped they'd think I was a simple Lithuanian peasant who could not contribute to their fascinating conversation. So I'm listening, but I don't believe what I'm hearing. Each is behind an official programme and every now and then one would have a little think out loud.

'Hey, I thought there were only *four* venues!'

'Did you know Oo-roo-goo-ay won the very first soccer World Series?'

'How do these group things work anyway?'

And, dear readers: 'Who was this Pele guy? Sounds like a hell of an athlete!'

I cursed quietly to myself in Lithuanian.

Then one of them – and I kid you not – stroked his goatee and said: 'Hey, how comes Scatland are called Ecosse in this brochure? I mean, it doesn't even *sound* like Scatland! Like, what's the point?'

'There's no point, man,' his mate confirmed, 'I dunno why they don't just stop messin' the hell round with English. Anyway, I dunno why the Brits have four teams in – like, they're all just regions of England.'

'Yuh,' said goatee boy. 'We don't get to put fifty state teams in.'

When I think back now, especially having met Bernie and Carol, I wished more than ever a country like Ireland had made it and phonies like the States had been back home playing silly boys' rounders like they do best. If they keep getting in, we should be allowed to play in their baseball World Series – if only so we could tap them on the shoulder at the Yankee Stadium and ask: 'Haw, Jim, what way are Scotland kickin'?'

Anyway, back to Lyon.

As first Bargeddie Boy then Bernie and Carol come and go from our lives, we realise it's ten minutes to kick-off and we still don't have Wilson Pickets. At most other games I'd been to this was the time the touts got desperate and gave them away at bargain-basement prices.

In Montpellier the night of that Italy *v* Cameroon game I was still ticketless as the noise of the teams coming out swelled in the dusk air. I was about to chuck it and go back into town to a boozer when I saw three kilted gentleman haggling with an Englishman. He was just about to get the spare Wilson they were holding for 500ff when I barged in: 'You guys got one for sale?'

'Aye – no problem. Four hundred francs okay?'

'Perfect – there's four-fifty, get yourselves a beer.'

'Want to join us at the game?'

'Okeydokey, amigos.'

And English Boy's left standing there with his jaw sweeping the pavement. 'Oi,' he said, ' 'ow come you wanted five hundred orf me but you took four hundred from 'im?'

Dear reader, if he didn't know there was no point explaining.

The boys were from Dundee and were sort of in between accommodation. Had I not been staying in a hotel packed with pressmen who wouldn't have understood the concept of helping fans out, they could have come back on the half-hour train journey with me and kipped there for the night. But instead we parted as mere business colleagues.

Buying tickets was the same at most games; there were always plenty, usually from the private stock of some obscure non-competing FA like Botswana or Wales, or from the squillions not taken up by corporate sponsors. And for all the hype about prices, you only got ripped off if you were stupid or English or both. Even a tad of an effort to speak French to the tout and you rarely paid more than a tenner over the face value.

Security? They never gave your ticket more than a glance. I went into the Denmark *v* South Africa game as Madame Lucille Lepetomane and they never cracked a light. That was the game when big Morten Wieghorst got sent off; how unlucky is that – the first tackle of your career and they red card you for it?

Anyway, back to Lyon again.

Time's running out and we're seriously considering a taxi back to town when a moustache approaches carrying an Iranian with it.

'Ccccchey – you ccccwant tickets?'

'Yes please.'

'Cccccccccokay – I have two and my ccccccccchum has one. You give us 2,000ff the ccccchhlot.'

We made a certain sign.

'Right, ccccchwait ccccchere a minute.'

And he goes into a massive argument with his mate that sounds like two Welshmen shouting placenames. Eventually he waves the back of his hand at his mate, takes his ticket off him and says: 'Cccccccokay, 1,000ff the lot.'

We give him 900 and he and his moustache go off muttering *acccccchhhachchchchchchch.*

Two of the tickets are property of the Iranian FA. Which is fine, because we look like we're from Broxburn, eh? Me in my Scotland top, shorts and pink tan and Craig in Sweden shirt and a kilt splattered with a fortnight's beer, mustard and other stuff that if he's clever and doesn't wash off for a few years could probably help impeach a president.

But here's the laugh. The third ticket, the one Clarky's got, is from Gillette. I mean, Gillette. How much business do *they* do in Teheran?

Anyway, the Gillette End was behind the furthest away goal, a stand full of corporate dudes and French neutrals. Craigy and I were smack bang in the middle of Nutter Central.

How can I explain the atmosphere in that end that night? Take a box of fireworks, drop in a few sticks of Acme cartoon dynamite, add a dash of nitro-glycerine, chuck in a lit match and then you're about a *fiftieth* of the way there.

Those Iranians made an Old Firm crowd look like the audience at an Over-eighties Sponsored Silence. They were tonto, completely and utterly hatstand. It was like the riot scene from *Indiana Jones and the Moustache of Doom.*

They would have been mental enough just at the thought of playing the Great Satan. But the fact that they were also able to have a right good barney among themselves made it Ramadan, Christmas and the first day of the January Sales rolled into one.

The deal was this. Half the Iranians were exiles who'd left the country for the US and Europe when the Shah was overthrown at the tail end of the '70s. The other half still lived at home and many of those were followers of a Communist leader who had recently been murdered. This was their perfect opportunity to publicise their anger away from the fist of the security forces in Teheran. So they sneaked in T-shirts and flags and banners with the boy's face on and yelled his name non-stop. This pleased the exiled Iranians not. They were furious that their biggest-ever football night was being hijacked by a political rally. So they told the protestors this and the protestors laid into them. The cops waded in and the protestors got in about *them* as well and suddenly a nice cup of Horlicks and *ER* with subtitles seemed appealing.

The cops tore the banners down and confiscated their flags and ripped the T-shirts off their backs. But once calm was restored, they just pulled out more flags and more banners. They must have had them up their sleeves like a magician's bunches of flowers.

This time they got tactical; a couple of hundred in one corner would give it yeehah and the cops would wade in; and while everyone was watching that, another pocket along the stand a bit would strike up. And so on round half the ground until the gendarmes were running around like blue-ersed flies, waving their truncheons at anyone who moved and just about anyone who didn't as well.

Then, just to hurl petrol on the already raging flames of passion, Iran only went and scored.

For a few minutes all their fans were as one. Exiles and homeys hugged and kissed and leapt and danced. Moustaches locked like velcro. The air was rent with the sound of frenzied *aaacccchhhh-chchchahhhhhhchhhh-ing*.

Soon, though, normal service was resumed as the T-shirts and flags and banners went up and the chanting restarted and the exiles screamed abuse and the cops waded in again.

The Yanks were baffled by it all. They thought the guy on the banners was the boy who scored. Well, he had the moustache, didn't he? Although it's debatable just how many of the Yanks actually knew what the score was. And most of those who did were waiting for the relief pitcher to come on and save the day.

Near the end Iran scored again and the roof almost came off. They could have got a third as the USA proved once and for all they haven't a clue about tactics in any sport where they don't let you have a direct headphone link with the coach.

And when it was over, *Allah almighty did they celebrate . . .*

Throw that lit match into the box of fireworks and nitro then heave the lot onto the nose of a nuclear warhead. *Cccccchhhhhh-kaboom!* Me and Craig had long since got separated in the mayhem, but kept in touch by moby so we could meet outside and make safe our escape under cover of the moustache worn by a particularly large Iranian.

We dodged into a nearby bar for warm beer in plastic cups until the hordes cleared and we could catch a cab back to the town. From the main square we wandered round to the Shamrock Bar, filled to bursting with Tartan Army boys, and hammered it until five in the morning.

The management put a turn on for our delictation, a woolly-looking Irish boy with an acoustic guitar and a nice line in Simon & Garfunkel. The lads got on stage and gave him a helping hand through his act, which was nice.

Last thing I remember is an American girlie with a camera asking three bruisers to lift their kilts for a picture. They turned and obligingly showed their backsides. But no no, she cried, the other way. So they flashed and so did she. Then she took the arm of the one in the middle and they wandered off into the night, a shining example of how it may be a small world, but a big Polaroid still gets you places.

THE EPILOGUE

We were right in line with Jim Leighton when the ball bent his fingers back like an angry teacher's belt.

From our nosebleed seats in the impossibly vertical Tribune Pierre Faurand, Big George and I almost felt we could reach out and grab it as it looped up and over his head. Instead, we watched hopeless as poor Jim turned and flailed like a drunk man chasing a balloon. And then we saw him take one last slow-motion swat with those Mickey Mouse gloves and flop into the back of the net. The ball lay and looked at him like a wasp which had outwitted its hunter.

Strange thing is, I don't recall any sound at the time; no groans or boos or jeers nor even the dervish cheering of the Moroccans. It was like watching the telly on mute.

I didn't turn to see the look on the big man's face and I don't suppose he looked at me either. We had both been there before.

In 1990, we'd been right in line with Jim when he pushed the shot out and Muller ran while the Scots defence froze, like the closing shot of every *Police Squad* episode. We sat, facing front, as Jim turned and hit the post a kick that sent a shower of raindrops flying like startled sparrows from a powerline.

Turin, St Etienne, Timbuk-bloody-tu. The venue makes no difference when you watch Scotland. The outcome is always the same.

As Jim scooped the ball, whose shoulders would still have been shaking with mirth had it possessed a pair, from the net and hoofed it back to the centre, I could only think one thing. *I want to go home.*

I wanted to be transported there and then from Row 34, Seat 238 to my bed in a cosy house in New Carron Village, Falkirk. To be cuddled up with Melanie and loved and protected from all the hurt that comes with being a Scotland fan.

It was no way for a trip like this one to end. It deserved a better send-off. It deserved to be laid to rest with full military honours, not shoved in a black bin-bag and tossed on a skip in the dead of night.

It shouldn't have ended with a man I admire and respect to the moon and back flailing crazily at a ball that did not want to come to him, in a stadium that gave me a sore head, on a night I wanted to start all over again yet also just to be over.

Officially, it didn't quite end there. Jim was beaten once more when a Moroccan's shot hit Colin Hendry's hambone thigh and whizzed past his ear. But by then we didn't give the square root of a chained-up monkey's.

In fact, I can now admit that when I filed the saddest thousand words of maybe a hundred thousand written over the campaign I forgot about that third goal. I think by then I was in denial.

Some, in the light of day, took comfort in the fact that had we beaten Morocco, Norway's jammy win over Brazil would have put us out anyway. They needed a slap.

On other occasions, I might have argued the toss with them. But not that day, the day after St Etienne. That day I didn't want to talk to anyone, not even to the lovely girl who had cleaned my room for three weeks or to the lady at reception whose husband was Jamaican or the *garçon* at the café up the hill who loved talking football each morning with the *Ecossais*. They could all go to hell and so could football.

Of course I got over it soon, because you're Scottish and you have to. As I said already, it's the only way to be. You just wonder sometimes why you choose to put yourself in the position of paying so much to be so unhappy.

This game has a terrible power over us, the power to make us sociable to the point of falling over or solitary to the point where men with long beards who live in caves ask who the miserable loner is.

If you don't understand why, then you're probably not reading this book, so that saves me explaining it. Which I couldn't anyway, so thanks for reading something else and saving me a hell of a lot of trouble.

EIGHT

366 REASONS TO BE CHEERFUL

(so you can be happy even in leap years)

1. King Kenny.
2. Naming your son after King Kenny.
3. Rangers 1 (Conn) St Mirren 4 (McLeod 4), League Cup, August 1972.
4. Kevin McAllister's goal for Falkirk *v* Hearts, Scottish Cup semi, 1998.
5. Alex Cameron being shunted by a police horse live on television.
6. George Best's goal *v* Sheffield United, Old Trafford, September 1971.
7. Seeing Cruyff and Gullit for Feyenoord at Love Street, 1983.
8. Hummel's white 'Alan Ball' boots, 1971.
9. Frank Worthington.
10. San Marino's goal in eight seconds *v* England, World Cup qualifier, 1991. God bless Davide Gualtieri.
11. Simon Stainrod's goal from halfway for Falkirk at St Johnstone, 1991.
12. Brazil 2 Italy 3, World Cup, 1982.
13. Carlos Alberto's goal to make it Brazil 4 Italy 1, World Cup final, 1970.
14. Coventry's brown Admiral away strip, *circa* 1978.
15. Pele.
16. Argentina 2 England 1, World Cup, 1998.
17. Norway 2 England 0, World Cup qualifier, 1993.
18. USA 2 England 0, friendly match, 1993.
19. Queen's Park's six-foot, seven-inch winger Alf Stamp, *circa* 1972.
20. Reading having a keeper in the 1970s called Steve De'ath.
21. Seeing George Best at Love Street for Hibs and Fulham.
22. King Kenny's goal against Spain, 1985.
23. The boy from Zaire running out the wall to knock the ball away before Brazil could take a free-kick, World Cup, 1974.
24. Haiti's celebrations when Emmanuel Sanon put them ahead *v* Italy, World Cup, 1974.

25. Jan Tomazsewski, Wembley, 1973.
26. Tomazsewski having a team-mate called Jerzy Gorgon.
27. Raith beating Celtic in the Coca-Cola Cup final, 1994.
28. Clydebank making it to the Premier League after only ten years in existence.
29. Hearts winning the Scottish Cup in our lifetime.
30. Archie Gemmill scoring the greatest World Cup goal of all time, Mendoza, 1978.
31. USA 1 England 0, World Cup, 1950.
31. René Higuita doing the Scorpion.
32. Roger Milla doing the first corner-flag dance.
33. Finidi George's peeing-dog celebration, Nigeria *v* Greece, 1994.
34. Brazil's 1970 strip.
35. The *Rothmans Yearbook*.
36. Clydebank 2 St Mirren 2, Christmas Day 1976.
37. Big Jim Holton.
38. Joe Jordan before he got an Italian accent.
39. Shug Hacker
40. Paolo di Canio.
41. Gazza when he sticks to playing football.
42. Every time a Scottish team wins in Europe.
43. Jock Stein.
44. Big Eck.
45. Airdrie in cup finals.
46. John Martin posing like a haddie for stupid pictures.
47. Michael Owen, English or not.
48. Celtic 1 St Mirren 2, Premier League, 29 September 1977.
49. St Mirren 1 Liverpool 1, Centenary Match, December 1977.
50. Allan McGraw.
51. *Scottish Football Today*, September 1992–May 1994
52. Alex Totten leading Falkirk out for the Cup final in a kilt.
53. Scotland 2 Sweden 1, World Cup, 1990.
54. Ireland *v* Romania, World Cup, 1990.
55. Being sick in the lap of an Englishman in a kilt, World Cup, 1990.
56. Newcastle 3 Barcelona 2, Champions League, 1997.
57. Gordon Strachan being too wee to leap a hoarding after scoring for Scotland *v* West Germany, World Cup, 1986.
58. Leeds keeping the ball for two and a half minutes *v* Southampton, 1972.
59. Denis Law holding his shirt cuffs.

60. The Johann Cruyff Turn.
61. Billy Bremner's face when we scored *v* Yugoslavia, World Cup, 1974.
62. Half-time *v* England at Wembley, Euro '96.
63. Coisty's winner *v* Switzerland, Euro '96.
64. Crying with Big George, Scotland 0 Holland 0, Euro '96.
65. Being in the Wembley press box when Southgate missed the penalty, Euro '96.
66. Craig Brown.
67. Both Jackie McNamaras.
68. Arthur Montford.
69. Hands Off Hibs.
70. David Hopkin with his teeth out.
71. Rob Roy of the Rovers (hopefully coming to a bookshop near you soon).
72. Alex Beckett's thirty-yard winner, Celtic 1 St Mirren 2, 1981.
73. Kevin McGowne's thirty-yard winner, Rangers 0 St Mirren 1, 1991.
74. Kenny McDowall going in goals, Dundee United 2 St Mirren 3, 1987.
75. Jimmy Nicholl.
76. Denmark 6 Uruguay 1, World Cup, 1986.
77. Dad getting me up at one in the morning to watch the 1970 World Cup on a black-and-white Ekco telly.
78. Proper-sized bloody Waggon Wheels.
79. Killie pies.
80. Playing *v* Rod Stewart's XI, Davie Cooper Fund match, 1995.
81. Being there when Albion Rovers won the Second Division, 1989.
82. Willie Pettigrew.
83. Listening to John Gahagan do after-dinner speeches.
84. QuizBall.
85. FIFA '99.
86. Subbuteo World Cup Edition (with floodlights).
87. Cammy Murray, St Mirren right-back of the '60 and '70s.
88. Tigana, Platini, Giresse.
89. Willie Ormond *v* Norway, telling Scotland's players to watch the blond boy on corners.
90. *Yabba Dabba Doo, We Support The Boys In Blue and it's Easy – Eeeeeaaaaaa-sy!*
91. Dundee United's run to the UEFA Cup final, 1987.
92. Raith leading Bayern Munich in the Olympic Stadium, November 1995.

93. Stevie Fulton's dad Norrie scoring goals for fun in the juniors.
94. Simon Stainrod's hat.
95. Robert Reilly's disco pants . . .
96. . . . They're the best, for they go up from his arse to his chest. Ask a Stirling Albion fan.
97. Hans Eskilsson's hair.
98. Gayfield when the wind drops.
99. Palmerston Park.
100. Clydebank's success against all odds, 1998–99.
101. And big Joe McLaughlin in particular.
102. St Mirren 2 Celtic 0, Scottish Cup final, 1926.
103. St Mirren 3 Aberdeen 1, Scottish Cup final, 1959.
104. Norrie McWhirter.
105. Paul Lambert winning the European Cup with Dortmund, May 1997.
106. Players chasing dogs round the pitch.
107. Winning a 50–50.
108. Not winning a 50–50 but taking a body anyway.
109. The feeling of putting a ball in the net.
110. Ivan Golac.
111. Newcastle's '79 midfield of Martin, Barton and Wharton.
112. Birmingham's 1972 change strip of black, red and yellow thirds.
113. Villa's '60s half-back line of Brown, Arce and Hole.
114. Wanderley Luxemburgo, coach of Brazil.
115. Clydebank 2 Rangers 1, first game after Souness was named boss, April 1986.
116. Man U losing at home and looking for someone to blame.
117. Peter Schmeichel's nose.
118. Johnny Watson doing Frank Macca.
119. Tony Roper in his strap-on Ally MacLeod nose.
120. The real Ally, making us all believe back in 1978.
121. Jamaica in the World Cup.
122. Killie 5 Eintracht 1, Fairs Cup, 1964.
123. Chic Charnley.
124. The Junior Cup final live on telly.
125. A goal for your team that comes from nowhere.
126. Nutmegs.
127. Backheels.
128. Catching one sweet on the volley.
129. A run, a cross, a bullet header, a goal.
130. James Sanderson.

131. Jimmy Sandison.
132. Terry McDermott flying in to head goal No.7, Liverpool *v* Spurs, 1978.
133. Hereford 2 Newcastle 1, 1971.
134. Paying £1 for a slice of Hampden turf and imagining it was where Fergie scored from.
135. Snatching a win out of nothing.
136. Sundays watching nothing but football from getting up until bedtime.
137. Reading in the papers that your team's made a new signing.
138. Standing on the terraces when a clearance drops right to you.
139. Wearing your team's strip.
140. Winning a derby game on their patch.
141. Manchester City, 1968–71.
142. Stoke City ending Leeds United's twenty-nine-game unbeaten run, February 1974.
143. *The Glory Game* by Hunter Davies.
144. Bill McAllister's radio reports on Highland League games.
145. Donny McDowall.
146. The late, great Bobby McKean.
147. Seeing No.146 and Donald Ford of Hearts score hat-tricks of penalties.
148. St Mirren and Hearts in Ajax rip-off strips, 1972–73.
149. Hamilton 3 St Mirren 8, pre-season friendly, 1978.
150. *They Used to Play on Grass* by Gordon Williams and Terry Venables.
151. Franco Baresi.
152. Manuel Agogo, Sheffield Wednesday.
153. Dan Petrescu's winner, Romania *v* England, World Cup, 1998.
154. Wembley '77.
155. King Kenny nutmegging Ray Clemence, Hampden, 1976.
156. Jinky Johnstone running round Hampden swamped in Shilton's shirt, Hampden, 1974.
157. Doug Baillie of the *Sunday Post*.
158. St Mirren 4 Dundee United 1, Scottish Cup, January 1977.
159. The Old Firm in the Anglo-Scottish Cup.
160. Andy Gray's diving headers.
161. Players with TV shows named after them. Like Dan Pet Rescue.
162. England 1 Scotland 5, Wembley, 1928.
163. Hughie Gallacher.
164. Bobby Clark's poses as the ball flew past him.

165. Andy Goram at his best.
166. Martin O'Neill.
167. Mark Fish.
168. Geoff Pike.
169. Harry Haddock.
170. Adrian Spratt.
171. Bert Troutman.
172. Sole Campbell.
173. Pilchard Gough.
174. Steve Guppy.
175. Scotland 2 Whales 0, Anfield, 1977.
176. Beating FA chief Ted Croker's Wembley ban on Scotland fans, 1981.
177. And then seeing John Robertson win it with a penalty.
178. Dundee United winning the league, 1983.
179. Brian McClair finally scoring for Scotland *v* CIS, Euro '92.
180. Carnoustie Panmure.
181. Bill Shankly.
182. Matt Busby.
183. Arbroath 36 Aberdeen Bon Accord 0, Scottish Cup, 12 September 1885.
184. Dundee Harp 35 Aberdeen Rovers 0, same competition, same day. How frustrating must that have been?
185. Peter Beardsley.
186. Kenny Black.
187. Jim Farry.
188. Sarcasm.
189. The musical montages at the end of live Sky games.
190. The first day of the season.
191. Midweek cup replays.
192. Tony Parks.
193. Being in a 100,000 crowd at Hampden.
194. Your neck tingling when you sing 'Flower of Scotland'.
195. The morning after a wonderful win.
196. Ian Durrant back playing at the top.
197. The Tennent's Sixes.
198. Sly Stallone as the goalkeeper in *Escape to Victory*.
199. The closing titles of *They Think It's All Over*.
200. Frank Skinner talking football without David Baddiel.
201. Scotland 3 Czechoslovakia 1, World Cup qualifiers, September 1977.

202. Ireland 1 England 0, European Championships, June 1988.
203. Marco van Basten.
204. England *v* Germany penalty shootout, World Cup semi-final, 1990.
205. West Germany *v* East Germany, World Cup, 1974.
206. Giuseppe Bergomi's single eyebrow.
207. Middlesbrough star of the '70s, Willie Woof.
208. Alan Ruff.
209. King Kenny Dogleash.
210. Spaniel McGrain.
211. Corgi Hagi.
212. Johann Crufts.
213. Willie Pedigree.
214. Your game passing a knife-edge pitch inspection.
215. The Kop swaying in its heyday.
216. Ray Kennedy.
217. Jimmy Case and his deaf-aid.
218. John Gregory.
219. Mickey Lawson and Whitehill Welfare.
220. Scotland 1 Brazil 4, Seville, World Cup, 1982.
221. Dave Narey's toepoke.
222. Toeing Jimmy Hill's erse.
223. And Gary Lineker's.
224. Not to mention Brian Moore's.
225. Davie Cooper.
226. Seeing Michel Platini play for St Etienne at Love Street, UEFA Cup, 1980.
227. Johnny Wark.
228. Brian Irvine.
229. Big Dunc's overhead kick for Scotland *v* Germany, 1993.
230. Berwick Rangers 1 Glasgow Rangers 0, Scottish Cup, January 1967.
231. Queen's Park staying amateur.
232. Barry Ferguson.
233. Mark Burchill.
234. Rab Douglas's monster throw-outs.
235. 2-3-5.
236. The smell of Wintergreen.
237. The feel of Wintergreen on your legs.
238. The pain fading after you've put a Wintergreen-covered hand down your pants.

239. Killie winning the league, 1965.
240. John Hewitt's dance after his winner, Aberdeen 2 Real Madrid 1, Cup-Winners' Cup final, 1983.
241. Jim Leishman going round the track like an aeroplane when Dunfermline won the First Division, 1989.
242. A perfectly observed minute's silence.
243. The Italian idea of applauding instead of having a minute's silence.
244. An unbeaten run.
245. Hearing a radio commentator who can paint a picture of the match.
246. Hearing a TV commentator who doesn't blab all the time.
247. Not hearing Archie McPherson.
248. Keeping your programme to read on the way home.
249. Billy's Boots.
250. Hot-Shot Hamish.
251. His American cousin from a religious cult, Hot-Shot Amish.
252. The thought of Macauley Culkin playing the lead in *The Joe Miller Story*.
253. Or Deputy Dawg playing Graham Kelly.
254. Or Giovanni van Bronckhorst as Mowgli in a live-action *Jungle Book*.
255. Andrei Kanchelskis as claymation dog Gromit's new master.
256. Simon Donnelly as the wee brother in *The Joe Miller Story*.
257. Seeing famous people at the game; I saw Eddie Izzard supporting Crystal Palace at the play-off finals. Sadly, he wasn't in drag.
258. Watching highlights on telly and seeing yourself in the crowd.
259. Watching highlights on telly and seeing someone you know but don't like in the crowd swearing and knowing they'll be in trouble with their mum/wife/boss.
260. Livingston youngster, surname Pevide de Serpa, first name Kevin.
261. Brian Rice.
262. Pat Rice.
263. Pakora Bonner.
264. Arie Naan.
265. Vindalou Macari.
266. Popadom Sullivan.
267. Istvan Korma.
268. *Washed down by* . . .

269. Ivo den Biemish.
270. Shandy Goram.
271. Dick Advocaat.
272. *And for the tee-totaller* . . .
273. Vimto Jonk.
274. Or Danny Lennon and Burdock.
275. East Fife winning the 1938 Scottish Cup when they were in the Second Division.
276. Richard Gough heading the winner, Scotland *v* England, Hampden, 1985.
277. Jim Baxter.
278. Jim Baxter taking the mickey out of Alan Ball, Wembley, 1967.
279. Wembley, 1967.
280. Ivan Zamorano screaming out the Chilean national anthem, World Cup, 1998.
281. Gianluca Vialli in his school cardigan.
282. Spain 0 Northern Ireland 1, World Cup, 1982.
283. The thought of the bus carrying the National Union of Cuddly Mascots to their annual conference going over a very steep cliff.
284. Scotland getting to the final of the 1989 Under-16 World Cup.
285. Knowing the Saudis who beat us then are now all old men with zimmers.
286. Arbroath fans in stick-on beards when Danny McGrain was manager.
287. Inflatable bananas.
288. Did I mention proper-size bloody Waggon Wheels? Well, it really gets my goat . . .
289. Your first-ever football strip. Mine was a 1970 round-collared Man U.
290. South African World Cup star, surname Buthalezi, first name Linda.
291. Tommy Burns at Cellicfooballclub.
292. Bradford City manager of the late '60s, Grenville Hair.
293. Gary and Phil Neville's dad, Neville Neville.
294. You've torn your dress.
295. Neville Neville.
296. Your face is a mess.
297. Games played on freezing cold, sunny days.
298. Old-time goalkeepers in polo-necks.
299. Getting hit with a Mitre Size 5 and having the maker's name backwards on your thigh for a fortnight.

300. Tommy Bryce in the *Guinness Book of Records* for the world's fastest hat-trick.
301. Billy Dodds saving the day against Estonia at Tynecastle, 1998.
302. David Francey.
303. Stevie Clarke being transferred from St Mirren to Chelsea the day my son was born.
304. Being glad you swallowed your pride and wore longjohns to the game.
305. And that you remembered to put trousers on as well.
306. Partick Thistle 4 Celtic 1, League Cup final, 1971.
307. Jimmy Bone.
308. Dennis McQuade.
309. Ian St John commentating on a dull 0–0 between Italy and Poland, World Cup, 1982: 'And this is what we at Liverpool used to call fannying around.'
310. Inter CableTel (Wales).
311. Uni Cluj (Romania).
312. Red Boys Differdange (Luxembourg).
313. Sporting Club BANG!!! 0 Nina Bayer Sager 0 (Channel 9, *The Fast Show*).
314. Young offenders in the park, car stereos for goalposts.
315. Forfar holding Rangers to a 0–0 draw, Scottish Cup semi-final, 1982.
316. And going home to eat bridies the size of hats.
317. Pictures of old games with bunnets as far as the eye can see.
318. Crawmill rattles.
319. Crawford Baptie.
320. Streets where they still let kids play football.
321. Dads and grandpas who get out there and join in.
322. Kickabouts in the park that end up 23-a-side.
323. Getting shouted in when it's already too dark to see your hand in front of your face.
324. Hearing The Skids do 'Into the Valley' when Dunfermline run out at home.
325. Or listening to 'Bobby Law's Burning' by The Ruts.
326. 'Andy Gray in the UK' by The Sex Pistols.
327. And The Clash with 'I Fought Denis Law (and Denis Law Won)'.
328. Jim Montgomery's double save that won Sunderland the 1973 FA Cup against Leeds.
329. Jim Leighton's single-handed salvage job, Scotland 1 Sweden 0, Ibrox, 1996.

330. Jim Duffy's baldy napper.
331. Dave Smith, the slaphead ex-manager of Dundee who did his team-talks in poetry.
332. Going to the game in a snorkel parka – first time round, in the '70s, before they were £120 and mega-trendy.
333. Celebrating a goal in a midweek Home International at Hampden and getting covered in dust from the old railway-sleeper terracing.
334. Standing on the Celtic End and watching the mushroom cloud go up like Hiroshima behind the other goal.
335. Dave Mackay.
336. Ally McCoist.
337. Zoltan Varga, Hungarian genius at Aberdeen in the early '70s.
338. Andy Ritchie's curling free-kicks.
339. Hugh Sproat and his razor-blade earring.
340. Rab Prentice on the wing for Hearts.
341. Peter Marinello before it all went pear-shaped.
342. Dougie Somner and Frank McDougall in tandem.
342. And Peter Weir setting them up.
343. 150,000 at two European semis in Glasgow on the same night.
344. 134,000 at Celtic *v* Leeds, Hampden, 1970.
345. St Etienne fans partying in Glasgow for the European Cup final with Bayern, 1976.
346. Crowds piling into cup finals without the Old Firm when the cynics sneered that they'd be ghost games.
347. Punters rallying round to Back the Bairns in their greatest hour of need, 1998.
348. Tony Fitzpatrick putting his job as manager on the line to stop Reg Brealy taking over St Mirren, 1998.
349. Players looking like ants from the long-lost Subbuteo Stand on top of Hampden's north enclosure.
350. Fans climbing floodlights to get a better view.
351. Marching to games abroad with the Tartan Army.
352. Peter Lorimer clapping his hands above his head after another volleyed goal.
353. Your hero running to where you are in the stadium after scoring.
354. The autographed photo King Kenny sent my Kenny.
355. That photo of Tom Finney aquaplaning through a giant puddle at Stamford Bridge.
356. Faroe Islands keeper Jan Knudssen in his Benny from *Crossroads* bobble hat.

357. Thinking what size of envelope you'd need to send a letter to the Venezuelan FA at: Federacion Venezolana De Futbol, Avda S.Erminy, Torre Mega II Pent House B, e/Sabana, y la Solano, Parroquia el Recreo, Caracas, Venezuela.

358. Especially if you then added South America, the World, the Solar System, the Universe, the Galaxy . . .

359. Michael Palin's *Ripping Yarn* about Barnstoneworth United's search for that elusive win.

360. The day they finally got it. We all knew the feeling.

361. Toshack and Keegan.

362. Jardine and McGrain.

363. Leighton, McLeish and Miller.

364. Herring and shortbread.

365. Don't worry about that one, my mum always said it when I asked what was for dinner.

and finally . . .

366. Football. Full stop.

Be happy . . .

THANKS . . .

To Kenny for being a top son and for carrying the torch at Love Street.

To Mum, Anne, Brian, Julie and Paul for always being there.

To Gordy Waddell for all his help in getting this book together and for being a mate. May Falkirk go one better next time and win the cup.

To Wolsty for letting me roam wild.

To Kevin McKenna at *Scotland on Sunday* for letting me loose on England.

To Joey Joe-Joe Junior Shabadoo.

To St Mirren for winning the cup and making it all worthwhile.

To Bert Paton, Dick Campbell, John 'Hey Sur!' McVeigh and all the boys at Dunfermline, and to Craig Levein.

To Andy Swinburne. Here's hoping 'Well do it again.

To Big Dan for the idea behind Chapter 1 and for inventing fresh-breath dog biscuits.

To Alasdair Campbell, bless his soul.

To every fan and every player and every manager of every club where football lovers are always made welcome.

But most of all . . .

To my wife Melanie for always believing it would all come together. All my love, all my life.